Anything Goes

JOHN BARROWMAN
Anything Goes
THE AUTOBIOGRAPHY

with Carole E. Barrowman

Michael O'Mara Books Limited

First published in 2008 by
Michael O'Mara Books Limited
9 Lion Yard
Tremadoc Road
London SW4 7NQ

A CIP catalogue record for this book is available from the British Library.

Papers used by Michael O'Mara Books Limited are natural, recyclable products made
from wood grown in sustainable forests. The manufacturing processes conform to the
environmental regulations of the country of origin.

ISBN (hardback): 978-1-84317-289-5
ISBN (paperback): 978-1-84317-299-4

1 3 5 7 9 10 8 6 4 2

Designed and typeset by E-Type

Plate section designed by www.envydesign.co.uk

Printed and bound in Great Britain by Clays Ltd, St Ives plc

www.mombooks.com

Contents

Author's Acknowledgements   7

1   'I Hope I Get It'   11
2   'Milly, Molly, Mandy'   21
3   'Defying Gravity'   37
4   'Journey of a Lifetime'   51
5   'Don't Fence Me In'   69
6   'New Ways to Dream'   79
7   'The First Man You Remember'   91
8   'That'll Show Him'   105
9   'No One is Alone'   119
10 'High Flying Adored'   129
11 'Love Changes Everything'   139
12 'Anything Goes'   149
13 'There's Nothing Wrong With Us'   165
14 'Nice Work If You Can Get It'   179
15 'Putting It Together'   191
16 'There's No Cure Like Travel'   205
17 'Being Alive'   217
18 'Together Wherever We Go'   229
19 'Live, Laugh, Love'   241

Timeline   247
Index   251

Author's Acknowledgements

I've always thought people would find a lot more pleasure in their daily routines if they burst into song at significant moments. So, if you're reading this while travelling on the Tube, standing at a bus stop, queuing at your local bookstore, or even sitting on the loo, don't resist the urge. As Mama Rose famously said in the musical *Gypsy*: 'Sing out, Louise!'

Musical theatre gave my professional career its start and musicals remain one of the unifying passions in my life, which is why I've organized this book according to songs from some of my favourite shows. As you'll soon discover, each chapter has a song for its title, representing a significant event, a life lesson, or a tale or two from a particular time. Like many of my favourite musicals, the narrative of my story avoids a straight chronology and shifts backwards and forwards through my life. When you've finished reading, I hope you'll have a clearer, more detailed picture of who I am as a person and as a performer than from anything else you've read about me.

To be honest, here's what I really hope – that by arranging the book in this way, you'll feel as if you and I are lounging in our pyjamas on the couch in my Cardiff living room, sharing a bottle of champagne or a pot of tea, with music on in the background, having a blether and a laugh about my life so far.

This book has been a collaborative effort with my sister Carole. She spent most of a summer and lots of iChat time listening, laughing, enquiring and reminiscing with me. I recorded my stories and memories on my iPod, and Carole gave them structure and shape. In order to achieve this, though, she thoroughly neglected her family for a while. As a result, Carole and I would like publicly to thank Kevin, her husband, the Barrowman Casey household's backbone and the one who keeps all of them in clean socks and hot meals. Carole also wants to give lots of hugs and many thanks to Clare and Turner, who have learned to put up with having a writer for a mother with humour and aplomb, and who can live without her for weeks without hurting each other or their dad.

Of course, like all good musical productions, this book owes a great deal to a supporting cast that I'd like to acknowledge before this show begins. Firstly, I'd like to thank warmly all the folks at Michael O'Mara Books for their patience, their commitment to the project, and their hard work in helping achieve its vision, especially Kate Gribble, Ana Sampson and Alison Parker. Thank you to my manager Gavin Barker, for all he does behind the scenes, and to my partner Scott, for keeping me grounded with a generous supply of love and support.

For their contributions to this production and all that they add to my life, a special thanks to my big brother Andrew, his wife Dot, and my nephew and nieces Andrew, Yvonne and Bridgett; to all the Gills; and an equally deep thank you, as always, to Bev and Jim Holt.

To my driver Sean, thanks for always getting me to the show on time, despite the distraction of yellow cars.

To my fellow cast members, crew and production staffs, past and present, whether on stage or on screen, thank you for sharing your stories, your talents and your friendship with me over the years. You're all the tops!

Finally, and most importantly, Carole and I would like to dedicate this book with love and gratitude to our mum and dad, Marion and John Barrowman, without whom there would never have been any stories to tell.

Now, turn the pages and sing along.

John, 2008

Chapter One

'I Hope I Get It'

The scene opens with a high shot of Covent Garden. Tourists are clustered around a street performer who has a sword balanced on his forehead and tea plates spinning on a tray in each hand. The weather is unseasonably warm for June, so a few of the foreign tourists wandering in the crowded, cobbled square are carrying colourful umbrellas for shade. From this lofty angle, it looks as if someone has tipped a box of Smarties on the ground below.

Enter our leading man stage left.

That would be me.

A soprano's voice rises from the cafe tucked underneath the open-air market, a cocky vendor scolds a shopper for ignoring his patter; all around, laughing children, honking taxis, boisterous students and the release of air from the brakes of a nearby double-decker tour bus blend to create a cacophony of sounds. This is summer in London's West End.

A teenage girl accompanies our leading man.

That would be my niece Clare, my sister Carole's daughter. Every year since they were quite young, she and her brother Turner have spent time with me during their school holidays; an invitation that's open to all my nieces and nephews when they're old enough to travel on their own.

The leading man and his niece are chattering away, despite the fact that she has to skip every few steps to match his stride.[1] After a beat, it becomes clear from the way our leading man is weaving through Covent Garden's busy marketplace that he's on a mission.

Oh, I was. I was between performances of Trevor Nunn's revival of *Anything Goes*, which was in full swing at the Theatre Royal Drury Lane. The matinee usually finished around five and that gave me an hour or so to myself before the evening performance. After nearly twenty years in theatre, doing eight shows a week, down time is personal time and personal time for me means shopping.

The camera zooms in for a close shot on our leading man and his niece, who are carrying packages while eating sandwiches from Marks and Spencer's.

Clare was devouring a chicken with lettuce on white, a bag of crisps and a Crunchie. She's short, but despite her sweet tooth, she's in good shape. I was scarfing down two avocado-and-spinach sandwiches, prawn crisps, and a bag of Percy Pigs. I'm tall and I was hungry.

The shot widens on the two as they approach Endell Street. We hear the leading man's phone ring. He fumbles his food trying to answer quickly. He stops frozen in his tracks. His niece walks up his heels. She looks at the leading man anxiously because he never stops moving ever, especially when he's shopping.

Cut to close-up of leading man looking stunned.

I was, in fact, gobsmacked. It wasn't so much the nature of the call itself that was shocking, but that it had come through so quickly. I've been to hundreds of auditions over the years and one of the

---

[1] Clare's short … well, she is.

basic tenets an actor can count on is the wait between the audition and the decision to give you the part or not. The time between you leaving that audition room and 'Congratulations, you've got the role,' or 'I'm sorry, but you're too young / too old / too good-looking / too tall'[2] can drag on for days or even weeks. Hours was simply unheard of.

Camera follows Clare setting the packages down on the pavement in front of a tea stand.

'Uncle John, are you okay?'

Leading man nods.

It was more of a grunt and a mad bob of my head, but that doesn't sound nearly as suave. In fact, I have very little memory of Clare talking to me at that moment, but she remembers everything in crisp detail. She said she could hear Gavin Barker, my manager and close friend, talking excitedly on the phone. She claims I was not responding coherently. She remembers hearing bursts of applause from the crowd gathered around the street performer and working hard to block it out.

What I remember is 'blah, blah, blah, blah, blah' because my brain stopped working at Gavin's first line: 'John, they want you to be Captain Jack!'

Camera cuts quickly to our leading man jumping off the ground, punching the air with his fists and letting out a rebel yell.

Actually, what I screamed was, 'I'm going to be in the TARDIS!'

Camera zooms in on Clare, who has no clue what the hell is going on, but is used to her uncle's antics and joins him in his manic celebratory dance. They leap and laugh and holler for a few minutes, and then the angle widens on our leading man performing a stunt that would make Keanu Reeves ask for paracetamol.

Here's what I did. I let go of Clare and I took a running leap up

---

[2] I've heard all of these comments at least once from casting agents or producers.

the side of the wall, did a kind of half flip and landed on the kerb, nearly knocking over an old-age pensioner, who was watching the scene from the tea stand. I managed to catch her before she toppled off her chair, and despite my heightened emotions and frenzied behaviour, I remember thinking that I was lucky she hadn't fallen, because I'd be late for the curtain if I had to wait for an ambulance.

Camera cuts to a close-up of the leading man apologizing to the elderly woman, while Clare gathers up the old lady's messages that have fallen over. 'Messages' is Glaswegian for groceries; as I am a Glaswegian by birth, it's one of the many Scottish words and phrases that, even after all these years, remain in my vocabulary.[3] However, of all the things I remember from this day – the time, the place, the going all *Matrix* on the wall – this pensioner's response to the entire scene still makes me smile the most.

She looked up at me and said, 'Must've been good news, eh, son?'

It was the best bloody news ever and it was the result of another phone call a few months earlier. I'd been lounging between scenes in my dressing room at the Theatre Royal, where I was playing Billy Crocker in *Anything Goes* for the third time in my career,[4] when the call came in. The Theatre Royal Drury Lane is London's oldest theatre and, because of this, its dressing rooms are bigger than most of those in younger theatres. Mine had enough space for a couch, a few comfy chairs and a full bar, which – despite what the tabloids may sometimes have fans believe – was actually used sparingly. I was watching the end of a DVD, something I often did

---

[3] Keep an eye out for the others. There may be a quiz later.
[4] I'll tell you about the other times later.

to pass the time, while my dresser, John Fahey, was preparing my costume for the next change, when Gavin rang.

'Andy Pryor just called me. He thinks there might be a role in the new *Doctor Who* you'd be perfect for,'[5] he said.

At this point in my career, I'd been on television in the UK and in the US. I'd been a presenter on *Live and Kicking* and *The Movie Game*, and I'd played a John F. Kennedy Junior type in Darren Starr's drama *Central Park West*, and a similar character in Aaron Spelling's short-lived night-time soap *Titans*; however, I was most known for my work in musical theatre. I'd starred in a number of Broadway and West End musicals, including Stephen Sondheim's *Company*, Sir Cameron Mackintosh's *Miss Saigon* and Lord Lloyd-Webber's *Sunset Boulevard*, and, in 1998, I was nominated for an Olivier Award for Best Performance of an Actor in a Musical for my role in *The Fix*, directed by Sam Mendes. I'd recorded two solo albums and a number of cast recordings, sung 'Springtime for Hitler' in Mel Brooks's film of *The Producers*, and performed 'Night and Day' in the biopic about Cole Porter, *De-Lovely*. To many West End producers, I was considered musical theatre's quintessential leading man and I loved all that this allowed me to do, but a part in the new *Doctor Who* would top all of that.

My sister Carole, who is eight years my senior, and my brother Andrew, who is older by five, had been fans of the Doctor since his inception on the BBC in the sixties, but I was too young to remember those original early episodes. I became a serious Whovian when I watched the series on WTTW Channel 11, Chicago's public television affiliate, in the late seventies and early

---

[5] Andy is a casting director for *Doctor Who* and *Torchwood*. Please do not send your tapes to him or he'll come after me.

eighties.[6] In case you're unaware of such things, *Who* fans are 'Whovians'; and I like to call *Torchwood* fans, 'Woodies'. *Doctor Who* ran on Sunday nights in a British package that included *Dave Allen at Large* and *Monty Python's Flying Circus*, but for me it was the Doctor I enjoyed the most … and I loved them all. Jon Pertwee, Tom Baker and Peter Davison ruled my Sunday evenings. I'd avoid homework, imagine eating Jelly Babies[7] and let myself be carried off to other galaxies. To this day, I'm a terrable (oops) terrible speller. I blame the Doctor.

The Brigadier and Sarah Jane, Autons, Cybermen and Daleks all flashed in front of me while Gavin gave me the details of the audition for Captain Jack.

Andy Barnicle, my acting teacher at the United States International University in San Diego, once told me that for an audition the key is to remember that producers don't always know how they want a character to be read, therefore the actor's job is to sell them his or her interpretation. So I imagined who Captain Jack might be.

I almost got it right.

The audition was in a room at the BBC in Shepherd's Bush, and the script from which I'd been asked to prepare was 'The Empty Child', written by Steve Moffat. The scene was the one where Jack first explains to Rose that he's a con man. Russell T. Davies, the executive producer and the creative force behind the new series, Phil Collinson, the show's producer, and Andy Pryor sat across the room from me at the audition.

After introductions, I began. I read the first part of the scene as an American, but when Jack reveals to Rose that he's not who he

---

[6] Stay with me, now. My family moved to the US in 1976. More on that later.
[7] You can't buy them in America.

appears to be, I switched to a Scottish accent and finished the scene that way. My reasoning was that a British character might have more impact and, therefore, I'd stand a better chance of being chosen for the role; after all, as far as I knew, there'd never been an American male cast as a regular character in any of the classic series.

'Can you do it again with an English accent?' asked Andy.

I could have done the entire bloody scene in an ancient Babylonian dialect if they'd asked. That's how badly I wanted the role. In the end, I performed the scene three times using three different dialects. Top that, Hugh Laurie. Eventually, the audition ended, but instead of leaving the room, the four of us ended up in a conversation sharing stories about the original *Doctor Who*, our favourite assistants, our scariest villains, our pick for best episode.[8]

From its start, I had a really good vibe about the audition and I knew my performance was strong – well, at least one of them. However, as any actor who's ever been in this situation will tell you, sometimes good isn't good enough. Plus, I was still a relative unknown in the British television market. Would they take a risk on an American? Would they see beyond the limitations that producers too often put on musical-theatre performers when it comes to working in another medium? More importantly, would they take a chance on me?

Yes, yes and yes.

At the best of times, I make a subtle first impression.[9] On the December day in 2004 when I walked on to the *Doctor Who* set in Cardiff for the first time, I was wired, bursting with energy and excitement, while Christopher Eccleston (playing the Doctor), Billie Piper (in the role of the Doctor's assistant, Rose Tyler) and the

---

[8] If you're interested, my picks are Sarah Jane, Davros and 'Terror of the Autons'.
[9] Just seeing if you're paying attention.

crew, who had been filming for months, were exhausted and ready to break for the Christmas holiday.

Billie and I hit it off immediately. Her smile and laugh are contagious and, let's face it, I don't need any encouragement in those areas either. She and I derived a great deal of pleasure from the press at the time: they were speculating wildly that Rose and Captain Jack would do more than flirt with one another. I knew from the beginning that Russell T. Davies had grander plans for Jack's character over the course of season one, but it was a kick, nonetheless, to read stories that completely underestimated the genius of Russell's imagination.

Russell had made it clear to me that Jack's character would be unlike any other in the classic *Doctor Who* series. As a result, the subtle sexual chemistry among all three characters – the Doctor, Rose and Jack – was always in play. Contrary to the tabloids' fixation, though, the relationships were by no means driven by desire. When the Doctor and Jack kiss goodbye in 'The Parting of the Ways', the episode that concludes the first season, for example, the kiss is full of fondness and respect, and absolutely no tongue. In fact, when the director Joe Ahearne called 'cut' at the end of that take, the crew whistled and applauded because the moment was not only a significant one in the annals of the series, but it was also a moment full of melancholy and loss for the characters. We all felt it.

My first day on the set of *Doctor Who* turned out to be long and draining, a trial by barrage balloon, and when we were finally ready for the last shot on the day's schedule, the adrenalin that had been fuelling my first few hours was seriously dissipating. The final scene to be filmed followed chronologically from the one I had performed for my audition. It's the London Blitz, and Rose and Captain Jack are sipping champagne while dancing on a Chula warship that's hovering in front of Big Ben.

In other words, the final scene of my first full day had to be performed while acting in what's called 'negative space'. This meant that for part of the take I had to act to nothing: no other actors, no other props, just John standing on a green platform in front of a large green screen. After the special effects had been added, the platform would become the Chula warship and the screen would transform into Big Ben and the surrounding London skyline. Achieving these dramatic images is a prolonged process under the best circumstances, demanding twice as many takes and set-ups, and with a special-effects team involved as well as the regular crew.

At this point in the day, everyone was so ready to go home.

Billie and I stepped up on to the small platform that would magically become the warship. The sparkling ginger ale that looks like (even if it doesn't taste like) champagne was poured. The lighting, hair, make-up, wardrobe and sound were checked and double-checked. The shot with Rose and Captain Jack was good to go.

According to the script, I was expected to waltz with Billie while giving a few lines, and then finish with a spin that would bring us around to a particular spot on the platform, where I would face the camera and conclude my dialogue.

'Do you want a choreographer, John?' asked the director, James Hawes.

Silence. I mean absolute utter silence – a silence so big a Chula warship could have towed a fighter jet through it and there'd still have been room for the TARDIS. The crew was knackered. Their day was pushing twelve hours. The last cup of tea was cold and the biscuits were all gone. I was fried, and I needed to get to London within the next two hours if I was going to make my flight to Florida, where my partner of fourteen years, Scott Gill, and I were spending the holidays with my family. To ask for a choreographer would slow down the entire process, and we'd run into overtime, to say nothing of what message my response would send to the crew about me as a performer.

I looked at Billie.

She smiled and shrugged. 'It's your call, John. I'll follow your lead.'

And so, on top of a Chula warship, I danced to my own tune, to my own steps, the way I've been dancing for most of my life.

Chapter Two

'Milly, Molly, Mandy'

The medieval artist Hieronymus Bosch's triptych[1] depicting the Fall of Man hangs in all its decadent glory in the Prado museum in Madrid. In 1993, on one of our first vacations together, Scott and I visited Madrid and Barcelona, and the Prado was a highlight of the trip. Bosch's most famous work, *The Garden of Earthly Delights*, has inspired the devoted and the disturbed for centuries. At the bottom right-hand corner of his renowned depiction of tortured souls trapped in the underworld, a tiny bawling baby is swaddled in a white shawl next to a fish-like creature devouring a man's leg. That baby is me. I was the baby from hell.

From the moment I was born on 11 March 1967, I cried constantly, screaming in a pitch my family claims has permanently damaged their ability to hear certain sounds. On the plus side, my parents never hear their doorbell when a salesman rings, and now, frankly, they miss most of what they say to each other.[2]

When my niece Clare was born in 1987, she too was burdened with the crying gene, yet somehow her screams solicited immediate

[1] It's always good to learn a new word. There will be more.
[2] Mum, I'm kidding. Really.

kindly attention from my mum and dad, who had the gall to suggest that their response to her crying was because she was the first grandchild. But these were just excuses, excuses, excuses. Deep down, I believe they were able to tolerate her squalling because my loud infancy had prepared them for whatever cranky colicky baby would come their way.

My dad claims that if I'd been the first one born, I'd have been the last one born. It didn't matter what my mum or dad did – the regular rocking on the chair next to the cot until tracks were etched deep into the floor, the soft music, the loud music, the lullabies, the threats and, eventually, in complete desperation and fear for their marriage and their sanity, a little whisky in the dummy – nothing calmed me.

Oh, get over yourself, don't tell me you haven't thought about slipping the little one a wee dram in the dummy in the middle of the night after four days without sleep and one-hundred-and-forty-two cups of tea, most of which you've ended up spilling on your pyjamas. Never having had any children of my own,[3] I hesitate to give any parenting advice in these pages, but I must ask the question: really, could I have been that bad?

Barrowman family lore is that I was worse than bad, and so over the years I've become okay with blaming my brother and sister for my insufferable infancy. My brother Andrew was five when I was born and Carole, the eldest, was eight. When my mum brought me home from the hospital and I was first introduced to them, they seriously freaked out. I know you're thinking that there's no way I can really remember these details from my infancy and early childhood, but in my family these stories are legendary. If you don't trust me, just ask my mum.

---

[3] Of this I know and I'll tell you how I know in a later chapter.

'Eeeew!' Andrew yelped, taking two steps back.

'He looks like Sooty,' Carole proclaimed with as much compassion.

Their reactions were based on the fact that my tongue, lips and most of the inside of my mouth were blue. I don't mean a dull, grey-toned, oxygen-deprived blue, which would've been bad enough. I mean a full-out periwinkle, the kind of blue that looks fabulous in a bold stripe on an Etro shirt, but not so gorgeous on a baby's face. My mouth was this odd hue because of an ointment used to kill an infection I'd contracted when I was born.

Blue mouth or not, I still think 'demon child' and 'freak of nature' were excessive responses from my own sibling flesh and blood. I don't care how old they were. Most other five- and eight-year-olds would have been much more adult and mature in their reactions. Therefore, it's my contention that I responded noisily to this initial tetchy sibling bonding and decided to punish them severely for it during the rest of my infancy. I believe I may have let out a loud wail at the exact moment they cried 'yuck' and I never shut my mouth again until I was … okay, I've never shut my mouth again.

According to my family, things only got worse. My constant crying sent my mum into desperation mode. My dad fared better during these years because he was at work all day. Regular double overtime, I bet. My mum began to pay Carole to take me for long walks in my pram around Mount Vernon, the Glasgow suburb where we lived, so that my mum could get a break and pamper herself a little. You know, get to the bathroom, brush her hair, bathe. Somehow, the walking seemed to stimulate my vocal cords even more.

Carole then did what any smart Scottish lass of eight would do. She outsourced the labour, paying one of the other kids in our cul-de-sac to walk me. To Carole's credit, this might have been successful, if not for Andrew, who did what any smart Scottish lad of five would do in similar circumstances, especially one who'd not been cut in on the deal. He went to the Big Man himself and told on her.

By this time, I'd been home for a couple of months. The blue mouth had faded, but I was still bawling. It was becoming painfully clear to my parents that at least as far as Andrew and Carole were concerned, the romance of having a baby brother had completely worn off. Drastic measures were called for.

After dinner one night, my mum told my brother and sister to go into the living room and sit down. A few minutes later, my dad carried me into the room concealed within a brown paper bag.

'Why's the baby wrapped up?' asked Andrew, puzzled.

'He's going in the bin,' my dad replied.

My mum stood stoically next to him and her performance was of Academy Award calibre, as good as Joan Crawford any day.[4] Mum even had props, clutching my little booties in her hands.

'But why are you putting him in the bin?' asked Andrew.

'Because you two don't seem interested in having a wee brother, and your mum and I think we should just get rid of him before we all get too attached.'

Even at such a young age, Carole was used to my dad's sense of humour. She'd survived his silly walks in public, his clownish falls in front of her friends, his dressing in drag at family parties,[5] and his elaborate games of hide-and-seek, where he would risk life and limb to be the last one found. Once, soon after my parents were married – 1954 in Shettleston, if you're interested – he left work early one

---

[4] Any comparisons to Joan Crawford from now on are purely for her acting ability and in no way imply any coat-hanger incidents in my childhood.

[5] Oh, trust me, that's another chapter.

night just so he could get home to plan a prank before my mum came in from her office job.

They'd recently moved into a flat in East Kilbride. When my dad got home that evening, he climbed into the coal bunker, which, in the 1950s, was often located in the hallway of a flat. He crouched inside that bunker for hours, until my mum finally came home, ate her tea, tidied up the flat and climbed into bed. All so he could scare her shitless by turning off the lights and throwing lumps of coal against the bedroom door.

He played jokes like this on her so many times that, one night, she sat in bed in the pitch dark for four hours, swearing at him for turning off the lights, yet refusing to get out of bed for fear he would drop zombie-like from the top of the wardrobe, which, in fact, he'd done once already to her (and has done since a number of times in my memory, too). As it turned out, that particular night East Kilbride had experienced a power failure and my dad wasn't even home. My mum was shouting over and over to herself for hours: 'John! Turn on the lights. I'm not getting out of bed. I know it's you. John!'

My dad didn't just contain his antics to his children and his wife. When my niece Clare was about seven and her brother Turner was four, they spent a weekend with my mum and dad. During the visit, Clare and Turner had to go to a neighbour for help to extricate my dad from a narrow basement cupboard, where he'd gotten stuck during a particularly competitive game.

So Carole knew better and she called my dad's bluff.

'You don't mean it, Daddy.'

But my dad was at the ready and began taping the paper around me until I was neatly swaddled in the brown bag. My dad was good. He had perfected the set-up, but it was my mum who threw the hook and finally roped Carole and Andrew in for the sting. From her pocket she produced a label with 'My name is John Scot Barrowman' already printed on it.

During my childhood, my mum regularly participated in my dad's elaborate cons and pranks, but she was always the one who, when it was clear the three of us were teetering close to a meltdown as a result of one of his jokes, would intervene with, 'That's enough, John,' or 'John, that's not fair, they're only wee.'

Like the time we were all on a caravan holiday in England. On our way south to the Isle of Wight, we stopped overnight at a campsite because it was raining so hard. As we were getting ready for bed, I noticed Dad was gone.

'Where did Daddy go?'

'I don't know,' my mum replied, innocently. 'Carole, Andrew, did you see what happened to your dad?'

They hadn't, of course, but now she'd amped the anxiety level because we knew some terrible, funny fright was coming. Suddenly, the lights went out, and then the clincher: footsteps on the roof of the caravan – yup, the roof – rapid, pounding and very scary.

'It must be ghoulies,' said my mum, eyes wide in mock distress.

The ghoulies were, in fact, our favourite Barrowman bogeymen. In our house they regularly loomed in dark corners, grabbed from under beds, fell from wardrobes, lurched from the back of dark closets, and howled at the moon.

In the caravan that night, I was the first to burst into tears. Andrew froze. Carole claimed it was 'just Daddy', but she still eased closer to my mum. By this time, the storm was blowing so hard that the caravan was shaking. The three of us started to scream.

'John, that's enough. John! They'll never sleep tonight.'

Then there was a heavy thumping at the door, followed by scratching against the metal of the jamb.

'You answer it, John,' said Carole and Andrew to me, in unison.

They shoved me toward the door, as they always did in these situations. I slowly opened it, and sure enough my dad fell like Frankenstein's monster on to the caravan floor. He was soaking wet, freezing cold, and his fingers were raw from climbing up on to the caravan's roof. To this day, it takes a hell of a lot to scare the three of us because nothing will ever be as terrifying as my dad's practical jokes.

When my mum began attaching the label with my full name to the brown paper bag, despite her bravado Carole broke first, followed quickly by Andrew. They promised to be better siblings and they agreed to stop trying to sell me to the highest bidder among their friends.

I'd like to say that this was the only time in my early childhood that my family tried to get rid of me, but, according to my dad, it wasn't and I 'just kept coming back'. My mum remembers one time when she and Murn, my gran on my mum's side,[6] were walking behind me in Argyle Street in Glasgow. I was driving a Matchbox car on the wall of C&A as I walked, lost in my own world, humming to myself. My mum grabbed Murn's arm and they ducked inside the store, leaving me toddling on ahead. They had a great laugh at my expense when I turned around and couldn't see them behind me.

In my humble opinion, they were damn lucky I always found them because, while I may have been a noisy wee so-and-so throughout most of my childhood, I was also the highlight of their parties.

My parents loved to entertain and among their circle of friends and neighbours in Scotland, and in Illinois after our move to the States, Marion and John Barrowman's parties were renowned. My

---

[6] Gran's name was really Marion Anderson, but she couldn't pronounce it when she was little. She'd say 'Murn Adden'. The moniker stuck.

dad, who was a skilled draughtsman, designed and built an extension on to the back of our house on Dornford Avenue in Mount Vernon just for their parties. The Extension – with capital letters as it came to be known – was off-limits to Carole, Andrew and me except when our parents were entertaining, which they did (at least in my childhood memory) every night.

Kitted out with a bar, modern leather furniture – and when I say 'modern', I mean seventies' 'pleather' chic – and room for dancing, The Extension was *the* gathering place in Mount Vernon. Before the party would kick into full swing, Carole, Andrew and I were sent to bed, or Murn and her sister, our Auntie Jeannie, would take us to spend the night at the 'high flats' at Sandyhills, where Murn lived. We called them the 'high flats' because everything around them was, well, low: post-Second World War prefabricated houses surrounded the flats.

My mum knew better than to feed us dinner on those nights because we were going to get sick on the sweets Murn would give us anyway, so why waste a good meal? The three of us would sit in front of the huge picture window in our living room and stare down the street, watching for Murn and Jeannie to appear round the corner with their goodies. Murn would bring Andrew some Walnut Whips, which – and I have no idea why this was the case, I'm thinking it had something to do with the nut – were considered adult sweeties in our house. Crunchies and Milky Ways were for the weans,[7] but Walnut Whips and Turkish Delights were for grown-ups. Murn would bring Carole packets of Maltesers or Cadbury's Flakes, while I'd inhale bags of Jelly Babies and Wine Gums.

'Ask Wee John[8] to give us a song before he goes?' someone at my parents' party would inevitably request.

[7] Which sounds like 'rains' – both common in Scotland.
[8] My dad was Big John, so I was Wee John. More about the burden of that name later.

They never had to ask me twice. I even had my own 'microphone': a stainless-steel drinks measure that I kept tucked behind some bottles on the bar.

My favourite parties, though, were the ones they threw at New Year's Eve, or for the Scots among ye, Hogmanay, which in Scotland is a night more revered and more publicly celebrated than Christmas. Until I was about six, I always thought Hogmanay sounded like 'hug many', which I still think fits the occasion and, in fact, ought to be a rule of life. I once read that for centuries the Scottish Presbyterian Church tried to ban excessive celebrating at Hogmanay, believing that it all smacked too much of paganism. Of course it did. Most good celebrations still do. Think Carnival in Rio, Mardi Gras in New Orleans, and a dinner party at Graham Norton's house. Hogmanay was an event to relish, and even as young as I was, I still have vivid memories of those evenings.

A neighbour whose name has long since left my memory would don his kilt, haul out his bagpipes, grab his bottle for first-footing,[9] and begin his descent down the hill of Dornford Avenue; a literal and figurative descent because very few adults were left standing by morning.

The night started with the ceremonial ringing of the local church bells, and then the aforementioned neighbour would stand at the top of the road, prime his sack, clear his pipe and proceed to wail. In case you're not aware of it, let me tell you, bagpipes are actually a bitch to play. Many years later, my parents bought me my own set and I attempted to learn. The damn things are impossible

[9] This ritual demands that the first person to put a foot across your threshold after the stroke of midnight on New Year's Day must carry a drink to share. Some Scots have been known to implement it on the occasional Saturday night in August. I'm kidding.

and I could never get more out of them than a sound like cats being strangled.[10]

The telltale wail of the pipes echoed down the street. Kids and adults alike darted out of their houses, falling in line behind him, and at the stroke of midnight he'd march down the road like a tartan Pied Piper, the sounds of 'Scotland the Brave' drawing even the crabbiest of our neighbours outside. (I'm not mentioning her name here. Her children will be adults now and likely in charge of processing parking tickets. Believe me, I need to cover my arse in that area.)

When I was allowed to stay up until the bells, the highlight for me was watching everyone crowd into The Extension and then the singing would begin. My mother has a beautiful voice and like the Barrowman party gene, this is a trait I'm glad to have inherited.

At family gatherings as well as parties, it wouldn't take long for someone to say, 'Gie us a song, Marion,' and she, like me, would always oblige. As a kid, I remember being impressed that she knew the words to every song she was asked to sing. If the party were a Barrowman gathering, one of my dad's brothers would harmonize with her. Each one had particular songs they liked to hear my mum sing. My Uncle Alex would add harmonies to a Sinatra number or something from the Big Band era, while my Uncle Charlie loved the more melodic, wistful numbers like 'We're Two Little Lambs'. My Uncle Neil would take off his shoes and hum.[11] After a few verses, the whole room would join in. This kind of evening was what I thought adulthood was all about. Family, friends and lots of singing. Okay, let me rephrase that. Family, friends, a wee bevvy and lots of singing.

---

[10] No actual cats were hurt in the creation of this metaphor.
[11] Couldn't resist. Sorry.

My mum sang at other times too, including Carole and Andrew's respective weddings, and in 2006 she performed at my civil union with Scott. Although age has diminished the range of her voice a little, it's still a big beautiful one, which is ironic given how quietly she entered the world.

My mum weighed only four pounds when she was born and at that time, in 1938, her chances of survival were slim and none, and none jumped on to the Glasgow bus and fled. My Papa Butler, whom, sadly, I never knew because I was only a year old when he died in 1968, refused to accept the prognosis that she was too tiny to survive. He and Murn brought her home to their corporation house in Shettleston, warmed up the cooker and – wait for it – placed her in the oven. She slept in the warmth of the stove until her weight rose above six pounds. She's still hot today.

All my grandparents were characters and throughout my childhood they were a significant part of my life. As a result of these relationships, issues of elderly abuse or just plain rudeness to an old person are the surest ways to rile me.

On Sunday afternoons, Carole, Andrew and I would leave on our 'itchy clothes', our name for our church clothes (sackcloth and woolly jumpers), and visit Emily and John, aka Gran and Papa Barrowman, for lunch. Gran Barrowman was an incredible baker and her sponge cakes were fluffy, airy masterpieces. I believe it's from her that I inherited my sweet tooth. Gran Barrowman's house was always freezing, but if you shivered and complained enough, she'd eventually – like Catherine Tate's hilarious character – say, 'Put another bar on, son.'

Murn was fierce and funny, and she loved to dance. When she and her sister Jeannie would take care of us on Saturday nights, Carole, Andrew and I would squeal with delight when their dancing would get wild, and Murn and Jeannie would hike up their skirts, birl like madwomen, and we'd get a gander at their bloomers. Murn also made the best fritters in south-east Scotland because she kept a jar of manky lard under her sink, reusing it whenever she deep-fried anything. One of her specialities was deep-fried Spam – just writing about it is clogging my arteries. And, man, her chips were the best.

Murn was from the 'gie them whatever they want' school of grandparenting. She was the kind of gran who would always have sweeties in her pinny pocket and could smother you in her soft chest with one hug, but she would have terrified the devil himself if he went after one of her kin. Because of a debilitating stroke in the 1970s, Murn lived with us for the last fourteen years of her life.

The year before my family emigrated to the US, I was eight, and my mum accepted a job outside the house. Hard to believe washing, cleaning and tearing around after three children and a husband wasn't all she wanted from her life. Her good friend Isabel Eusebie and her husband Joe owned a beauty salon on Shettleston Road, and next door to the salon they opened a record shop, which is where my mum worked, serving at the music-store counter.

Top of the Pops with Jimmy Savile was the barometer for hits back then, and although the shop had a wide array of albums from every genre, my strongest visual memory of the store is the walls lined with 45s, which were listed in numerical order according to their weekly chart standings.

After I finished for the day at Mount Vernon Primary School in the afternoons, I'd head straight to the record shop. My mum usually wouldn't be able to leave, so I'd sit on the counter and she'd let me play any records I wanted. Pretty soon, I was standing on the counter singing and customers were coming in just to request a song for 'Wee John' to perform.

This was the era of unforgivable, I mean unforgettable, novelty songs, ditties such as Rolf Harris's 'Two Little Boys' and The Scaffold's 'Lily the Pink', which, believe it or not, is about a real person, Lydia Pinkham, who invented cures for all sorts of female ailments, including 'flatulence and fertility'.[12] My favourite song from this era, though, was Glenn Poole's 'Milly, Molly, Mandy', a song that today can make my fillings ache.

It soon became clear to all customers in the record shop that watching 'Wee John' belt this song out, dimples and all, was worth a stop. Before too long, I was a fixture in the store, a permanent presence on the counter.

Sadly, the record shop no longer stands. During renovations years later, the building collapsed while a customer and Joe Eusebie were still inside, making that one last cut, selling that one last record.

Carole was at Bannerman High School by the time our mum got her job, and Andrew had football practice, so neither was around much to look after their little brother. When my mum couldn't pick me up after school, I'd ride the bus with Jeannie or Murn down to the record shop. One afternoon, as Murn and I were waiting at the Sandyhills bus stop for our trip to the store, she noticed I'd been crying.

'What's the matter, son?'

'My teacher keeps hitting me on the back of my head for no reason.'

Two points are important to note here. The first is that in 1973 corporal punishment was all the rage in UK schools. Secondly, if you have children or even know a child just a little, you'll appreciate that the likelihood was high that there *was* a reason. In retrospect, I'd have slapped the hell out of me too if I was singing that fucking 'Milly, Molly, Mandy' all the time.

---

12 Really makes you wonder why Jennifer Eccles, who had lots of freckles, was actually being called all those names. I dare you to listen to the song if you don't get this reference. You'll have it stuck in your head for months.

Murn was quiet for most of the bus ride and eventually I forgot that I'd told her anything about the teacher's slapping. Until two days later, when someone knocked timidly on the door of my Mount Vernon Primary School classroom. My teacher, She-Who-Shall-Remain-Nameless, was a bit startled by the knock, but asked the person to come in. In marched Murn.

With her hat pinned on her grey hair – the front curl of which was tinged with the telltale yellow from smoking – her handbag caught in the bend of her arm and her wool coat pulled tight across her ample chest, except for the nicotine curl she looked a lot like the Queen after a bad day with her corgis. Without so much as a 'How are you?' or 'I'm John Barrowman's gran,' she walked right up to the teacher and hit her across the back of her head several times, punctuating each slap with a word: 'Don't. You. Ever. Lift a hand. To a wean. Again. Ye auld bitch.'

The moment remains one of my most compelling memories. How could it not? The class was instantly silent; the teacher too stunned to move. The whole classroom became a blur to me. After Murn marched from the room, a few of my classmates started to giggle, and then their laughter became all-out babbling excitement at what had just happened. I was completely embarrassed for about ten minutes, while the teacher tried to settle us down. What I remember most about the incident is that, once I got over the initial shock, I was terrified that the teacher would call the police and Murn would get arrested. Fortunately, though, like Roxie Hart in *Chicago*, Murn escaped the law.

For some, childhood memories may be the result of wishful thinking or perhaps, tragically, the uncovering of repressed experiences that have suddenly been exposed. Neither of these things shape my memories of my childhood and I'd like to believe that for more rather than less of us this is true. When I think about what it meant to grow from a 'wean' into a 'wee boy' in Scotland, the meaning I draw from my memories as a man are defined by my family's lessons about love and laughter, and singing, lots and lots of singing.

Chapter Three

'Defying Gravity'

Our house in Mount Vernon, where I lived until I was nine, had a fenced yard for privacy and for restraining Pagan, our family dog, a mournful-looking beagle who liked to wander. When I was four years old, I figured out how to jimmy the lock on the fence's back gate, and one afternoon I decided to visit Murn at her flat in Sandyhills, about four miles away. Of course, I walked in the wrong direction and ended up in the middle of the Hamilton Road, a busy street that eventually becomes one of the main roads connecting Glasgow and Edinburgh.

The traffic whizzed past on either side of me – horns blaring, tyres screeching – until a man about my dad's age at the time realized that the obstruction the cars were swerving to avoid was actually a wean trying to cross the road. He skidded to a stop, darted from his car, and yanked me to safety. I didn't know my address, but I was able to tell the stranger my name, which he recognized. Mount Vernon in the early 1970s was still a relatively small community of middle-class homes and had not yet morphed into the sprawling Glasgow suburb that it has since become. Families who'd lived in the area for generations – as both my mum's and dad's had – knew of each other.

Leaving his car in the parking lot of The Woodend, our local pub, the stranger gripped my hand and walked me back home, where my parents and most of our neighbours were combing the streets and nearby park in a frantic search for 'Wee John'. I learned later from my mum that the stranger then proceeded to 'gie them laldy', which is to say he tore into them for not paying closer attention to a curious toddler, fenced yard or no fenced yard. To my parents' credit, they stood under their carport in front of many of their neighbours and accepted the dressing-down because they knew he was right.

I suppose it would be easy to see this experience as having some kind of symbolic significance in my life. I could've been roadkill that day, turned into mince by a Corporation bus, or, just as terrible, abducted, but since neither of those outcomes occurred, I could imply that from this incident I learned early in my life that there's a fine line (in this case a double white one) between life and death. But that'd be a load of bollocks. The experience has remained one of my most vivid early childhood memories not because of its possible figurative connotations, but because it was my first manifestation of the Barrowman risk-taking gene.[1] Over the years, that gene has shaped many of my personal and professional choices.

Anyone who grew up in Tollcross or Shettleston in the 1940s knew Emily Barrowman's boys: my dad John, and his three brothers, Neil, Charlie and Alex. Emily herself was a formidable woman and in another era she might have found herself in a position of corporate power or even practising medicine, but instead Emily was forced to leave school at fifteen to help run her family's billiard hall at

---

[1] Along with the party gene, this one is hot-wired into my system.

Parkhead Cross, which may explain another genetic cord – to this day, whether it's pocket, nine or shooter, your balls are not safe on my table.

I'm sure raising four sons often put Emily's intelligence and organizational skills to the test, especially since her husband was a meek man. My Papa Barrowman was a good father, but he was happiest with a pint in his hand and a pound in his pocket for the bookies. Like many working-class women who came of age between the world wars, Emily was essentially a single parent, and so it wasn't surprising that the exploits of her sons sometimes escaped her.

My dad and his brothers had reputations for being 'wee rascals' who grew up to be 'big toerags', and although each of them eventually became a successful professional in his own right, even as adults they never outgrew their mischievous natures or their willingness to take chances. With the exception of a mysterious fire in a Tollcross warehouse – that may still be an open case, so I'll write no more about it because I'd like to keep my dad out of Barlinnie Prison – the Barrowman boys' antics were generally harmless, but nonetheless legendary. Years later, during Barrowman family dinners, usually when we all gathered at Gran Barrowman's house in Springboig for New Year's Day dinner, my poor gran would often get a taste of her boys' adventures with her steak pie. She had never known the half of it.

I think as a result of this strand of my heritage, I have an addiction to adrenalin-fuelled activities. Over the years I've skied in the Alps, snowboarded in the Rockies, driven fast cars in Monte Carlo, sailed the Aegean, dived in the Caribbean, flown on Concorde multiple times and kite-surfed across the Straits of Gibraltar. I've gone scuba diving during a solar eclipse in Turkey, canoed inside a volcanic crater near Santorini, and I've even chanced a few Friday nights with Jonathan Ross, which can be a terrifying experience.

I've been in great shows, good shows and a few so-so shows, and even in the failed endeavours, I've never regretted my decision to accept the role because I've always gained something from chancing the experience. Once, during the short-lived London production of the musical *Matador*, in which I starred with Stefanie Powers and which ran for only three months in 1991, I learned a valuable lesson about what it meant to close a company with dignity.

One afternoon, Stefanie and I were called to a meeting with the producers to hear officially that we were closing and the financial implications of that decision. I was an emotional wreck, close to tears and feeling very sorry for myself. On our way into the room, Stefanie pulled me aside.

'Don't you say a word,' she said, her face so close to mine I could feel her breath on my cheek. 'Stop being so pathetic, John. This is not about you. Do you understand? It's about the show. Let me do the talking.'

I did as I was told and the meeting's outcome was far better than it might have been if I'd charged in with crumpled tissues in my hands. Our contracts were honoured, and she and I made it clear we were not happy with the way things were winding down.

I also took some professional grief for agreeing to participate in *Dancing on Ice* – the ITV programme on which celebrities learn to ice dance – for choosing to put myself out there in the public eye in such a physical manner and in a reality show, no less. In the acting profession, reality shows can be seen as the gigs you do only if your career is in a slump and your visibility needs a boost; it's generally thought you would never choose to do them when your career is ascending, which mine was at the time, as I was fresh from appearing in the first series of *Doctor Who*. While that perception may be true for some, I chose to be involved with *Dancing on Ice*, and later *How Do You Solve a Problem Like Maria?*

and *Any Dream Will Do*,[2] because they had high entertainment values and I'm an entertainer. These shows were far removed from the kind of 'car crash' voyeurism that can be the attraction of too many programmes; programmes that I'll admit I'm not above watching.

Agreeing to be a judge on *Maria* and *Joseph* also appealed to one of my professional values: those of us who've made it up the ladder of success should reach down when we can and offer a hand to others. *Dancing on Ice*, meanwhile, had broad audience appeal – and I wanted to show that audience, some of whom had probably not seen me in anything else I'd done, that I could entertain them.

As it turned out, poor Papa Barrowman would have lost his pound if he'd bet on me, because although the bookies had me as the favourite after the first round, I was voted off mid contest. I was crushed. When I got home that night, I ignored the messages on my answering machine from family and friends, and instead felt sorry for myself for a while. Then I got over it – because this is showbiz and a thick skin is a necessary accessory.

Despite being voted off part-way through the series, I don't regret the decision to perform at all. I learned how to skate from the masters, Torvill and Dean, made a good friend in my ice-dance partner Olga Sharutenko, and I left the show with the hardest bum I'd had in years.

Despite the risk-taking in my genes and the bravado in my actions, I'm not above worrying about death or on occasion being gripped by fear. Oscar Wilde is reported to have gasped on his deathbed that, 'Either that wallpaper goes, or I do.' From what I've

---

[2] Aka *Maria* and *Joseph*, the BBC's talent quests that I helped to judge in 2006 and 2007 respectively. The programmes searched for undiscovered performers to play the lead roles in the West End productions of *The Sound of Music* and *Joseph and the Amazing Technicolor Dreamcoat*.

read about him, Wilde's death wasn't the least bit funny, yet he never lost the ability to laugh at himself or the world around him. Now, whether or not I can be so glib when actually facing death remains to be seen in the very far-off future – everyone, on the count of three, touch wood, spin, spit and throw salt over your shoulder[3] – but in June 2007, when I was asked to participate in the launch of the Royal Air Force Tattoo, the thought that I might die in a ball of blazing jet fuel crossed my mind more than once.

Even when I'm in the comfort of first class, I'm a nervous flyer, keeping myself occupied with music, movies and any other distraction that I can legally embrace from take-off to landing. It's rarely enough, though. I can count on one hand the number of times I've flown when I've successfully managed to distract myself so that I haven't thought about the plane plummeting through the clouds to the ground at 500 miles an hour ... and bear in mind I fly a lot. However, one of those rare times of calm was on an American Airlines flight from California to London in 1992, when I was seated next to Dame Shirley Bassey.

'Dahling,' she said, in her distinctive drawl, when she noticed how nervous I was, 'nothing can happen when you're with Shirl!' Then she burst into the opening lines from her signature number, 'Goldfinger'.

The first-class cabin wasn't busy and by the time the plane reached cruising altitude, she and I were bosom buddies. In the years before 9/11 and the financial troubles the tragedy forced on the aviation industry, American Airlines used to serve caviar in its first-class cabins. An hour or so before we were due to land, Shirl leaned into me and said, 'Dahling, you know they have to throw the caviar out before landing. They're not allowed to bring it into the country. Why don't you go and ask them for what's left?'

---

[3] More about my superstitions and phobias later, I promise.

I did, and she and I devoured the remaining caviar and most of the champagne before landing. You might therefore think that my fondness for this particular flight has something to do with how smashed I was when the plane finally landed, or the fact that I'd eaten so much caviar I had gills, but you'd be wrong. My fondness was a direct result of Shirl's presence, because she's the woman, the woman with the calming touch.

The RAF had invited me to be part of the Tattoo launch partly because Captain Jack is in the RAF. Additionally, since I have dual nationality in the United States and the UK, they thought I'd be the perfect person to represent the sixtieth anniversary of the US Air Force and the RAF working and fighting together. I must admit I had a couple of personal motives for accepting this particular request out of the hundreds I regularly receive.

First of all, a serious motive. The British Armed Forces in general have allowed homosexuals to serve since 2000, and the RAF in particular has worked in partnership with the gay-rights organization Stonewall to reshape their recruitment strategies to include gays and lesbians. In 2006, I'd won Stonewall's Entertainer of the Year Award. Their positive association with the RAF factored into my decision to participate that afternoon.

My second reason was way cooler. The launch events for the Tattoo included the opportunity to fly in a Hawk fighter jet, and I'm a man who loves big, fast, loud toys.

Luckily, I get to play with a few on the *Torchwood* set. After we'd shot the first few episodes of the first series, Burn Gorman, who plays Owen on the show, made it clear that he did not like stunt driving for the team (he'd only ever driven manual cars before, and the sleek *Torchwood* SUV is an automatic). I couldn't wait to get my hands on the wheel. Eve Myles, who plays Gwen, thought she'd picked the short straw with this new arrangement, though. She doesn't like it when I drive too fast – but hey, it's TV. It needs to look good. Plus, scaring the hell out of her is a side benefit.

When I arrived at the Ministry of Defence base at Salisbury Plain that June morning, a security detail marched over to my car. As I was about to be led away, my sister Carole, who was visiting me at the time, jumped from the back seat to give me a kiss and a hug, which scared the hell out of me. She figured if I were about to plummet to my death at 500 miles an hour, our mum would have wanted her to have said a special goodbye. After prying her fingers from around my neck, I was swept away under the security detail's watchful guard. To what, I wasn't sure, but I was convinced that touching wood wasn't going to help me anymore. In all honesty, I was scared shitless.

The dread had settled in the day before, while I was sitting in my trailer on the *Torchwood* set. I'd been watching the Hawk fighter jet safety DVD that the RAF had sent me, and when I ejected the disc, my hands were clammy and my mouth was seriously woolly. Last time I'd felt this way was when Janice Dickinson marched toward me backstage at *Friday Night with Jonathan Ross*.

There were so many bloody things to clip, fasten, touch and not touch. The DVD even pointed out stuff I thought I already knew, like where to put my feet, where not to put my feet, what to do if I had to eject from the plane, and what to do so I didn't eject prematurely. But the most intimidating piece of advice was how to avoid blocking my oxygen mask with my own vomit. The answer: swallow it.[4]

For the rest of the day, I walked around the set mumbling all the things I was supposed to remember to do and not to do. My co-stars on *Torchwood*, Eve and Burn, knew something was seriously wrong

[4] Stop it. It's not that kind of book.

when I missed an opportunity to sing a dirty limerick with them during a camera set-up and instead sulked off silently to our artist chairs and sat down. By the time I returned to my flat in Cardiff Bay that night, I was seriously freaked out.

I called my manager Gavin, and told him I would still participate in the launch, but I wasn't going to fly in the Hawk no matter how fucking fabulous I'd look in the flight suit.

Gavin was quiet for a second and then he said, 'You know Connie Fisher[5] is flying in a Hawk tomorrow too? It seems her grandad was an RAF man during the Second World War and her mum had some connection as well.'

'Ye bastard!' I exclaimed, because there was no way Maria was flying high above the hills while Captain Jack was quivering in his boots.

So, despite some rumbling in my lower intestines, I arrived at the RAF base and marched off with my escort to be prepped for the flight. Connie and I were told we'd eventually land at an RAF base in Fairford, Gloucestershire, where at least sixty members of the press were waiting, including photographers and TV journalists, as well as a number of British and American Armed Forces personnel. But before we could even suit up, we had to undergo two hours of medical checks and safety preps.

Then a surprising thing happened. When the tests and preps were over, I felt much, much calmer. Two things helped my mood considerably. The first was that the pilots who were helping Connie and I kit up were so matter-of-fact about the whole experience that I figured they were not planning on dying that day.

The second was that right before the final suit checks, one of the

[5] The star of the West End's *The Sound of Music* and winner of *How Do You Solve a Problem Like Maria?*

pilots got down on his knees in front of me, pulled out a long hose that ran along the inside of my thigh and blew hard into it. By the time the air was circulating round my G-suit, I wanted to spoon with him.

Two hours later, Connie and I were finally prepped and ready. We stepped out on to the tarmac looking like we should be in *Top Gun*, but rather the musical version, where I get the hot guy in the uniform and my own fighter jet.

I climbed the portable steps into the gunner compartment, where Squadron Leader Gary Brough fastened me in, reminding me of a few last-minute safety points.

'Don't vomit into your oxygen mask.'

'Check.'

'Don't pull the yellow lever prematurely or you'll die.'

'Double check.'

We were good to go.

'Fear lend me wings,' I mumbled, channelling Clint Eastwood in *Where Eagles Dare*, one of my dad's favourite Second World War films. Frankly, any film about the Second World War is a favourite of his.

My dad has advanced degrees in business and engineering, and from 1954 until 1963, he worked at the Rolls-Royce plant in East Kilbride, a town on the south side of Glasgow. He started out working on the Merlin piston engine. He eventually moved to the design shop, where he was part of the team working on the Griffin engine that was originally in the Spitfire, and he worked on the design of the other Avon engines that made millions for Rolls-Royce in the 1950s and 1960s. My dad's love for and fascination with planes and engines have fuelled my own passion for machines of all kinds, which is why, as I sat in that Hawk with the engines roaring to life beneath me, my eyes started welling up. When he was a young man, my dad would have loved the chance to fly in a plane like this.

After release from the tower, Squadron Leader Brough engaged the throttle and we lurched forward. Through the intercom system in my helmet, he explained, 'John, the most dangerous time to fly a plane like this is at take-off and during the few minutes in the air before we reach our cruising altitude.'

'Okay,' I replied, my pulse quickening once again.

'If we need to abort before take-off, I'll yell "abort" and you need to slam both your feet on the brakes. Okay?'

'Okay,' I replied, my heart now lodged securely in my throat.

'Finally, John, if we need to abort when we're in the air, I'll yell "eject", but if that happens, you need to pull the yellow lever immediately. Don't wait for me, because if you look up and I'm already gone, it'll be too late. Got that?'

'Got it,' I rasped, my hand immediately gripping the yellow lever.

'Good man. Now, would you like to taxi this bird?'

'Thought you'd never ask,' I croaked.

The rudder pedals were at my feet and they were surprisingly fluid. I taxied the plane for a hundred yards or so[6] until we got the go-ahead to fly. When we lifted off the ground, Connie's plane was directly next to us and we rose into the clouds side by side, a duet of the finest kind.

At 15,000 feet, the Hawk was in cruise mode, and the risk of an aborted flight was now minimal. I unclenched my butt cheeks, and turned my head to ease my knotted neck muscles.

'John, are you interested in a civilian flight or a pilot's flight?'

I hesitated for only a beat. 'A pilot's flight.'

With my permission, the pilot banked the plane and we flew under and then over Connie's Hawk, eventually flipping upside

[6] I'm not a pilot, but I play one on TV.

down so that I was looking down on Connie. We could almost touch each other through our respective cockpits. The planes then swooped, banked, dived, flipped and soared, as they replicated fighter manoeuvres above the British countryside.

Our flight path took us along the southern coast of England to Cornwall, and then over the city of London. I was in awe of Gary's skill and the majesty of what I was seeing beneath us. A number of times, he pulled the plane completely vertical, and with the pressure from the G-forces pinning me hard against the seat, I could see the curve of the Earth. Fighter jets aren't allowed to fly over villages of a certain population in the UK, and so every time one loomed on the horizon, the pilot zigzagged around them, as if we were the Millennium Falcon cutting into the Death Star and I was Han Solo.

Of course, puking was inevitable. The aerial acrobatics with their resulting G-forces finally did me in. I could no longer control my rising nausea. Like most virgin flyers, I had actually paid attention to the safety instructions and with very little fumbling I managed to get my oxygen mask off in time, vomiting neatly into one of the sick bags supplied in my flight-suit pocket.

'Are you okay, John?'

'I'm brilliant,' I replied, and I really meant it.

Meanwhile, miles away, two other fighter jets had landed at Fairford to whet the press's appetite, followed quickly by a huge pug-nosed carrier. Finally, everyone looked up into the clear blue June sky and waited for the stars to appear.

When Connie and I finally streaked across the sky, we were once again flying in unison. Our Hawks banked at about 400 miles an hour, their wing tips almost touching, and then they crossed the sky from separate directions, touching down smoothly and safely.

I eventually emerged from the Hawk as if I'd been doing this all my life, which in Captain Jack's world, of course, I had. In my world, though, this was the experience of a lifetime. In fact, I was so high from the adrenalin rush and so in awe of the Hawk itself, I was almost speechless.[7]

Despite my best intentions, I did finally crash that day. After all the interviews were completed, I changed back into my civvies, climbed into my car, and collapsed. I was physically a wreck. My equilibrium was shot. I couldn't hold my head up without tidal waves of nausea washing over me. My complexion turned Daz white with a hint of Palmolive green under my eyes, and because of the G-forces my chest and legs felt as if they'd been pummelled with a baseball bat. To make matters worse, the drive back to Cardiff was through narrow, winding country roads, where trying to keep perfectly still was like asking George Michael to stay out of public toilets. Not going to happen.

Yet if I was ever asked to do this again – in fact, if I was ever asked to repeat any of my experiences – I'd have to say, fuck it, bring them on. I've no regrets.

This is what it means to be alive.

[7] Well, almost.

Chapter Four

'Journey of a Lifetime'

My favourite novel when I was a young teenager was S. E. Hinton's *The Outsiders*. The novel opens with the narrator, Ponyboy Curtis, saying, 'When I stepped out into the bright sunlight from the darkness of the movie house, I had only two things on my mind: Paul Newman and a ride home.' When I was Ponyboy's age, I actually had three things on my mind: a love for all things *Star Wars*, becoming an American boy, and an infatuation with the television show *Dallas*.

In a curious way, all three were related, each one a result of my dad choosing to accept an executive position in America with Caterpillar Inc. in 1976, when I was nine. Although I didn't realize it at the time, I can see now that each one of those youthful passions represented a piece of the man I was to become.

I was ten years old when *Star Wars* was first released. As it was for many boys of my generation, the film became one of a handful of defining cultural moments. I collected *Star Wars* figures, *Star Wars* ships, *Star Wars* books, and other bits and bobs from the *Star Wars* universe. I had *Star Wars* curtains in my bedroom, *Star Wars* sheets on my bed, every *Star Wars* action figure I could get my hands on and, of course, my very own lightsaber. When I wasn't playing with my figures, I stored them in their assigned compartments in the official Darth Vader Carry Case, which I kept on a shelf next to my model X-Wing Starfighter and my full size Tauntaun. I could, and still can, quote the exact classic line Boba Fett says in *Episode V* – 'He's no good to me dead' – tell the difference between a Sandcrawler and a Landspeeder, and deduce that the acronym TIE, as in TIE Fighter, stands for Twin Ion Engine. And like any true *Star Wars* geek, I got tongue-tied when I had the chance to talk to the Force himself, George Lucas.

The opportunity arose when I was performing at the Cannes Film Festival in 2003. I was there as part of the promotion and premiere of the biopic of Cole Porter's life, *De-Lovely*, which starred Ashley Judd and Kevin Kline. I had a few lines in the movie, but along with a number of other musical performers, including Robbie Williams, Alanis Morissette, Sheryl Crow, Natalie Cole and Elvis Costello, I also performed a Porter song in the biopic, in my case it was 'Night and Day'. At one of the many Cannes parties, I found myself literally speechless as I stood with a glass of champagne in one hand and my jaw in the other, trying to sound like a grown-up having a conversation with George.[1] Now to be playing a character like Captain Jack, who's part of a similarly iconic cultural phenomenon is, to say the very least, a bit mind-blowing to contemplate sometimes.

My family's permanent move to America in 1976 was not our first time in the US. When I was three, in 1970–1, Caterpillar, where my dad now worked, transferred him to Aurora, Illinois, for a year's stint. My dad kept a journal of this entire year, and many of the experiences we had as a family were detailed in the pages of that book (which came in handy when I came to write this one). Back then, my parents

[1] Mister Lucas to you.

embraced the trip as an educational experience, a sort of 'Barrowmans' Excellent Adventure', but with much better diction, dude. Whenever my dad managed to get an extra Friday or a Monday off work, we'd pile into the leased station wagon, a wide berth woody,[2] and we'd take advantage of the long weekend to explore the country. On each trip, my parents extended the range in different directions, covering territory that many of our neighbours in Aurora had never ventured into – which I think may be typical if you live in a city with a tourist economy. How many of my colleagues in Cardiff have actually been inside Cardiff Castle? Gareth?[3] No? It's a date, then.

One weekend during Barrowmans' Excellent Adventure, we found ourselves in the Motor City: Detroit, Michigan. We were all so busy gawking out the wagon's windows at the tall buildings, like refugees from Planet Lame, that my dad didn't realize he was driving at 5 miles an hour and holding up the traffic until he spotted flashing lights in his rear-view mirror. A cop pulled us over. Now when I say cop, I mean cop. This was not a police officer, but a true-blue, American city cop in all his lovely leather motorcycle glory. My dad weaved over to the kerb amidst a cacophony of car horns and raised middle fingers from drivers accelerating around us. Carole, Andrew and I pressed our faces against the back window, amazed and slightly terrified.

The cop pulled up directly to our rear. He touched his fingers to his forehead in a mock salute, grinned, and slowly unzipped his leather bomber jacket, exposing his black T-shirt straining tight against the line of his abs, the weight of his gun belt sitting on the edge of his muscular hips. He carefully removed his helmet.[4]

'John, we're going to get a ticket,' said my mum to my dad.

[2] Puhleeze. That's what they're called in the States.
[3] Gareth David-Lloyd, who plays Ianto in *Torchwood*.
[4] Truth, schmooth. This is my memory.

'No, we won't. Let me talk,' said my dad to my mum.

The cop stepped up to the driver's window.

'You're driving a bit erratically, sir. Is everything okay?'

'Officer, I'm sorry if we were holding up traffic, but I think we're lost,' replied my dad, in a Glaswegian accent so broad Billy Connolly would've barely understood.

'Well, goddamn, sir! You really are lost.'

We did not get a ticket. What we got instead was our own personal motorcycle escort guiding us back to the motorway.

Then there was the weekend my dad borrowed a friend's RV pop-up trailer, the kind of camper that's quintessentially American, so we could take a trip deeper into the Midwest, in particular to Springfield, Illinois, the state's capital and President Abraham Lincoln's birthplace. The camper was one of those toppers that hooked over the cab of a truck, where my parents sat, and it was fitted with a double bed over the cab, where Carole, Andrew and I stretched out in glorious but dangerous accommodations. Seriously, think what would have happened if every family in the 1950s through the 1970s had to stop suddenly. No seat belts, no air bags, no children's faces …

When the trip to Springfield began, Carole, Andrew and I felt like we were part of *The Brady Bunch*, one of my favourite television shows then and later, but by the end of the expedition, we were lucky not to have become a bunch of roasted chestnuts.

The three of us spent the journey sprawled above the cab laughing, yelling and taking potshots at each other. My mum banged on the roof to settle us down when the squabbling got out of hand, or when I'd start screaming that Andrew was threatening to roll me off the bed and on to the Formica table below.

And then we all noticed the smell.

Now, if you've ever travelled any long distances with anyone, I don't care if it's with your family, your friends or your co-workers in your carpool, eventually there's a smell. And when you can no longer seriously continue to blame your brother / sister / driver / dog or the shit spread on the fields outside, you need to turn inward to the car itself.

'Smells like something's burning,' said my mum, who on these trips was never without her knitting, which was why, come Christmas Day, the entire family would receive a home-knitted jumper, cardigan or socks[5] along with our toys and other presents.

'Andrew let off,'[6] I exclaimed.

'Did not.'

'Did too.'

Andrew attempted to roll me off the bed on to the Formica table.

'Mu-um, it's getting worse up here,' Carole whined. 'I'm going to be sick.'

'No, you're not, young lady!' shouted my mum. This ability to control random acts of fluid loss on car trips was one of my mother's superpowers. Her other special gift was the use of eyes in the back of her head, which I've heard is common among all mothers.

She turned to my dad. 'We should stop.'

'Where? There are no lay-bys in America.'

According to my dad, metaphorically, this became the mantra for the entire year my family spent tooling around the US non-stop, frantically packing in as many sights as possible in short bursts of time; however, my dad was also literally correct. There are no lay-bys in America. If cars need to stop, unless it's a mechanical emergency, they have to wait for a corporate-sponsored

---

[5] I kid you not. With toes, too. They gave new meaning to 'sweat(er)y feet'.

[6] For the toffs among you, 'to let off' means 'to fart'.

food stop or a state-sanctioned rest area. None of us had seen either in miles. Finally, my dad took an exit ramp off the motorway and pulled over.

When we all climbed out, the smell was smothering the entire camper.

'Andrew stinks.'

'John, be quiet.'

My dad walked gingerly around the camper, Andrew following him. While my mum gripped my arm, holding me back from the traffic, Carole sat on the grassy verge.

'It smells worse back here,' announced my dad.

'That's 'cause Andrew let off.'

'John, enough!'

My dad decided to crawl underneath the camper, which in retrospect was probably not the smartest thing to do because what he discovered solved the problem of the smell, but later that evening almost got Carole, Andrew and me killed.

'It looks like tar,' my dad explained. 'I must have driven through it when we passed that construction earlier.'

The mystery of the smell solved, we all climbed back inside.

As had been the case when we holidayed with our caravan in the UK, finding a place to stop and park for the night with the camper was always a test of my dad's mechanical fortitude and my mum's patience. She'd have to entertain three overly tired cranky kids, while he'd hook the vehicular beast to its various lifelines. In the campsite we found on this particular night, my dad had to string the electrical connection from the roof of the camper across a grassy area and round a couple of big trees in order to connect it to the electricity pole supplied by the camp ground. He'd just finished doing this and was walking back toward the camper, where my mum had hustled the three of us inside, when there was a loud pop, a blinding flash, some sparking wires, and a flaming current shot from the electricity hook-up near the trees and raced along the wire toward the camper.

My dad sprinted to the camper like a bat out of hell. My mum screamed, 'Get Out Of The Camper!' And for once in our lives, we listened the first time she yelled. Carole, Andrew and I came flying out of the door as the shot of electricity hit the vehicle and the entire camper lit up.

Thankfully, the fire was minor and the electrical damage to the camper minimal, but the trip was over. Neither my mum nor my dad trusted the vehicle anymore, so we headed to a motel for the night. We later realized that if the camper's faulty wiring hadn't been masked by the smell of the tar, the real culprit for the bad stench might have been discovered.

During this year of Barrowmans' Excellent Adventure, my parents met a couple, Madelyn and Glenn Brown, whom to this day remain close family friends. Glenn worked at Caterpillar with my dad in Aurora. Once or twice a week, whenever we weren't on one of our road trips, my parents would have dinner or drinks with Maddie and Glenn.

One night, they were at the Browns' home in Oswego, Illinois, enjoying an after-dinner drink in their study. I was playing with my Matchbox cars on the floor at their feet. Also on the floor was a full-size bearskin rug, a real one with the head stuffed and lounging stoically against the hardwood floor. I was asked politely to drive my cars far away from the rug.

Imagine this. I'm about three years old. I'm playing cars. I have a large dead animal spread across the floor next to me. What would any self-respecting child do? Exactly. And that's just what this child did. According to my mum, I began to rev my cars and drive them nearer and nearer to the rug.

'John, get your cars away from that bear. Now!' called my mum before I could get too close.

I wheeled my cars across the floor again and then, when I thought the coast was clear, I crept closer. On this occasion, my dad grabbed me by the collar and pulled me out of reach before I could actually touch the bear.

This time, I stayed away a bit longer, but the bear was calling to me – 'John, John, touch me' – and pretty soon I was inching closer again. My parents had had enough. My mum picked me up, carried me into the hallway and deposited me on the floor. She gathered up my cars, and she and my dad said their goodbyes. But just as Maddie opened the front door, I turned around, sprinted back into the study, and with all my might kicked the bear hard on the side of its head.

My parents were furious. The next time we were at the Browns, the rug was nowhere to be seen. For the Browns and for my parents, the incident with the bear has become one of those moments when adults believe they see the spark of some future personality trait in a child. Thankfully, for all concerned – including wildlife – the story has had more to do with my mischievous and stubborn streak than with my choice of career.

Barrowmans' Excellent Adventure ended with our return trip to the UK via the *QE2*, a voyage where I participated in my first talent contest, winning first prize – not because of my voice, but because of how cute I looked in a bikini. Seriously. My dad dressed me up, stuffed my boobs, dolloped on generous amounts of make-up, and put a banner across my chest that read 'Queen of the Nile'.[7]

The Excellent Adventure turned out to be a prequel to our emigrating to the States five years later, when my dad accepted the

---

[7] So it's my dad's fault.

position of Manufacturing Manager at Caterpillar's Aurora plant. With this move, I officially became a legal alien.

Murn had her stroke soon after we returned from the Adventure, and subsequently moved in with us. As she was already living with us in Mount Vernon when my dad landed his new job, she too came to America. For her, the trip was both more and less of an ordeal than it was for the rest of us. For one, we were her family, my mum her only child, and Carole, Andrew and I her only grandchildren. For that reason, the move was a no-brainer for her; however, she was in her sixties, debilitated from the stroke and had never left the UK, so psychologically I know it had to be a tough move.

The stroke had left Murn with speech difficulties and she seemed to regress to a childlike state at times, but I never had any problems understanding her. She never lost her sense of humour or her sweet tooth. When she'd go to bed at night, our dog Pagan and I would follow her. I'd climb into bed next to her for a wee 'coorie',[8] while Pagan would climb up on to the bed, salivating a little because Murn always kept a secret stash of sweeties in her night-table drawer.

Eight years after we emigrated, in 1984, Murn passed away. The morning she died, I was supposed to be picked up from high school by my mum. We had planned to go into Chicago for an audition for a television commercial. I stepped into the school's parking lot and saw my dad's secretary Leota standing next to the car instead of my mother, and I knew something was wrong. I didn't say a word or utter a cry until I got home, where I went straight to the kitchen to find my mum. As soon as I saw her, we both collapsed against each other. We were devastated – the whole family was. My siblings and I felt the loss especially, because Murn had been a major part of

[8] The kind of cuddle that only mums and grans can give you.

our lives since birth. At that time, Carole was teaching in South Dakota and Andrew was living in Chicago. They both came home immediately.

Although Murn had left Scotland with us in 1976 – and always thought she'd left behind all her friends – I think the number of people who attended her memorial service in Joliet would've moved her. I was then a member of Joliet West High School's swing choir and the choir sang at the funeral. In her lifetime, Murn had travelled with my mum to all of our concerts. After the service, my mum remained behind at the church, while Carole, Andrew and I went with my dad to the crematorium, where we stayed with the coffin until it was out of our sight.

In the last years of her life, Murn was convinced Lake Michigan was the Atlantic. Whenever my mum and I went into Chicago with her, Murn would insist on sitting on the boardwalk, where she'd stare across the water with a bittersweet longing. A few months after her death, my mum and dad carried Murn's ashes back to Scotland, sprinkling some on the grave of her husband, Andrew 'Papa' Butler; the rest they sprinkled near Loch Lomond.

The Barrowmans arrived in the United States as permanent residents in the May of 1976. When I started school in Aurora, Illinois that September, my Scottish accent became an audible characteristic of difference and the easiest way for others to taunt me. So, I adapted. Over the course of the next couple of years, I became bidialectical, a term Carole uses to describe our ability to switch dialects. A few have suggested that there may be something a bit schizophrenic about this vocal-code switching; my response to that is bring on the padded suit, because it's the least crazy thing about me. My sister mastered this dialect switching for similar reasons and she does it effortlessly too. My brother Andrew's accent, though, is more a blend of Scottish and American. His voice sounds pretty much the same no matter who his audience; whereas Carole and I talk with our Scottish accents to each other and to our parents, but with American accents to everyone else. My mum and dad, on the other hand, still sound as Scottish as the day they climbed on the plane at Prestwick.

Carole was seventeen when we emigrated, Andrew was fourteen, and they were not happy campers. Actually, this is an understatement. They were pissed. They hated leaving their friends and did not want to rethink their futures, which as teenagers they had already planned out in considerable detail. But my parents pulled a slick move on them. They cut a deal. Give it a year, my parents said. If after that either of you still wants to return to Scotland, then you may.

Of course, they knew what would happen. Carole went off to university in Illinois, finished degrees in journalism and English, and met her husband, Kevin Casey, in a postgraduate history seminar. She's now a writer and a Professor of English at Alverno College in Wisconsin. Carole and Kevin have two children, Clare and Turner, and they've been married since 1982.

Someone tossed a ball at Andrew and that's all it took for him. He became the kicker for his high-school football team,[9] a leader on Aurora University's soccer team, and he was invited to play on the US Olympic soccer team in 1980 – sadly, the year the US boycotted the games. He's now in sales management for Nicorp in Illinois. In 1997, Andrew married Dorothy (Dot), and they have a son, Andrew,[10] whose soccer skills may well rival his dad's, and two beautiful and feisty daughters, Yvonne and Bridgett.

As for my opinion of the emigration, I was nine when we left Scotland and my main concern was that the only way to get to

[9] American football, of course.
[10] Both Andrews, my brother and my nephew, are named after my mum's dad, Andrew Butler.

America was on a plane – I was seriously freaked about flying, a phobia that still plagues me despite my stunts on Hawk fighter jets and frequent trips on Concorde.

The area in which my parents bought their first house in America was Prestbury, a suburb of Aurora. It had a private swimming pool for the residents and as soon as we moved in, my parents made a rule. Lifeguard or no lifeguard, I couldn't hang out at the pool until I learned to swim. Every day after school, I'd ride in the school bus from my grade school to swimming lessons at the nearby high school, and every day this large spotty dick of a kid would get on the bus and at some point on the journey he'd climb over the seats and sit on me, flicking my face with his dirty fingernails.

As a child I had a few phobias, and as an adult I've added a couple more – okay, I've added a lot. Then and now, I can't stand anyone touching my face or my neck. Obviously this is a bit of a challenge when I have to wear make-up for TV or photo shoots. I've learned to suck it up and be brave. My *Torchwood* make-up artists, Claire Pritchard-Jones and Marie Doris, have tricks they pull when they need to chunk my hair or use their fingers near my face or neck, distracting me with shopping catalogues, sweeties or cute bums when they need to. When I played Che in a concert production of *Evita* in Oslo, Norway, I loved the show, but it was torture every night having a beard glued to my face. My immediate family shares this peculiar phobia for face and neck fondling. Being able to use this odd trait to annoy my big sister was one of my great triumphs as a little brother.

When Clare and Turner were young but old enough to use this power wisely, I taught them how to harass their mother this way. Think of me as Obi Wan to their Luke and Princess Leia. Whenever we get together as a family, Carole is on edge for a while because she knows at some point, usually early in the morning, usually right after Kevin sneaks out from the room, Clare, Turner and I are going to attack her with our ferocious morning breath and lick every inch of her face and neck.

So, in grade school when Spotty Dick began to sit on me daily and violently rub my face and neck, I made a decision to do something about it. Even at nine years old, I knew that bullying happens for lots of reasons, ones that are usually more complicated for the bully than for the bullyee,[11] but knowing this never made the face-flicking and the chest-sitting any less painful. I knew exactly what I needed to do to make it stop. I had to get off that fucking bus.

After dinner one night, I excused myself from the table, went downstairs to the basement and dug my swimming trunks out of the laundry, where I'd tossed them when I'd come home from lessons that afternoon. They were still damp, but I didn't care. I stripped off my clothes, pulled on the damp trunks, grabbed a towel from the rack in the bathroom and snuck out of the house. I ran to the Prestbury swimming pool, where I climbed the locked gate, and then I chucked myself in at the deep end.

My plan was to sink or swim. After a handful of lessons, I believed I knew enough of the basics to figure out the necessities, but no matter what happened, I wasn't getting on that school bus with Flicka ever again. After thrashing wildly for a few panicked moments and swallowing gallons of water, I finally figured out a rhythm and within a half-hour I was gliding effortlessly – at least in my mind – up and down the pool.

I learned later that my clandestine getaway to the pool was not as stealthy as I'd hoped. My parents had followed me, my dad fully prepared to dive to my rescue at any gagging moment.

---

[11] My book, my word.

I went from grade school into junior high while we lived in Prestbury and it was at this time, like Ponyboy in Hinton's *The Outsiders*, that I experienced the first real challenges to my identity and the boy I perceived myself to be.

I chose to play the flute in the junior-high band because I loved listening to Jean-Pierre Rampal and James Galway, and because Juleen and Nadine Johnson, the daughters of close family friends, also played. The other boys in the school band played the bigger, brassier instruments.[12] Before going into band practice after school, the band director would line us up according to our sections: wind and strings on left, brass and percussion on right. John on left, most of the other boys on right.

During this time in my adolescence, my love of music was channelled through playing the flute. I stayed with it and continued to play in the band all the way through junior high and into high school, at which time I realized, during my high-school freshman year, that my voice was a better, stronger instrument for me. Although I was never great on the flute, I was good enough to play at Carole and Kevin's wedding in 1982 and I still love to listen to a flute played well.

In the course of my first year in junior high, someone somehow learned that my family nickname was 'Wee John'. This became a regular taunt as the boys in the brass section strutted down the hall to get in line. Years later, after we'd moved to Joliet, Illinois, where my dad became General Manager of Joliet's Caterpillar plant and I was a student at Joliet West High School, one of my best friends in Aurora, Laura Mickey, invited me back to Aurora for a high-school dance. We walked up to the table, and there with his date sat one of the Brass Boys who'd regularly harassed me in junior high.

---

[12] Even then, it had something to do with where I put my mouth.

Top left: Me aged seven.

Top right: My brother Andrew, sister Carole and me on the day we left Scotland for Barrowmans' Excellent Adventure in America.

Above left: In The Extension, about to perform.

Right: Dressed up as the 'Queen of the Nile' for a talent contest.

Don't mess with us: the Barrowman family, circa 1976.

Left: Living in my swimming trunks in Prestbury. The lady in the blue hat is Murn.

Right: Me and Pagan The Transatlantic Pup.

Left: John the flautist at my sister's wedding.

Above: Laura Mickey and me at the high-school dance in Aurora, Illinois.

Left: Performing in *Camelot* at Joliet West High School.

Above: Performing with Marilyn in *The Boyfriend* at USIU.

Above: In action in Opryland. This was the night of the Nashville kiss. Those are also the infamous white polyester trousers.

Right: Me, erm, dressed as a tap-dancing penguin.

Below: At Carhenge with our nephew Gabriel.

Above: Dragging it up with Turner and Clare one Hogmanay.

Below: With Clare in Santorini.

Above: My nieces and nephews *(from left to right)*, Turner and Clare *(top row)*, Andrew, Bridgett and Yvonne *(bottom row)*.

Below: Scuba diving with Scott in Mexico.

Above: On holiday at a spa in Scotsdale, Arizona.

Right: With Scott Gill, the love of my life, in Mykonos.

Left: Scott and me at our civil partnership ceremony on 27 December 2006.

Below: With our dogs *(from left to right)*, Lewis, Penny and Tiger.

Above: With my manager and friend, Gavin Barker.

Right: With my brilliant mum and dad.

Below: Posing with Carole and Andrew.

After some inane conversation, he finally broached the subject and asked, 'Why did you never fight back, John?'

I shrugged. 'I figured one day, you'd regret it.'

He was quiet for a few beats. My pulse quickened. I wasn't sure which way the night was going to go. I'd managed to avoid wrestling with him all through junior high; I really didn't want to take him now. Oh, I could have. But as much as I loved *West Side Story*, I'd rather this particular dinner avoided musical plot lines.

Finally, he looked a bit sheepishly at me. 'You know, everyone now calls me "lawn boy"[13] and I hate it.'

We ended up having a great night.

In junior high, the bullying began because I sounded a bit different. I didn't fully embrace my bidialectical nature until I was in high school. I continued to be bullied during those years because I was interested in doing things that didn't appeal to most American boys. Yet I still wanted to become a real American. I think this is one of the reasons Hinton's *The Outsiders* was such a profound read for me as a boy. Not because I felt like an outsider, I honestly never did. I had lots of friends and a close adoring family, but I was struggling during those years to figure out what it meant not only to be an American, given my Scottish heritage, but also what it meant to become a young man.

Hinton's novel is all about male friendships, some destructive, some not, but at its heart the book is about Ponyboy, the narrator, trying to balance peer pressure with personal integrity. Who among us hasn't been there? Although Ponyboy's rite of passage is violent and heart-wrenching, to this day Hinton's book continues to inspire me, and can still make my eyes moisten and my heart swell.

Of course, so can a shiny pair of new shoes.

---

[13] His dad was in landscaping.

Personal integrity aside, even as a youth I managed to get back at the Brass Boys and the other Spotty Dicks who taunted me. First payback was the best. I was always popular with girls. Need I say more? Second payback was a biggie, too. During my last year of junior high, aged thirteen, I was asked to be the school's drum major, which meant I had to lead all sections of the band, including the Brass Boys. I marched in front of the band with military precision in an outfit that looked as if Mr Humphries had designed it in collaboration with Liberace, but 'Seventy-Six Trombones' never sounded so fucking good.

During those years, I did establish some traits that have remained with me into adulthood. I've never forgotten my Scottish roots, and I'm proud to be an American. I no longer collect *Star Wars* stuff, but I've a nice collection of *Doctor Who* memorabilia. I love to swim, and I love over-the-top night-time soap operas, an infatuation that started in my youth with the American TV show *Dallas*.

On Friday nights, when the Barrowmans lived in Prestbury, we would go out to dinner at a local Moose Lodge – a name that thankfully had little to do with the menu or the type of customers it welcomed – with our friends Kay and Paul Johnson and their daughters, Juleen, Nadine and Loreen. Afterwards, we'd all gather in our TV room at 8 p.m. to have *Dallas* parties. I loved the glamour, the glitz, the outrageous behaviour and the general campiness of the Ewings' lives, and I was completely besotted with Victoria Principal, who played Pam Ewing.

I even spent an agonizing few hours after one of our *Dallas* nights expressing my adoration to 'Pam' in a fan letter – which I eventually sent and, in return, received an autographed picture. For years, I kept the picture on my desk next to a framed calligraphy of Robert Frost's poem 'Nothing Gold Can Stay', which features in *The Outsiders*.

Almost two decades later, I was entrenched in meetings for my upcoming television show *Titans*, which ran for half a season in the States starting in the autumn of 2000, and was produced by the TV legend Aaron Spelling. I was killing time in Aaron's office (which looked like a sitting room), chatting on the phone with my mum, when Aaron announced that someone he wanted me to meet had just dropped by: the actress who would be playing my screen mother in the new series. The next moment, in walked Victoria Principal. I couldn't believe it. I screamed into the phone, 'Oh my God, Mum, you'll never fucking believe this. Pam Ewing is my mother!'[14]

'I'm going to like you, John,' laughed Victoria. We did end up becoming friends, enjoying dinner together on lots of nights and spending many days conspiring over how to keep Yasmine Bleeth from her destructive behaviour. While filming *Titans* in 2000, I bought a condo in West Hollywood near LeMontrose Hotel, and Victoria and I were neighbours for a time.

When you're young, the periods of hurt and intimidation and the awkwardness of adolescence can seem all-encompassing. But then, suddenly, you're an adult, and you realize that if you 'stay gold, Ponyboy,' as Hinton's novel says, sometimes the gay guys, I mean the good guys, do win.

---

[14] For those of you keeping track for a future *Friday Night Project* trivia game, my character's name in *Titans* was Peter Williams, but in the initial script it was Mason Williams and my real-life mum's middle name is Mason.

Chapter Five

'Don't Fence Me In'

The summers of my American youth were glorious ones. By the late seventies, Carole no longer lived at home. She was a student at Northern Illinois University. Andrew was in high school with his own circle of friends, so he wasn't around the house much either. I don't want to suggest they had been cramping my style, but it seemed like overnight I went from being the baby in the family to becoming essentially an only child, and I experienced the kind of childhood everyone deserves.

We were living in Prestbury at that time and I spent May until late August in my swimming trunks. I'd pull them on in the morning, grab a towel, and head to the pool, where I'd meet two of my best friends at the time, Laura Mickey and Mike Molina. The lifeguard was on duty at the pool until 6 p.m., but we'd hang around later and whenever any adults came in, we'd ask if they'd let us swim with them taking charge. They always agreed. Prestbury was a secluded community at that time so everyone knew each other, but today, sadly, no matter how private and quiet the neighbourhood, no one on either side of the Atlantic would take on the responsibility of watching someone else's children, never mind leaving them alone at a private swimming pool.

When we lived in Scotland, Carole, Andrew and I always had set bedtimes and curfews. Naturally, Carole was allowed to stay up the latest, Andrew went to bed an hour earlier and so on. Problem was, I didn't need much sleep. As a result, I'd be sent to bed first and I'd still be wide awake, singing to myself in bed, reading or playing long after Andrew and Carole were fast asleep. Therefore, once my parents had adjusted to the cadences of an American summer, bedtimes and curfews shifted and were enforced only when my parents needed to lock up the house and go to bed themselves.

Did I take advantage of these loosened rules? You bet I did. My friends and I were little hellions, and not just in the summer. The roads and pavements of all the homes in Prestbury were bordered by a concrete culvert for water run-off and, during the winter of 1977, I learned how to ice skate on the narrow channel, which circled the entire neighbourhood and then drained into Prestbury's man-made lake. Skating on that lake in the winter was like skating through Narnia. The ice was punctured with trees piercing through its smooth surface, and I'm sure my friends and I looked as if we belonged in a Christmas special as we'd swoop along the culvert in a line and then burst one by one on to the expanse of the lake, breathless from laughing and skating so fast. I learned some of my best moves on the Prestbury lake in the seventies, although when I first skated for Olga during training for *Dancing on Ice*, she wasn't nearly as impressed with them as I was. Somehow, they seemed more spectacular when I was ten.

In the spring, when the ice melted, the water would run off into a creek that ran behind my friend Laura's house. From there, it flowed into a more secluded section of the culvert, through a concrete tunnel under the road, and finally, in a rush, it would recycle into the lake. In the late spring and early summer, when the water draining into the creek was at its fullest, Laura, Mike and I would sneak behind her house, throw ourselves into the rushing creek and let the current carry us along the culvert into the tunnel – where the water would be flowing so fast we'd pick up speed, get flipped over a few times, swallow a few litres, pop to the surface and then ride the speeding current out of the tunnel into the lake. This became our own personal water slide. If I ever thought one of my nieces or nephews was getting up to something like that, I'd have them grounded for life. But, hey, it was the late seventies and children played with reckless abandon.

Maybe a bit too much abandon at times. Once, through a rather unfortunate baking incident – you read correctly, baking – I had an early experience with the highs of, let's say, 'organic materials'. One afternoon, I was at a friend's house and we unwittingly ate a whole batch of laced brownies that a much older sibling had left on the kitchen counter to cool. My friend and I treated ourselves to the entire plate of chewy delights – and then spent the rest of the afternoon stoned out of our fucking minds, watching *Scooby Doo* cartoons and thinking they were the best episodes we'd ever seen. Even Daphne looked good to me. I remember going home that night and hoovering every morsel of food off my plate at dinner and a few off Murn's too. My mum and dad had no clue what was wrong with me, and for most of the duration of the accidental high, neither did I.

It was during one of my idyllic Prestbury summers that I was finally able to take revenge on my brother for his years of tormenting me with a song he'd made up when we lived in Scotland. I know it sounds a bit *Monty Python*ish that the biggest threat he could inflict on me was to torment me with a song, but it's true. Andrew would sing his ditty, 'Up the park, there was a man, and his name was—' and then he'd stop. The man need never be named because whenever Andrew wanted to blackmail me into doing something for him, he needed only to sing those first few lines. Singing the song served as a warning that if I didn't do what he asked, he'd snitch to my parents about something I'd done 'up the park' while we still lived in Scotland. This song haunted me all the way across the Atlantic.

Let me explain. One afternoon, when we lived in Mount Vernon, I was playing with a frisbee in the swing park at the top of Dornford Avenue. I can't remember now what the provocation was, but for some reason one of our neighbours confiscated my toy and so I screamed at him to give me back my 'fucking frisbee', or something close to those words. I was about six or seven at the time, and it didn't matter that I'd probably learned the phrase from Andrew in the first place. I was too wee to swear and certainly the offence was further aggravated by the fact that I'd said it to an adult.

Andrew witnessed my verbal outburst and he swore he'd never tell Mum and Dad. He was my brother and, of course, he kept his word. Yeah, right. In retrospect, I'd have been much better off telling my parents, but I made the mistake all younger brothers make at least once in their childhoods: I trusted that my big brother had my best interests at heart.

For years, and I do mean years, any time Andrew wanted me to do something for him, he'd begin to sing 'Up the park, there was a man, and his name was—' to a tune of his own making. After a while, he didn't even have to finish the phrase. He'd just open his mouth and say 'Up' and I was his slave. That is, until the summer of '77, when revenge was mine – and it tasted oh, so very sweet.

Andrew was in his mid teens when 'Episode III: The Revenge of the Sib' occurred. He and his friends often borrowed[1] Prestbury's pontoon boat, a boat that anyone – well, any adults that is – could use. Andrew and his mates would let the boat drift over to the island

---

[1] I use the term loosely.

at the centre of the lake, where they'd spend long chunks of their summer days drinking and smoking. How did I know? Because my friend Mike's brother often hung out with them on the island and he had a big mouth.

On the lazy summer afternoon when I finally got my revenge on Andrew, my brother and his buddies were on the Prestbury island as usual, when Andrew decided to show his friends how well our family dog, now known as Pagan The Transatlantic Pup,[2] could swim.

Before I go on, I must take this opportunity to offer a caveat,[3] especially for my younger readers. Boys and girls, there are three things you should never ever do if you've been drinking – actually, if you're a boy or a girl, you shouldn't be drinking in the first place, but I'm digressing in my digression:

Never drive.

Never get a tattoo.

Never take your dog swimming. This rule also applies to cats, hamsters, little bunnies, and anything in the furry rodent family.

Alas, Andrew had not learned the third lesson. After considerable fanfare, he chucked Pagan The Transatlantic Pup into Prestbury's lake. Andrew and his buddies cheered and then they cheered again in anticipation of Pagan The Transatlantic Pup bobbing up from the watery depths and paddling across to the island to be duly congratulated. Problem was, no one told Pagan that was the plan, so that after about thirty seconds, it was clear to Andrew and to all his friends that Pagan wasn't bobbing anywhere except maybe under a floating gravestone.

Andrew jumped into the lake at the same spot he'd tossed the dog.

[2] Pagan had emigrated with us from Scotland, thus the new name.
[3] A Latin word! I told you there'd be more cool vocabulary.

Down he went, frantically searching for Pagan The Transatlantic Pup. After five minutes of fruitless hunting, Andrew was in full-blown 'I'm so screwed' mode, as were his friends, who were quickly evacuating the scene of the crime. Sadly, still no sign of Pagan The Transatlantic Pup.

What Andrew didn't know – and I did because I was watching all of this from the opposite shore – was that Pagan The Transatlantic Pup did indeed have exceptional swimming skills and like any smart hound he'd decided, quite rightly too, that he'd had enough of Andrew's game. After getting chucked in, he swam directly under the boat, surfaced on the other side, paddled to the shore, spotted me, accepted a quick rub of his ears, shook himself off, and then trotted home.

At that very moment, a song broke into my head: 'Up the park, there was a dog, and his name was Pagan The Swimming Pup.' Whistling the same tune as Andrew's song, I turned from the panic on the lake and followed Pagan The Transatlantic Pup home.

A few years later, when I was about thirteen, my dad accepted a promotion to become General Manager of the Joliet Caterpillar plant, and we were on the move again. He and my mum tried hard for my sake to find a neighbourhood that matched Prestbury. The closest they could find was Timber Estates, which was lovely, but it lacked any private neighbourhood water amenities. To make up for this, my parents joined a club that had a pool. In Prestbury, my circle of friends had always included a fairly even mix of boys and girls, and in Joliet the same was true. Our escapades at the club were limited only by my dad's charge account – and even then, not until the damage had been done.

My friends and I would hang out at the pool all day, swimming, diving and sunbathing, and I would order vodka tonics for the entire group; our age didn't seem to be a great concern. I was signing for lavish lunches and decadent desserts ... until my dad cottoned on to this, which wasn't hard for him to do since one week I charged over $1,000 on lunches alone. My dad's charge number at the club was 007 and, man, did he use his licence to kill that day.

It was the summer before we moved to Joliet when I realized for sure I was gay – although I'd really known I was in my gut, or thereabouts, since the age of nine, when I'd seen my first girly magazine and been more interested in the male bits than the female bobs. I'm not saying that coming of age as a gay male in the late twentieth century wasn't difficult for many boys, but, honestly, at least for me, it was no big deal. I'd grown up with parents who were sure of themselves as individuals, very comfortable in their own sexuality, and open and frank in how they approached the issue with their children. They raised Carole, Andrew and me with the knowledge that we were valued human beings, loved completely and unconditionally, and nothing we'd do would ever be so bad that we couldn't come home. When the time came and I needed to say the words 'I'm gay' aloud, I flew home to my family to say them.

It was 1992 and I was playing Raoul in Andrew Lloyd Webber's *The Phantom of the Opera* in London's West End. I was ill. I had a persistent cough, a low-grade fever, and stomach cramps twisting my gut every few hours. I'd been sexually active. I panicked and feared the worst. I headed home to America to face up to the truth. My parents and I sat at the kitchen table and with very little preamble I said, 'I'm gay and I need an HIV test.'

I then told them that no matter what happened, I knew I was going to do great things with my life and I hoped they'd continue to be an important part of the journey I was on. However, if they couldn't accept that I was gay, I would leave and do it all without them.

My dad was quiet for barely a beat. He looked at my mum, who was still reeling a bit from the HIV part of the statement, and then he leaned forward and said, 'John, honestly, it's none of my business what you do in your bedroom, just as it's none of yours what we do in ours, but I have to say that we're hurt you'd think that because you're gay we'd not want to be part of your life anymore.'

That night, we went out to dinner and they both admitted that my news had not really been a revelation. The next day, I had an HIV test. As the doctor was a family friend, he put a rush on the results. Nonetheless, the wait was interminable. Sheer panic kept me from sleeping more than a couple of hours at a time and dread was a brick sitting in the pit of my stomach.

While I waited for news, I travelled north to Milwaukee to visit Carole and Kevin, and to spend some time with Clare and Turner, then aged five and two. They had just moved house and the rooms were filled more with boxes than with furniture. I stayed the whole day and played hide-and-seek and kick the can, then Clare, Turner and I made forts with the boxes, and to round off the fun we ate pizza sitting on the floor.

I briefly explained to Carole and Kevin that I was home because I was sick. I told them I was having some tests, although I didn't elaborate as to what kind of tests or why. I withheld this information, in part, because it was clear to me that they really already knew. The other reason was that Clare and Turner wouldn't leave my side for a minute and there was no opportunity for any real discussion. When I left, I promised to call with the results.

During the long wait, I also phoned my brother, who was at a business seminar, and had a similar conversation with him to the one I'd had with my mum and dad. Like them, Andrew's response was very much: 'It doesn't change anything.'

Ultimately, the test came back negative for HIV. I did, though, have a gastric infection and a chest infection, and both were working together to create my general exhaustion. I called Carole and told her I was going to be fine. Then I admitted what the test had really been for, and the reason I'd been so worried about contracting the virus. Her response was pretty much, 'Ho hum – and what else is new?' It seems all my family knew I was gay before I told them – so much for my bombshell news.

The next day, I flew back to London in time for the following evening's performance of *Phantom*. Those few days of sheer panic taught me a tough but valuable lesson – and not just about practising safe sex. It was one of those moments in my life when I realized information and awareness can save lives, and everyone should have equal access. I began my association with a number of AIDS/HIV charities at that time, and I continue to be an advocate for West End Cares, the Terrence Higgins Trust, Stonewall's education campaigns and others.

Many things shaped my identity as a young boy: a strong self-worth (something that was instilled in all three Barrowman siblings by our parents), my immersion in theatre and music, and my DNA. I was born gay. It's not a choice I – or anyone else who is gay – made. If it were, why on earth would anyone choose to be part of a minority, part of a group that in so many cultures and countries, even in the twenty-first century, is regularly blasphemed, hounded and worse?

Happily, during my childhood years in Prestbury, when I first realized my sexuality, my being gay was no more an issue for my friends Laura and Mike than Laura and Mike not being gay was an issue for me. I didn't act on my newfound awareness in any way that was different from how Mike and Laura were responding to their emerging sexuality. We were all equally confused, equally goofy and equally self-conscious about that aspect of development. I was a child and I was still doing pretty childish things.

So what's changed? You ask. Not much, except now my toys are bigger.

Of course, in adolescence, there's a fine line between ignorance and innocence. Did Mike and Laura know I was gay? I don't think so. Did my other high-school friends? Perhaps. Does it matter? Probably not. Laura is now a lawyer for a firm in Chicago and Mike lives in South Carolina with his daughters and his dogs. I still consider them to be friends and I know that if I'd felt it necessary to say openly to them when I was young that I was gay, nothing would have changed in our friendship.

The only incident I remember from those summers, when I made a decision to do something because I was gay, was when I agreed to crew for a neighbour and his wife in their sailboat because I thought the husband was hot. On the other hand, Mike was interested in the crewing job because to him the wife was equally gorgeous.

Gay or straight, our dicks were driving both of us.

Chapter Six

'New Ways to Dream'

Noël Coward once told an interviewer that a person could learn as much about acting from 'a bad matinee in Hull' as a West End show. Beverly Holt, who was the musical accompanist for Joliet West High School when I was a student there and who has since become my close friend and musical director, once said something of similar pithiness[1] to me. 'Listen, bozo,' she said, 'sometimes you need to play crap theatre to know good theatre, and you can learn a lot from both.'

At the time Bev made this pronouncement, it was 1984 and she was trying to cajole this bozo into trying out for the Joliet Drama Guild's Bicentennial Park production of *Anything Goes*. I was a senior in high school and I was resisting her urges to audition for this community theatre production. However, like most of Bev's advice to me then and now, it was advice worth following, and so, almost six years before my big break in the West End production of the same show, I ended up auditioning for and getting the part of Billy Crocker.

A number of teachers have been, in the words of Cole Porter, 'the purple light of a summer night' in my life and, as the saying

---

[1] Of course it's a real word!

goes, if you can read these pages, you should thank a teacher too. Along with Bev, Mark Wilson, my English teacher at Joliet West High School, was inspirational. He was responsible for putting me in the gifted English class and introducing me to Forensic Competition.[2] I also owe a huge debt to David Dankwart, who was my high-school choir director – and the first professional to recognize I had a 'voice'.

I was in a music practice room at high school one afternoon, struggling with a piece of flute music I needed to learn for the school band. I began to sing the piece aloud to help me get a grip on it, when David walked past the room. He knocked and stuck his head inside.

'Was that you singing?'

'Yes.'

'Do you think you have talent?'

'Yes.'[3]

'Are you arrogant?'

I wasn't sure exactly what he meant by this, but I said 'yes' anyway.

'Good. Those are both qualities I like in my performers. Come to the theatre and try out for the school musical.'

Not only did I audition, but – much to the chagrin of the juniors and seniors who also tried out – I got one of the lead roles in my freshman year, at the tender age of fourteen. It was my first real part in a musical, playing Barnaby in *Hello Dolly!* This high-school

---

[2] I'll explain what this is in a couple of pages. In the meantime, rest assured it had nothing to do with examining crime scenes.

[3] Although my audiences up until this point had mostly comprised family and friends – and the few odd characters who had wandered into the record shop back on Shettleston Road in Scotland to listen to me sing – I still knew in my heart and in my head that this answer was true.

production was my first time singing to a real, live, sitting-in-seats-in-front-of-the-stage audience.

It was during this production that I first met Bev, who, along with her husband Jim, from that moment on became a second family to me. She'd sometimes bring her children, Jennifer and Michael (both now adults with their own families), to rehearsals and when I wasn't on stage, I'd babysit them. I recorded my first solo album in Bev's living room, on a borrowed soundboard with two duct-taped mikes. Given its amateur quality, it's probably just as well that we made only enough copies for family and a handful of friends. Bev has since worked with me on most of my subsequent albums. She also accompanied (in a musical sense) my parents and me when we performed at several Burns Suppers in Chicago.

These annual celebrations to the Scottish Bard are held on the anniversary of Robert Burns's birth, 25 January, in Scotland and in every country with populations of transplanted Scots. Typically, the evening is organized around a number of traditional performances of Burns's poems and songs, with lots of bawdy stories about his exploits thrown in for good measure, all washed down with a dram or two of whisky. Dressed in our kilts, my mum and I would each sing one or two songs, while my dad would present a tribute to the poet himself, called 'The Immortal Memory', which – next to the whisky and the Toast to the Haggis – is the most important part of the traditional Burns Supper.

When I started attending Joliet West High School in 1981, I'd been living in America for about five years. Although the transition had been a bit bumpy at times, for the most part I was settling into my new life pretty comfortably. However, it was during that freshman year in high school that I first came face to face with what I like to call the 'Dues and Don't Syndrome',[4] which generally seems to have affected groups of my fellow performers, but not casting directors with any talent. Later, this syndrome followed me into my early experiences at college, but by that time I was prepared for it.

During my high-school freshman year, I kept up with my flute and I continued to enjoy playing in the band, but after getting a taste of performing in *Hello Dolly!*, I knew I wanted to join in the school's swing choir. Under Bev's guidance and encouragement, I was now singing regularly for any organization or church in Joliet that needed a soloist, so I was increasingly experienced. Regardless, it seemed there was a pecking order at school that needed to be followed, and I was told my talents wouldn't be considered. I hadn't been forgiven for disrupting the hierarchy by landing the part of Barnaby, and so I was to pay the price in harassment from a few of my peers for a long time.

After a school assembly concert one afternoon, Bev found me backstage, alone and close to tears.

'What's up, John?' she asked, sitting down next to me.

'Why are some of these choir kids mean to me all the time?'

A few of them had taunted me in the wings that day, as they often did before or after concerts.

'John,' she said, 'they're jealous of you, and you may not believe this right now, but some day you'll get the last laugh.'

Bev's response to me that afternoon was not the first time I'd heard those words; my mum and dad had certainly said them to me many times since I'd started high school, as I'd shared some of the choir incidents with them. For some reason, though, that afternoon Bev's words sank in. It was one of the first times that I can remember

---

[4] This can be summarized as: 'You haven't fully paid your *dues*, so *don't* even think you should get a chance, no matter how talented you are.'

thinking to myself: 'She's right. This is what you love. Get the last laugh.' It fuelled me with determination.

Despite the initial obstacles, the following year I did become a member of the school swing choir. I loved everything about the experience; the combination of choreography and choral singing was simply irresistible. With persistence and – I'd like to think – charm, I even managed to win round a few of my detractors in the group ... eventually.

They say that you never forget your first kiss[5] or your first car. Mine was a Ford Escort XR3i and it cost me £10,000. I bought it the first month I was in *Anything Goes* in the West End in 1989.[6] I'd like to add winning your first acting award to this list of unforgettable things. Although I've been nominated for and won many awards over the years – including a number of Theatregoers' Choice Awards, a Welsh BAFTA nomination for Best Actor, and Best New Drama for *Torchwood* at the *TV Quick* Awards in 2007 – the first award still retains a special place in my heart. There were no free goody bags when I won it, back in high school, but it has remained a truly memorable experience, especially given all the grief I'd taken from some of my peers during my freshman year.

My English teacher Mark Wilson was the first to encourage my involvement in Forensic Competition, which is basically a kind of academic *X Factor*, where students from across the country compete in local, regional and then state competitions in events such as storytelling, oratory, acting and public speaking. I'd never done anything like it before, but I was up for the challenge.

I signed up to compete with my friend Barb Eagle in the Dramatic

---

[5] Oh, I'll get to that later, don't you worry.

[6] My first real dream car was my Jaguar XJS Insignia, a model I had wanted since I was a wee boy, when I used to play with a Matchbox version; I bought the Jag when I was in *Sunset Boulevard* in 1994.

Duet Acting category. We chose to perform a scene from *The Lion in Winter* by James Goldman. Barb was Eleanor of Aquitaine and I played the role of Henry the Plantagenet. Our first competition was held at Plainfield High School, in a neighbouring town close to Joliet. As Barb and I watched our competition, I grew more and more nervous. The other teams were really good, and although we had rehearsed, there were a couple of places in our scene where I hadn't completely memorized my lines. Times like this have taught me a lot about myself as a performer – and this time showed me that if I let my nerves get a hold of me, I dry up, my head goes blank and I forget everything. To this day, whether it's in front of a live television audience or at a Royal Variety Performance, the key is not to let my nerves take over, but instead to channel that adrenalin into my performance.

Barb and I were sitting anxiously at the back of the classroom where the competition was being held. The judges were either drama teachers or other Forensic coaches. When they called Barb and my name, we had a few seconds to prepare. The protocol was that we'd perform, and then walk to the corner and bow our heads: a signal that the scene was over. In the category of Dramatic Duet, we were allowed two props. We had a chair and a desk.

For the first part of the scene, I sat behind the desk, while Barb, as Eleanor, stalked behind me, ranting about my flaws as a king and a human being. About halfway through the scene, we switched places – jeez, we were so creative – and I paced up and down in front of 'Eleanor' and returned her jibes in kind.

About a minute after I stood up, I went blank. I had nothing. Nada. Zip. Instead of speaking my lines, I started to stomp in front of the table, gesturing wildly, grunting and sighing loudly like Darth Vader on steroids. At one point, I believe I pounded the table while exhaling. I was really giving it big time. Barb was just gawking at me in sheer terror.

I suddenly made up a couple of the lines and then the rest of them popped into my head. Barb fed me a line and I finally got back on track. In my head, my lexical dry spell felt like it had lasted twenty-five minutes, but in reality it was only about thirty or forty seconds. Barb gave her last line. We moved to the corner. Heads down. End scene. Very dramatic.

Despite having blown our performance, Barb and I were good sports and along with all the other schools' teams, we attended the awards ceremony. My friend Mike Bryson was teamed in another category with Andy Dick, who was a year ahead of me in school and who is now famous and infamous in his own right. Andy is a successful actor and an eccentric comedian. In his stand-up act, Andy does a little slapstick, tells a lot of raunchy stories, and sings songs like 'Dip Your Cock in Vodka' (readers, please don't) and 'A Great Day for Drugs' (it's not usually). Andy also played the quirky oddball character in a terrific US sitcom that ran in the late 1990s, *NewsRadio*. The sitcom also starred the late Phil Hartman, of *Saturday Night Live* fame, comedian Dave Foley, and Maura Tierney, currently playing a doc in *ER*.

Andy is the only person I know who even in high school made self-deprecating humour an art form. He came to school one day dressed as a superhero and called himself 'Super Dick'. If I remember correctly, he ran for Homecoming King on that same platform. Of course, I voted for him. He was pretty much a nutcase and, guess what, he and I were often nutcases together. Once, at a school concert, we performed 'Sing' from *A Chorus Line*, and for each of us it was one of our first standing ovations from an audience.

One of the cool claims to fame that Joliet West High School's theatre department can make is that in the school's 1983 production of *Oliver!*, the cast included three performers who've gone on to become very successful and accomplished actors and entertainers.

Andy played Dr Grimwig, I played Mr Bumble and Anthony Rapp, who has since appeared in films like *A Beautiful Mind* and *Six Degrees of Separation*, TV such as *The X Files* and *Law and Order: SVU*, and who created the role of Mark Cohen in the Broadway and film production of *Rent*, played Oliver.

In the Forensic Competition of 1985, Andy and Mike performed a comic scene from *The Importance of Being Earnest*. They took third place in their category. Up until that point, Joliet West had won nothing all evening, and we certainly weren't holding out for any more prizes. I'd already told the coaches what had happened during my scene with Barb. Given that it was my first competition, they expected me to learn from it and move on. Good advice.

When our category was called, Barb and I decided to get really into the spirit of the awards show experience, regardless of the outcome. We had the whole faux excitement thing going on, holding hands and squeezing each other as if we even had a chance. Whether we did or not, we wanted to look like we had some confidence left and we hadn't completely given up.

In reality, I felt utterly defeated.

In our category, my favourite to win was a scene from Lillian Hellman's *The Children's Hour*. Two girls from a suburban Chicago high school had performed the scene and, given the lesbian nature of the work, I'd thought it was pretty risky for high-school students to tackle. During the performance, these girls were gutting it and sincerely so – unlike yours truly, who made a dry spell look like a category-five storm.

Then the judges announced, 'Second place in the Dramatic Duet goes to —' and the Hellman girls took second.

'First place,' continued the judges, as the girls returned to their seats, 'to Joliet West High School's John Barrowman and Barb Eagle for *The Lion in Winter*.'

Even as Barb and I were yelling and whooping it up, in my head I was thinking, 'This is crazy.' I'd bullshitted my way through half of that scene. I'd chewed up the furniture and spat it out – and we'd still won.

The next week in practice, Barb and I really hammered into our scene because at the next competition, usually held the following month, we would be the reigning champs and we'd have something to prove. We worked all my grunts and sighs and table-pounding into the performance and at the next competition, we won again – and at the next one, and the one after that. It got to the point that at the awards ceremony, as the judges would begin to announce our category, they'd say 'and in first place' and the audience would yell in unison, 'Joliet West High School!'

Barb and I took our performance to the Illinois Forensic finals and, in the end, we took second with *The Lion in Winter*, finally losing to the two Hellman girls and *The Children's Hour*.

A slew of trophies from all of my various Forensic wins, state choral awards and solo singing competitions are now packed in boxes in my parents' condo in Brookfield, Wisconsin, where my mum and dad now spend their summers. One year, I was awarded the First Tenor for the State of Illinois, an honour that required competing at a variety of state-endorsed contests, gathering enough first- or second-place wins to compete at the state level. Another year during high school, I was in the top three in jazz vocals. All of this was possible, in part, because a teacher took a minute to listen at a music-room door.

Along with my peers, including Barb, Mike, Andy, Anthony and others, we brought as many, if not more, state first trophies to Joliet West High School than all the sports teams combined. Yet we'd get a passing mention in the school's morning announcements, while the football and basketball teams would get pep rallies, cheerleaders, and a huge mahogany case for all their trophies. Am I bitter? Abso-fucking-lutely! And mostly because I don't think much has changed since I was a student. If anything, support for the performing arts may be worse. Sports continue to rule in many high schools in the US, while the arts and music programmes are regularly losing funding. Yet I'd bet more young people go on to use the skills and abilities they hone in theatre classes, choirs and bands in their professional and personal lives than go on to play sports beyond high school. While I was a student, the funding for the arts was seriously slashed, but the football team always had new uniforms when they needed them.

This funding gap in high-school programmes was one of my initial reasons for starting Dreamers Workshop, my scheme of non-profit performing arts workshops for young people. A staunch belief that theatre skills are lifelong skills, regardless of the profession you end up in, was the second reason. Oprah was the third.

In the spring of 1998, I was visiting my parents in the States when I caught one of Oprah's shows on the box. She was spotlighting people who 'pay it forward' in their community, using their wealth or their talent to give something back. Bev Holt and I had talked for years off and on about organizing a series of classes or a camp of sorts, where students could come and learn from professionals about acting, singing and performing. I called Bev before Oprah's show was over, and that very afternoon, Dreamers Workshop was born.

Bev and I conducted the first Dreamers Workshop the following summer at my old stomping ground, Joliet West High School. The week consisted of lessons in performing, voice training, acting activities and practice, practice, practice. The event culminated in a performance from all the students, with Bev and I doing a couple of numbers too. Whatever profits the workshop generated after Bev and I had covered our expenses, we put into a scholarship fund that supported the following year's students who couldn't afford the cost. We successfully conducted the classes at Joliet for three years in a row.

We were planning a fourth workshop when the administration for the school at the time made a decision that, in all honesty, hurt me, and that I felt was a serious slap in the face from an establishment I'd tried hard to repay in my promotion of its arts programmes by bringing Dreamers Workshop to it in the first place. After all, this was the school that had turned me on to musical theatre. However, when Bev began her planning for the fourth year, the administrators insisted the workshop pay for the rental of the facilities, the hiring of janitorial and security staff, and a number of other costs that Bev and I thought were unreasonable and just too much.

Instead, Bev and I held a successful workshop at the University of St Francis in Joliet and, the following year, at my old Forensic rivals' lair, Plainfield High School. Both institutions kindly gave their facilities and support for free. Since Bev and I only ever had our expenses covered, this meant we were able to give more students scholarships, and even cover lunches for participants who needed the extra help.

Application to the workshop was always via a letter describing why the student wanted to take part. As far as I can recall, however, we never once turned down an applicant. During those five years, we gave back to well over a hundred students, many of whom returned in the following years to help out with the new crop of participants. A few have even remained in touch. One is now pursuing her dream to be an actor in New York.

Before my work demands made continuing Dreamers Workshop impossible, Bev and I took it on the road to Dallas, Texas, where a fan and a friend, Barbara Thomas, generously helped support the workshop for her school district. Our final road trip was to the northwest to the Spotlight Theatre for Children in Eugene, Oregon. I cherish the memories of those workshops and some day I'd like to organize one or two more, perhaps even bring the seminar to the UK.

The 'pay it forward' ideology that led to me starting the Dreamers Workshop in the first place was also part of my motivation to become a judge on *Any Dream Will Do* and *How Do You Solve a Problem Like Maria?* Although I have to admit, both shows were also the most fun I'd had doing live television for a long time. I love live television because it's a lot like theatre. The energy from the audience coupled with the eagerness and enthusiasm from the contestants creates an adrenalin rush that's intoxicating. I revelled in the opportunities to improvise with the other judges and Graham Norton – and who could turn down the chance to mock a peer of the realm?[7] Add to all of this the chance to kick-start the career of a young talented performer and I couldn't resist.

Any Dream Will Do and *How Do You Solve a Problem Like Maria?* were my Dreamers Workshop writ large on the small screen. I'd do another show along those lines in a minute, because whether you're a fifteen-year-old trying to come out of your shell, or a nineteen-year-old desperate for a break, in the words of lyricist Christopher Adler, 'to dreamers, the real world can be unreal.' Everyone needs a boost up the ladder sometimes – and I'm always happy to extend my hand.

---

[7] Good-naturedly, of course. Lord Lloyd-Webber took it all in his stride.

Chapter Seven

'The First Man You Remember'

In 1985, after my graduation from Joliet West High School, I went to the University of Iowa in Des Moines to study drama and music. The landscape of Iowa is a lot like Paris Hilton: incredibly flat with no visible curves. In fact, Iowa is the one state in the United States that even Alabama taunts. But Iowa doesn't seem to care. It's firm in its Midwestern values and strong in its resolve that if it wasn't for the Hawkeye State,[1] there'd have been no John Wayne, no *Field of Dreams*, and a lot less corn in the world. The University of Iowa had a strong music department, and they created a financial package that was hard for my parents and me to turn down. Consequently, I accepted a place to study there.

Unfortunately, I hated the university, and ended up leaving after only one term. Unlike the host of good teachers and mentors who'd taken an interest in me up until then, the faculty at Iowa didn't seem to give a shit about me. I was one of approximately 25,000 students, and instead of asking me what I wanted to do with my talent, the music faculty insisted they knew what I should do with it – and

[1] That's Iowa's nickname, in case you didn't know.

what they wanted was to train me as a classical opera singer. Even then, Gene Kelly, Fred Astaire, Ginger Rogers and Noël Coward were more appealing to me as performers, but I think they were too déclassé for U of I's music department.

Speaking of Ms Rogers, another special moment on the highlight reel of my life, which is up there with meeting George Lucas at Cannes, was meeting Ginger at an American Cinema Awards dinner in 1996. Sadly, I never got the opportunity to dance with her, since she was in a wheelchair that night, but she and I spent a few minutes chatting and the glow of the moment stayed with me for days.

The American Cinema Awards were an annual event designed to celebrate the work of older Hollywood stars. In 1996, I was in LA working on a project for David Gest, who was also producing the awards show. He asked me if I'd escort actress Angie Dickinson to a pre-awards dinner. Of course I agreed. I was staying at the Beverly Wilshire Hotel and Angie picked me up in her Mercedes. I climbed into the car and because her skirt was split high on the side, I noticed her great legs immediately.

'Wow!' I gushed. 'Your legs still look great. I remember when I was eight years old and watched you on *Police Woman.*'

She stared at me for a moment and then she said, 'Would you like to put your other foot in your mouth now or wait until later?'

I began to babble an apology, but she cut me off with a genuine smile and a flick of her wrist. We had a great time at dinner and the next day our 'date' was all over the tabloids, with headlines screaming that I was her 'Boy Toy' – which was just rubbish.

Notwithstanding my general disappointment with the University of Iowa, during my time there I did manage to get one musical gig. I performed with the Old Gold Singers, the university's swing choir, which turned out to be the only memorable part of a mostly unmemorable semester.

But guess what? The 'Dues and Don't Syndrome' struck again. I was the freshman, the newbie, and I was given the smaller singing parts in the choir. Merit be damned. It was all about seniority. I felt as if someone had hit rewind and I was back in high school. I really didn't want to go through this again, but I craved the performance experience, and on the whole I enjoyed travelling with the group (though admittedly that could well have been because I had a crush on one of the other singers, Jim Brucher). I sucked up my pride and stuck it out. In the end, my merit kicked their seniority in the balls.

Many people believe that as individuals we're the product of some preconceived plan, some grand design that God, whatever you may call Him or Her, has predetermined for us, but I've always believed that was rubbish. I am who I am firstly because of genetics, and, running a very close second, because of choices: ones my parents made, such as choosing to emigrate to America; ones their parents made, like my Papa Butler opting to ignore medical advice and instead warming my mum in the oven to keep her alive; and very conscious ones that I've made for myself.

I made the decision to get out of Iowa at the end of the term, but in a show of group loyalty, I agreed to go along with the university's Old Gold Singers to Chicago, to audition to be a summer performer at Opryland, USA.

In the eighties, Opryland was a popular tourist attraction in Nashville, Tennessee, and the theme park was considered the 'Home of American Music'. A company called Gaylord Entertainment – I kid you not – owned the park, and although it boasted a few roller coasters and other rides, it was best known for its fabulous musical shows. Sort of Broadway meets Blackpool, but bigger and with more twang.

The night before the auditions, the Old Gold Singers all stayed at my parents' house in Joliet, which was roughly halfway to Chicago from Des Moines. Seriously, Cardiff is closer to Chicago than Des Moines in terms of its cultural cache and coolness. Until the wee hours of the morning, the house was alive with the sound of music. Singers practised in the living room at the piano, a few gathered in the dining room around a tape player, and the rest sang out from the rec room in the basement. But not one of the voices was mine.

At about 10 p.m., I came into the kitchen, poured myself a glass of milk, and kissed my mum goodnight.

'John,' she called after me, 'shouldn't you be practising with the rest of the group?'

'I can practise in my head.'[2]

Later, I learned from Andy Barnicle, my acting teacher at United States International University in San Diego, that to practise in your head is a proven rehearsal technique. According to Andy, 'If you can see yourself doing it, you can perform it.' But, to be honest, it wasn't just that. I really didn't want to let the other members of the choir hear what I could do. In all the time I'd known them, they'd never been much interested in discovering my talent, so why give them a preview now? I went off to bed, letting my competition for Opryland serenade me to sleep.

For the first round of auditions, all of the Old Gold Singers performed in the same room. I was the last one to be called. Now, although I'd taken a couple of ballet lessons while in high school, Billy Elliot I was not. Most of my dancing experience at this time had been the few steps I'd picked up during performances and my own raw skills. I was, however, athletic, and could and still can flip, jump and kick with the best of them. For my Opryland audition, I did a number that would have made Gene Kelly proud. I included a couple of high kicks, some serious tap, a little soft-shoe and then

---

[2] Back then, my head wasn't so full. There was rehearsal space.

my big finish. I closed with a standing back somersault, which I landed perfectly, never missing a beat or losing the final notes.

I looked up at the panel of judges and I knew I had them. I looked at the other Old Gold Singers, watched them readjust their jaws, and knew I'd got them, too.

At the close of this round, Jean Whitticker, one of the casting directors and choreographers for Opryland USA at that time, pulled me aside. 'We're not making the callback announcement yet, John, but we know right now that we want to hire you, so don't go anywhere.'

I didn't. I said goodbye to the Old Gold Singers and the following summer I went to Nashville.

My work at Opryland during the summers of '86 and '87 dominates my memories of this time in my life, even though the Nashville shows were not the only performing I did back then. After I left the University of Iowa, I took acting classes in Chicago and I auditioned for commercials and other small jobs to occupy my time in the months between my summer gigs at the theme park.

As it turned out, well into the 1990s I regularly received residual payments from one of those early jobs. It was probably the worst ice-cream commercial ever for Baskin-Robbins. A commercial shoot that was supposed to take a morning stretched into an entire day because I completely overacted and looked like I was having an orgasm instead of enjoying an ice-cream treat. Some day, I know the commercial's going to show up; when it does, please remember I was very young and be kind.

While performing at Opryland, I met one of my best friends, Marilyn Rising. We hit it off instantly. For a start, she looked almost as cute in chaps as I did. She was small and bubbly, with a big voice and lots of charm and energy. We shared the same passion for the performing arts and a similar outrageous sense of humour. We once spent an entire road trip to Illinois with cockatiels, real ones, on our shoulders,[3] wearing rubber masks that looked like old-age pensioners' faces. A trucker followed us for miles trying to figure out if we were nuts or just, well, fucking nuts. Another time, as my mum and dad's plane was leaving San Diego International Airport, Marilyn and I climbed out on to one of the observation decks (this was pre-9/11), and dropped our jeans in tribute. According to my mum and dad, the passengers cheered wildly when the pilot announced that 'someone was getting a royal send-off.'

In my second summer at Opryland, Marilyn and I were assigned to a show called *Way Out West*. A number of the songs we performed were from *Oklahoma!* – and, trust me, after singing songs from that musical day after day, it's easy to see why 'poor Jud is dead.'

The summer before, after I'd finished my show, I'd walk across the park to watch another performer, Michael Clowers, dance in a different production. He was probably one of the best dancers at Opryland and he had an incredible smile. I thought he was sexy and for the longest time I never flirted or approached him in any way, I just watched him dance. Occasionally, I'd catch a glimpse of him at one of the gay clubs in Nashville – a place where many of the Opryland performers gathered to watch one of our wardrobe guys do his drag show, a wicked 'Le Jazz Hot' from *Victor Victoria*. The show was brilliant, but he had to perform in the worst area in Nashville in order to distance himself from any direct association with Opryland, which was a lovely slice of irony because it seemed to me that almost everyone who worked at Opryland was gay anyway.

Living in such a gay community was, in fact, a kind of liberation for me. Although I never felt as if I'd been 'in the closet', I was conscious of being truly myself for the first time in my life. I do think that being part of a group where, gay or not gay, we accepted

---

[3] The birds were originally my flatmate Midge's. More on Midge in chapter nine.

each other and marked territory by our talent not our sexual preference made all the difference. Having said that, those years of puberty and adolescence were never really years of keeping myself hidden; instead they were all about growing comfortable with all parts of myself, and my sexuality was only one of those parts.

When a group of my closest high-school friends came to Nashville to visit me, I kept my Opry friends around and did not change who I was becoming. I remember thinking that my life so far was turning out okay, and my schoolmates would either accept me or they wouldn't; we'd either stay in touch or we wouldn't. With a couple of exceptions, we have.

The Nashville summer nights saw my Barrowman party gene kick in, and with a little help from my friends I threw some great bashes. We were all between eighteen and twenty-one years of age, all far from home, and there wasn't much we didn't do. At one of these parties, I finally plucked up the courage to ask Michael Clowers if he wanted to go swimming in the apartment complex's pool.

I was a tit bipsy, I mean a bit tipsy, and so was he. In the still of the Nashville night, the stars shimmered like sequins. I kept my eyes on them even as I sensed Michael gliding slowly across the swimming pool toward me. The water rippled slightly as he slid on top of me and cupped his hand under my head. Then it happened: my first gay kiss. To this day, it remains one of the most romantic kisses of my life. As far as I know, the recipient of that slow sensational snog is now a choreographer for the Radio City Music Hall, but in 1986 he was in my arms in a swimming pool in Tennessee. It hadn't taken much flirting on my part to get him into the pool, and that kiss led to, well, let me just say, 'Uh oh, those summer nights ...'

The sad part was that, despite both of us being comfortable with being gay, the threat of HIV and AIDS loomed large in the late eighties, and so taking the plunge, so to speak, and participating in the complete sex act scared the hell out of us. He and I still had a lot of fun, though, and that night in the pool led to a few more romantic evenings under the stars. It was my first real summer fling and, as such, holds a special place in my memories.

I experienced lots of firsts at Opryland. Getting a real pay cheque for performing in a musical was another one. I did four shows a day in either a morning or an afternoon time block. It was hard work, but I loved every minute of it. I was getting paid to sing and dance on stage, wearing outfits that made my drum-major uniform from junior high look drab.

While performing at Opryland, I learned how to be part of an ensemble, and how to project my voice into the wind without losing volume or damaging my vocal cords. I learned how to dance my ass off in 100-degree temperatures and never let the audience see me sweat. In *Way Out West* I played Marshall Dillon, a character from a popular American TV show in the fifties. After each performance, the entire cast had to return to the stage, where we were expected to chat with the audience as they filtered out of the amphitheatre. When you're already soaked with sweat and 500 people or more are filtering past you, shaking your hand, asking questions, taking your photograph, you quickly learn all about interacting with an audience, staying focused, and appreciating the feedback. Still, to this day I think the most important lesson I learned at Opryland was how to leave the stage gracefully with shit trickling down my white polyester trousers.[4]

You've probably heard from other sources that I can be a bit of a prankster. I have, on just one or two occasions,[5] embarrassed my friends and family in public. Once, when Bev and I were in New York to premiere my cabaret at Arci's Place in 2002, I was in need

---

[4] Stay with me, now. All will be revealed shortly.
[5] Maths was never my strong point.

of a little retail therapy. We headed to Fifth Avenue and the Louis Vuitton store. I was looking for a dog collar for Penny, my beloved golden cocker spaniel, who sadly passed away in 2007 at the age of seventeen. I was dressed in my off-hours uniform: shabby chic jeans, polo shirt and trainers. For at least ten minutes, not one assistant in the store made eye contact with me – until I pulled out my LV wallet. Suddenly, three of them were on us.

'May I help you, sir?'

'I'd like a dog collar.'

'What size?'

'To fit her,' I said, and pointed to Bev. At least I didn't ask for a leash too.

Given this predilection to pranks, I'm always prepared to accept when I may be on the receiving end of one. When I was recording my third solo album, *John Barrowman Swings Cole Porter*, in 2004, Bev arrived early at the studio with me to hear, for the very first time, a few songs on the album after they'd been fully mixed. The sound engineer adjusted his tracks, the orchestra swelled, the music rose gloriously, and then my vocals filled the room. I couldn't believe it. I sounded fucking awful. My pitch was too high and I had a lisp. I sounded like Pinky after Perky had punched him in the throat. My stomach jumped into mine.

'Oh my God, Bev, is that how I really sound?'

She was too stunned to reply, which confused me even more. Ever since Bev first accompanied me to a high-school vocal competition – where I wanted to sing 'My Heart at Thy Sweet Voice' from Camille Saint-Saëns's opera about Samson and Delilah, which is a song sung by Delilah, and Bev agreed to let me do it – she has been my biggest supporter. Over the years, Bev has gone from comforting me backstage during that fateful high-school concert to accompanying me on the piano for any of my solo endeavours, as well as assisting with song arrangements and the necessary production matters for my cabaret.

Bev's silence spoke volumes. The producer cut the tape. Gradually, giggles and then guffaws of laughter from the musicians filled the studio. They'd deliberately manipulated my voice in the mix as a joke. Dirty bastards!

All of this is to say that I can take as good as I give; however, the 'polyester pants' prank that was pulled on me by a fellow performer at Opryland was not nearly so kind. In fact, I've always suspected the so-called 'practical joke' may have had a malicious motive. The performer to whom I'm referring had lost out to me as the lead in many of the troupe's numbers, and I think he was hoping to put me out of commission for a few days, perhaps to get the spotlight he believed he so deserved. Consequently, before I went on stage that hot summer's day, he laced my water with ExLax, a very potent laxative. Since the tropical Nashville temperatures required constant hydration, I'd gulped at least three healthy doses by the time I was ready for the final number.

As anyone who's worked with me over the years knows, I've always followed Robert Burns's advice that 'where 'ere you be, let your wind gang free,' so it wasn't unusual for me to release a little 'wind' during a performance when the urge presented itself. Unfortunately, when the urge suddenly presented itself that morning, it was not a little toot that escaped but a full-blown trumpet voluntary. What made things even worse, oh yes, there can be something worse than diarrhoea filling your underwear, was that I was not even wearing any underwear. My pants were white and skintight, and I had to perform three high kicks in a row, through which I fired spurts of shit at an elderly couple sitting in the front row.

Mercifully, for them as much as for me, I managed to nudge a fellow dancer into my forward position in the line, and eventually I was able to make my escape off stage.

Every now and then, I wonder how long it took the couple from the front row to notice the stink as they were driving home. Because at some point on a road trip, as I've mentioned earlier, there's always a smell.

Another first for me during those summers was turning down a show with Disney. This happened in 1986, during the first year I performed at Opryland. It was not long after Bev – together with her husband Jim and their two children, Jennifer and Michael – had visited me in Nashville. During their stay, Bev had faithfully come to the show a number of times. After one performance, she'd pulled me aside.

'John, knock off the stupid antics as you're leaving the stage.'

She was referring to my occasional tendency to drop my pants or lift the skirt of a fellow performer, usually Marilyn (and always with her full knowledge), as we exited stage left.

'What if someone comes just to see you?' Bev continued. 'They'll see everything and they may not be impressed.'

'We do stuff like that all the time, Bev.'

But she wasn't having any of it.

My *Torchwood* family can attest to the fact that, to this day, I remain partial to an occasional 'full moon' to shine the way when the set is feeling dark and the crew's morale is a bit gloomy – and sometimes even when it's not. Once, when Carole and her husband Kevin were visiting me in London when I was playing Raoul in *The Phantom of the Opera* at Her Majesty's Theatre, they got lost on their way to the venue. Carole called from a phone box on Regent Street.

'I know I'm close,' she said.

'Keep going until Charles II Street, then turn left,' I replied. 'You'll see the sign as soon as you turn.'

Carole and Kevin came round the corner – and saw my bare bum hanging out the top-floor dressing-room window, a shining beacon in the night for weary travellers.

It has to be said that I'm not shy about showing my behind on screen, either. In the late 1980s, one of my first film roles was in Brian De Palma's *The Untouchables*. My few seconds in frame were as an uncredited extra in the scene where Sean Connery is recruiting Andy Garcia at the police academy. I'm on camera from the rear, standing in tight grey sweats with my hands folded behind my back. It was a 'butt part'.

Of course, as always, Bev's advice to me in Opryland that summer afternoon was spot on. There's a time and a place for your bum to shine, and, as it turned out, the time and the place that her point was carried home to me was the very next day.

I'd just stepped off the stage without pulling anyone's pants down, even my own, when I was stopped by a man who introduced himself as the Head of Casting for Disney. He'd come to Opryland to see me. He offered me a job for the following summer, performing at Disneyland in Orlando, Florida. It was a show, he explained, that they'd write around my talents as a performer.

I thought seriously about this for a long time, even though I'd already signed a contract to return to Opryland the next summer. After talking to my parents, I knew that if I decided to go with the Disney offer, my dad would find a way for me to break the contract. Nevertheless, in the end, I chose to honour my commitment and return to Nashville. Why? Perhaps it 'bares', ahem, repeating here that I've always followed my own tune and danced to my own steps. Furthermore, although loyalty played a part in my decision, my main reason was that I knew I still had things to learn that Opryland could teach me.

When I called Disney to tell them of my decision, I received an unexpected reply.

'John,' the then Head of Casting said, 'the performers who turn us down are usually the ones we later see with their names in lights. Good luck to you.'

I've always thought that was a generous and unselfish thing for him to say and I've always tried to follow his lead. When in similar situations, whether advising others or evaluating a role for myself, I try to remember what it felt like to have someone support the risky decision. I really have no time for sour grapes or for individuals who want to dim someone else's light because it's shining brighter than theirs.

Honestly, the world can be a dark enough place. Light it up.

Chapter Eight

'That'll Show Him'

A boy can learn a lot from the back seat of a car, but for the few months I spent regularly crawling into the rear of mine while it was parked in the South Loop of Chicago, sleep was the only thing I got to know really well.[1] Chicago is sometimes referred to as the 'City with the Big Shoulders', so it was only appropriate that for a few months during the spring and autumn of 1987, I hauled my padded ones into the city, where I occasionally went to acting classes, frequently wandered in Boys Town[2] and, when the desire struck, slept in the rear of my car until it was time to drive home to Joliet.

The reason for my excursions into Chicago was because I couldn't audition for the Performing Arts School at the United States International University (USIU) until December 1987, which meant I couldn't take classes there until the following term. When I finally packed up my belongings and my parents drove me out to San Diego, California to start my new degree, I felt as if an exciting stage in my life was about to begin. I was thrilled about a lot of things in this move, not the least of which was that I was finally

---

[1] Disappointed?

[2] A gay district of Chicago.

studying what I really wanted to learn. Goodbye opera, hello dolly!

Since my programme at USIU was built around the performing arts, I was in a much better frame of mind to take on the role of newbie once again. I had no problem working my way up the ladder when I knew that each rung would lead me to something I wanted to learn. I was a human sponge, soaking up techniques, advice and anything that I believed would help to get me a job as an actor when I graduated. I learned a lot in those two-plus years, with the help of dedicated educators who shared their time and expertise in and outside the classroom. My friends from Joliet were thrilled about my move to California and so was my family, both very aware that this was finally a university where I'd be happy.

There was only one fly in the ointment. Another student, Peter Prick,[3] who was already in the programme at USIU and quite comfortable with his leading-man status, seemed to feel threatened by my arrival on the scene. Thus began the tale of what I perceived to be Peter Prick's petty professionalism and personal posturing – sorry, I was on a roll – all of which ended in a parking lot full of fake Nazis almost twenty years later.

The rift started one afternoon as the full cast of the theatre department's production of *42nd Street* was rehearsing the big tap number for the song '42nd Street'. This was my first university show. I was in the back row of the chorus – if you're old enough to remember the original movie, think Dick Powell, only younger – and I was wired. I'd never taken a tap-dance lesson in my life, but I was athletic and nimble, and what I lacked in knowledge, I more than made up for in confidence. The closest I'd ever come to dance training was my high kicking at Opryland and a handful of ballet

---

[3] Of course, that's not his real name.

classes in high school, but 'shuffling off to Buffalo' was a whole different kind of fancy footwork.

The chorus had already run through the big Busby Berkeley number a couple of times, and for me the sound of dozens of taps snapping against the floor and the occasional loud exhales from my fellow dancers was inspiring. Suddenly, Jack Tygett, the show's director and someone from whom I learned a lifetime's worth of stuff, yelled, 'Stop the goddamn music!'

On a good day, Jack's voice sounded more like shaved granite than gravel. That afternoon, he'd been shouting at the chorus so much he sounded like Harvey Fierstein after three shots of raw alcohol. The shuffling and murmuring slowly ceased, and Jack got right to the point.

'I just want everyone to know that Barrowman's in the back row and he doesn't know a goddamn lick of tap, but he's selling the number better than any of you. He's goddamn selling it!' Jack roared. 'And not only that, but the scene where Barrowman's the bartender, he's stealing that from the principal actors too – because he's taking nothin' and makin' it into something.'

No one turned round and stared, especially not the leads, one of whom was Peter, but they didn't have to. I could feel their glares through the back of their heads. With respect to the famous line from the original movie, I was 'so swell' I made them hate me. Of course, after the cast finished rehearsing, most of the chorus who knew me were congratulatory and not the least bit put out by my enthusiasm. This was showbiz, even if it was only in its early stages for many of us. No one had time for back-stabbing, and most theatre performers I know still don't.

Over the years, I've learned that back-stabbing always leaves blood on your hands, no matter how slick you are with a blade. I've no time for it. In fact, in television and in theatre, I've earned a reputation for being unabashedly forthright and honest in professional matters. I may be a bit of a raunchy lad on set, backstage, and even in real life,[4] but when necessary, I say what I think: no bush beating, no word mincing. If I'm angry about something, you'll know. If I'm happy, you'll know that too, but the work comes first. Once, when Noël Coward was facing some criticism for his personal escapades, he wrote, 'It is discouraging how many people are shocked by honesty and how few by deceit.'

The scene to which Jack was referring in his admonishment of the cast was a relatively small moment in the musical, where the two leads are having an argument in a bar about who's in love with whom or something trivial like that. I'm in the background tending said bar, but instead of standing there with the towel draped over my arm looking professional and appropriately disinterested, I decided to empty drinks into the potted plant on the edge of the bar, wipe the mahogany with foppish flair, and generally ham it up a bit. My acting wasn't pulling from the scene's focus – well, maybe a wee bit – but it was giving some realism to the background and adding some much-needed humour. I mean, have you ever seen *42nd Street*? Was I playing it up a bit too much? Maybe. Did I mention this was showbiz?

Over time, Peter began to get fewer of the male romantic leads (they went to yours truly), and Marilyn, my best friend from Opryland who had encouraged my enrolment at USIU and was in the theatre programme herself, was regularly cast as my female lead more often than Peter's regular co-star.

Admittedly, Peter was a much better dancer than me, but I was a better singer, and since USIU now had two pairs of strong male and female leads, the directors would cast us in different plays running in repertory. They'd do a show and we'd do a show. However, this kind

---

[4] No need to skip ahead – the stories will be there when you are.

of professional trading off didn't stop Peter crossing the line from professional rivalry to personal wankerdom,[5] as far as I was concerned. As in high school, though, what I thought of as his jealous behaviour simply made me even more determined to succeed.

Throughout my years at USIU – the string of shows, the post-performance parties, the hard work, Marilyn becoming my girlfriend, the workshops and classes ... what? I've not mentioned the girlfriend part yet? A quick digression, then.

Over two summers and the seasons in between, my friendship with Marilyn deepened. Since up to this time I had experienced only one real gay relationship – and, as you've learned, even that never went beyond the secret handshake – Marilyn and I decided to try out the boyfriend/girlfriend thing. I have to admit there were lots of things I enjoyed about it, including an increased appreciation for the softer parts of the female form, but in the end it simply confirmed to me that I was a fully committed player for the boys' team.

Obviously it was never going to last, given my sexuality, but the best thing about the whole affair was that Marilyn and I remained dear friends. A few years after we officially broke up, she got hitched in my native Scotland at Gretna Green. Marilyn had fallen in love with Scotland when she'd toured it with my parents and me in the summer of 1989, the year of my big break in the West End. I had a traditional Scottish wedding cake specially made for her celebration.

To this day, Marilyn has the honour and, dare I say, pleasure of being the only woman I've ever seriously snogged, and I mean seriously – but that's all I've ever done with a woman. My boys and I have never gone where no gay man should ever go. And now you know how I know that I've never sired children.

---

[5] Derived from the Latin phrase *wankerus non wankeri*, meaning 'once a wanker, always a wanker'.

During my studies at USIU, Andy Barnicle, my acting teacher, would deliberately piss me off as a way to challenge me. From the first class I took from him, he read my nature correctly, recognizing that my competitiveness was equal to my professional pride and my thirst for learning – and he exploited this to my benefit. In class Andy would say, 'If you're a working actor, you're a successful actor,' and I let that motto shape many of the career choices I made in the years before the success of Captain Jack. When last I checked, Andy was the Artistic Director for Laguna Playhouse in California. Whenever I'm in a West End show, Andy makes a trip to London to visit me.

Trips to the West End in London were, in fact, part of the USIU course. Every year, faculty members from the Performing Arts School travelled with a group of students for a semester in England to study Shakespeare, and to see shows and plays in and around London. My class and Peter's were scheduled for this trip in 1989. Peter and I were even assigned as room-mates, but as things turned out, I was to spend my nights with Reno Sweeney at the Prince Edward Theatre in the West End, and Peter would be rooming alone.

In all the stories I can tell you about my life and my career, the one about how my big break in theatre came about is still one of the coolest, because it has so many of the characteristics of a musical. Here's the rough plot. A successful West End show needs to find a replacement for its American leading man – and quickly. A handsome young boy walks off a street in Glasgow, auditions for the role in said successful West End show, and is flown to London for a callback audition, where he meets and has an instant connection with the already famous leading lady. Cue orchestra. Sing.

In the summer of 1989, before beginning our course on Shakespeare, Marilyn and I went to Scotland to visit my relatives in Glasgow. One afternoon, my dad's eldest brother Neil heard an announcement about an open casting call for *Anything Goes*, which was running at the Prince Edward Theatre in the West End. The auditions were being held at the Royal Scottish Academy of Music in Glasgow. According to the announcement, the producers were looking for a young man with an American accent who could sing and dance. I knew the perfect person.

As it had before and many times since, my Barrowman risk gene burst into life. I figured I had nothing to lose and a hell of a lot to gain. Thanks to Bev's advice about doing community theatre, I'd already played Billy Crocker, the role they were looking to cast, once before in 1984, so despite not having any sheet music with me on the trip, I knew Billy's character and I knew I could sing Cole Porter.

Before the audition, I went to a restaurant near the Academy to prepare in private. I started warming up my voice in the restaurant's bathroom, but I was forced to vacate the space in the middle of practising my scales, when an old man banged on the door and yelled, 'I dinna ken what yer on, Jimmy, but if it's good for piles, I'll huv some a' it!'[6]

By the time I'd finished my song in the audition, Larry Oaks, the resident director, was no longer slouching in his chair and I knew I'd hit all the right notes. Larry went on to become a friend and a significant mentor during those early days. He'd show up in my dressing room after every performance with a page of notes, advising me on everything from how to hold my hands in certain scenes to which way to tilt my head in others. No detail ever escaped him. I'm a better performer today because of his keen eye and generous spirit. Larry even let me stay at his house until I found a place of my own in London. Years later, while I was judging *Any Dream Will Do*,

---

[6] Once again for the posh among you, 'piles' are haemorrhoids. No matter what you call them, they're still a pain in the arse.

there were many times when I felt as if I was channelling Larry, especially when one of the Josephs would call me at home for advice and encouragement. I always gave them plenty of both.

I sang a second song from *Anything Goes* in the audition, and when I'd finished, Larry asked, 'Can you do an American accent for us, John?'

Now, keep in mind what I've already told you about me being bidialectical. As I'd been travelling for the past couple of weeks with my parents, visiting relatives in Glasgow and revisiting my roots, I'd come into the audition speaking with my Scottish accent.

'I'll try,' I said.

I went off to read the script alone for a few minutes, came back into the room, and then read a few lines as an American.

'Thank you very much, John,' said Larry. 'We'll be in touch.'

I learned later that the casting team immediately called Elaine Paige, exclaiming, 'We've found him!' Elaine, who was playing Reno Sweeney in the production, was also one of the show's producers, so she was involved in the audition process. Elaine's own West End debut had been in *Hair* in 1969. By the time she starred as Eva Perón in Sir Tim Rice and Lord Lloyd-Webber's *Evita* in 1978, she'd become the First Lady of the West End.

When I got back to my cousin's house after the audition, Larry had already left a message, asking if I could fly to London immediately for a callback audition and a meeting with Elaine. Her opening line when I walked on to the stage at the Prince Edward Theatre the following day was, 'He's pretty, but let's see if he can sing.'

Once I'd convinced her that I could, she asked to see me dance. *Anything Goes* is a dancer's delight, with lots of show-stopping numbers and tons of tap, so it requires strong all-rounders in the lead roles. The whole musical is a fast-paced romantic comedy set aboard an ocean liner sailing to America. Reno Sweeney is the ship's nightclub star and Billy Crocker is a young lovesick businessman (and Reno's ex) who stows away on the ship so that he can be with Hope Harcourt, a beautiful young woman with whom he's fallen in love. The rest of the ship's passengers are a bunch of wonderful eccentrics, including Public Enemy Number Thirteen Moonface Martin and his girlfriend, who are posing as a minister and a missionary. The show is full of mistaken identities and misunderstood motives. All those high-energy dance numbers make it demanding for the principal performers, though. It was not surprising that as Elaine climbed up on to the stage during the audition to dance with me, she admitted her legs were a bit tired.

Now, one of the things I hope this book has already demonstrated is that my mother did not raise an impolite lout. My only excuse for the following speech is that I was nervous.

'Don't worry, honey,' I said aloud to Elaine Paige, leading lady extraordinaire and the woman who quite literally held my fate in her hands, 'I'll keep you up. I'll keep you in time!'

Elaine stared at me for a moment, and then she laughed, a big, throaty, 'you've got something' kind of laugh, and that was the start of my professional career and the beginning of a beautiful friendship with Elaine. I landed the role and the rest, as the saying goes, is history.

During the next few months of my professional debut in the West End, my class from USIU remained in London studying Shakespeare and going to the theatre, while I was learning on the job from Elaine and Bernard Cribbins, who was playing Moonface Martin. I couldn't have had a better pair of mentors. Bernard has been in television and film since the 1960s, with credits in a number of the *Carry On* comedies. Bernard was also the narrator for one of my favourite animated children's shows, *The Wombles*. My absolute favourite role of his, though, was as the spoon salesman in *Fawlty Towers*, whom Basil Fawlty mistakes for a hotel inspector. Bernard is a terrific musical comedian and his recording of the song 'Right Said Fred' is one I remember singing along to on the counter of the record shop in Scotland.

Most of my peers from USIU were thrilled for me on the day I announced to all of them that not only would I be missing class during the 'Shakespeare' semester, but I would not be returning to San Diego with them when their time in England came to an end, because I'd gotten a job as the leading man in a West End show. At first, Peter Prick appeared to be pleased for me too, but after a few weeks, our rivalry raised its head again, with him saying he believed me to be 'a one-hit wonder'. Incidentally, that damning phrase was not only apparently employed by Peter, but also Peter's father, who used it to describe me to my own dad, when they happened to run into each other the following year at a show in Chicago. Despite Peter's seeming sour grapes, however, whenever he could, he'd show up at the Prince Edward Theatre and want to schmooze with all the stars.

By the time my class was ready to return to USIU without me, friends like Marilyn were still important in my life, but I'd taken Elaine Paige's advice and flushed out 'the Negative Nellies'. Peter and some of the others had long since been stopped at the stage door.

That wasn't the only tip I took from Elaine. Over those few months, Elaine and Bernard became my surrogate parents, and I've never forgotten the gist of their professional advice. 'Don't do things just because other people want you to do them, John. Do them because you want to, because even if you fail, you'll still be satisfied, because when you look back on it, it was your choice to take part.'

When I think about that time in the West End, I'm surprised I remembered to eat. Everything was new and exciting and incredibly hectic. Along with Elaine and Bernard, a fellow actor Ian Burford, whom I met when we were both performing at a Jerry Herman concert at the Royal Palladium, and his partner Alex Cannell, were a second set of surrogate parents to me. After a long day at the theatre, Ian and Alex always made sure I had company when I wanted it and a bowl of the best chilli whenever I needed it.[7]

So, Peter and my peers returned to California, time moved on, and so did I. Then one afternoon, almost ten years later, while I was in New York performing in Stephen Sondheim's *Putting It Together* with Carol Burnett and Ruthie Henshall, I came out of the stage door at the Ethel Barrymore Theater and literally crossed paths with Peter. We were surprised to see each other, but we were older and more mature and so we shook hands and went to dinner at Joe Allen's restaurant.

Peter was working in New York choreographing a Broadway show and we chatted about the things we'd done since we'd parted ways in London. Our dinner was perfectly amicable, but – as always – I felt that Peter's jealousy was so present that we might as well have been at a table for three. We weren't boys anymore. I decided I would rise above the sourness I suspected. We finished our meal, he offered to pay, I refused to let him, and we went our separate ways once again.

That is, until the summer of 2004, when I found myself once again in New York and walking toward Peter on Ninth Avenue. This time, I was blond[8] and – even if I do say so myself – looking pretty

---

[7] Incidentally, Alex and Ian were the first gay couple to record their relationship in London's Partnerships Register in 2001, and in 2005 they were one of the first couples to take advantage of the Civil Partnership Law. They've been together for over forty years.

[8] I totally freaked my family out the first time I emailed them pics of me as a blond.

hot. The dye job wasn't done on a personal whim; it was related to an exciting film role. A few months earlier, Mel Brooks and Susan Stroman had come to see me in Trevor Nunn's revival of *Anything Goes* at the National Theatre on London's South Bank. In my dressing room after the performance, they'd asked if I'd be interested in taking the lead tenor role in the song 'Springtime for Hitler' in the upcoming film of the hit Broadway show *The Producers*, which Stroman was directing. I agreed immediately – partly because I'd been a fan of Brooks for years, especially *Young Frankenstein*. Once, during a long plane trip back to Scotland from America, Carole and I had recited entire scenes from that movie, much to the annoyance of most of the passengers around us, except Murn, who every time we said 'lovely knockers' would laugh and heave up her ample bosom.

'Oh my God, John, look at you,' exclaimed Peter.

'I'm in town for *The Producers*,' I informed him.

'I am too,' he said. 'I'm here all week.'

At that instant, my own personal Jiminy Cricket jumped on to my shoulder, his soft little voice saying, 'Tell him the truth, John. Tell him you've already been here a week working on the big finale. Tell him you have your own dressing room right next to Uma Thurman's. Tell him you've been chatting with Will Ferrell. Tell him, John. Be a real boy.'

Ah, hell. I flicked the cricket to the ground.

'I'm here all week too,' I said.

A couple of days later, I was up in my dressing room having my hair tinted, which they had to do every day so my dark roots would not show on camera. Matthew Broderick, Nathan Lane and Mel Brooks were with me, when Mel suddenly let out an almighty howl and sprinted from the room.

Through the window, we could see over a hundred supporting actors in Nazi uniforms gathering in the parking lot of the warehouse where we were filming – and may I just interject here and note how fabulous all those gorgeous men looked in their costumes; did you know that the designer Hugo Boss was the original creator of the Nazi's SS uniforms? The supporting cast of 'Nazis' were rehearsing these big, stomping, Busby Berkeley-like routines, 'heiling' this way and 'sig heiling' that way, when all of a sudden Mel darted out into the parking lot, screaming at an assistant, 'Get them fucking in here now or we're all gonna get shot!'

The warehouse was in the heart of an Hasidic community in Brooklyn, and from the vantage point of my dressing room, Mel had seen small groups of bearded dark-clothed men gathering around the fences.

After some subtlety was returned to the parking lot and I'd rehearsed the first part of the 'Springtime' number, I decided to go outside to do a bit of flirting, to see a few folks I recognized from other shows and, of course, to check in with Peter, who I knew was out there.

I spotted him and made my way through the crowd of gay Nazis to where he was sitting. Peter looked at me, shocked. 'Where the hell have you been, John? You're really late. We've been rehearsing all morning.'

I couldn't resist. This 'one-hit wonder' took out his knife. It may have been a butter knife, but I really wanted to savour the moment.

'Oh,' I said, prolonging my explanation, 'I've been inside rehearsing with Uma. I'm fronting the "Springtime for Hitler" number.'

He looked as if I'd whacked him with my nightstick. He recovered quickly and we said our goodbyes. I went back inside, humming to the tune of 'Springtime': 'Payback for John in the parking lot / Barrowman is happy and gay!'

Chapter Nine

'No One is Alone'

My friend Midge was twenty-nine when she died. There was no public funeral, no memorial service, no flowers, no obituary – in fact, no overt acknowledgement of her death of any kind. Even today, ten years later, I'm angry and incredibly sad about what happened to her. Midge was a friend during my high-school days – not an especially close one at that time, but still a friend – and later, at the United States International University in San Diego, we were flatmates. Midge's life mattered to me and, despite her problems, I think it should have been far more important to those closer to her. I've thought about Midge a lot over the intervening years and given what happened to her, Midge's story deserves to be told.

In my opinion, Midge was not so much her family's black sheep as she was its wild mare. To her family, she seemed hard to contain, difficult to control, and she jumped their fences whenever she could. To her friends, Midge partied with gusto, played with heart, and had a passion for animals that was boundless. And did I mention she was gorgeous?[1]

Midge's family was part of the professional aristocracy in Joliet,

---

[1] I'm gay, not blind.

and since my dad at that time was the plant manager of one of the biggest employers in the area, I guess the Barrowmans had moved into those heady ranks too. Of course, none of us 'shites scented soap', as Murn used to say, and my family never forgot that. After all, it wasn't too many decades ago that my dad was filling cream cakes at a bakery in Tollcross, and my mum was making ends meet at the end of the month by serving tripe and mashed potatoes for dinner.

In case you don't know, tripe is a Scottish delicacy made from a sheep's stomach – mmm, yummy! – and onions, all of it served – get ready for this – in a warm milky base. The only joy to be found whenever tripe was on my mum's menu was that Carole, Andrew and I were allowed to eat with trays in front of the television, and we were not required to sit at the table with my parents. Frankly, I think my mum did this not as a reward for eating the tripe, but so that she didn't have to see the pain she was inflicting on us as we tried to swallow the chewy, tasteless concoction. If William Wallace had served tripe to the English, they'd have turned and fled, and we'd be singing 'Scotland the Brave' at coronations.

Midge's parents, on the other hand, seemed convinced their farts were fragrant. They were neighbours of my mum and dad in Joliet and they quickly became friends. Although my mum and dad were significantly more liberal than Midge's parents, the four of them shared similar passions for music, theatre, travel, good food, a wee drink, and throwing a hell of a party, which they did regularly.

I must admit that after our move to America, it wasn't just my family's social status that improved. My parents' soirees took a step up from Saturday nights in The Extension. Their parties were now held in a fully kitted-out basement, which included an area for dancing and a full bar that would have made Dean Martin drool (not that he needed any help).

Although the time and place had changed significantly, some

essential things had not. Whether the parties included my dad's business associates or just friends from the neighbourhood, whenever possible I was the nightly entertainment, and although I wasn't singing 'Milly, Molly, Mandy' anymore, I was still the main event. Thanks to the many high-school performances and Forensic Competitions I was getting under my belt in Joliet, I was a more polished performer. I was even a bit more confident in my dancing ability, which was the part of my repertoire that, back then, I felt was my weakest.

The other big difference was that instead of getting my cheeks pinched by adoring aunties and family friends, I was now getting my bum pinched by someone's wife or girlfriend who'd occasionally hit on me. Naturally, I'd share these incidents with my mum and Murn, when she was still alive, over toast and tea the next morning, and we'd cat about them for days. I mean, what good's a grope if you can't get some decent gossip from it?

Although Midge and I went to different high schools in Joliet, when our parents were socializing together, we would hang out. As was the case with most females when I was growing up, Midge felt as if she could talk to me and I to her, so we, like our parents, became friends.

After high-school graduation, though, Midge and I went our separate ways. I headed off to the University of Iowa for fun and games with the Old Gold Singers and Midge attended college in Florida, but we stayed in touch. She visited me in Nashville a couple of times during those intervening summers, and she continued to call me when she needed someone to talk to.

After two full summers working at Opryland USA, I transferred to USIU in San Diego. When I made my decision to move to California, Midge, who had dropped out of Florida for reasons I didn't learn until later, insisted that her parents let her move too.

My mum and dad always instilled in Carole, Andrew and me

the value of higher education – and they put their money where their mouths were, funding room, board and tuition for each of us. Even in the late eighties, it was expensive to live in California, and to make it possible for me to study, audition when I wanted to and perform when I needed to, my parents came up with a pragmatic financial solution. They bought a condo in LaJolla, California with Midge's parents, and while we attended university, Midge and I lived in the apartment. When I left USIU to play Billy Crocker in *Anything Goes* in 1989, Midge's mum and dad bought my parents out.

The flat had two bedrooms and a balcony. By anyone's standards, not just a student's, it was lovely. For a while, living with Midge was a terrific arrangement – until, that is, she began to fall apart.

At first, she and I had a blast. Midge's sense of humour was both outrageous and ever present. Remind you of anyone else? We also shared a similar taste in cheesy sitcoms and campy dramas. We'd stay up for hours watching reruns of *The Love Boat* or *Happy Days*, or playing drinking games with my friends from university. When we cleaned up after our frequent parties, she and I would act out scenes from our favourite shows. It was during these housework sessions that I began to perfect my Cher impression, an impersonation that has since brought me wild applause, especially once when I performed it while riding the escalator at Munich's International Airport. Even Germans thought it was funny.

Whenever Midge had any kind of chore to do, she'd do it in style. Sometimes she'd dress up as Snow White, dusting and vacuuming while dancing around the room singing 'Some Day My Prince Will Come'. Sadly, Midge's never came. In the end, I think it would have taken much more than a kiss to save her if he had.

Midge was gorgeous and gregarious, but like many young women she was worried about her weight, worried about her hair and worried about her skin. Ironically, despite her looks and her sense of humour, she had trouble fitting in and never had any real friends of her own – that is, except for me. I realize now that this should have been my first clue to her troubles, but I was young and away from home and stretching my proverbial wings – and I do mean stretching. As I've said, I've undoubtedly inherited my parents' party gene.

The more I got to know Midge, the more I witnessed her using her insecurities to manipulate those around her, especially her family. After experiencing years of Midge's unpredictability, it seemed to me as if they'd taken to throwing money at her, giving in to her every whim in an attempt to keep her consoled and out of range of their lives. Midge rarely tried to manipulate me and so our friendship survived, despite her occasional bitchy tendencies. Her behaviour was actually a symptom of something much more serious, but no one was really paying attention.

Because Midge had a difficult time making friends, I often included her when I had plans with mine. I even set her up with one of my friends from university, Thorsten Kaye, who is now a well-established television actor in America, most recently to be seen in the soap opera *All My Children*, and father to two daughters. Their first few dates went fine, but soon Midge began to rant about their relationship, in a manner that I thought verged on paranoia.

It was at that time that I learned from another friend that Midge's reasons for leaving her last university had to do with her destructive, obsessive behaviour with an ex-boyfriend. I pulled Thorsten aside one night, when he and Midge returned to the flat, and I told him to back away. Thankfully, he did.

Midge was both naive and world-worn at the same time, so she was easy prey for scams. Once, she was persuaded to sign up for modelling classes that most of us knew were not legit, but Midge wouldn't listen, and the modelling agency had just enough legality to stay in business without raising too many red flags. The agency published its own so-called magazine and the deal was that after taking the required make-up, hair and wardrobe classes, the sucker, erm, I mean model, could purchase an ad in the magazine to promote herself. The company guaranteed dissemination of the magazine to all the biggest agencies and fashion designers in the country. Midge attended the necessary classes and at the end of the course she was given the option to buy either a quarter-, half- or full-page ad. Midge insisted on a full page, and so Midge got a full page. The tab for the entire experience was $10,000. In the mid eighties, that was a hell of a lot of money. It still is.

She charged it to her American Express card without telling her parents, and when they did find out, they never acknowledged the outrageousness of the cost nor the stupidity of the decision to participate in the first place, which I believe was what Midge had really wanted. She was desperate for a reaction, and if she couldn't get a positive one, negative would have been fine, too. Even if it meant that her parents cut off her credit card, flew her home and screamed at her for a month. My parents would've dragged me home by the scruff of my neck and fed me tripe for weeks.

It was right after this incident that Midge's behaviour became even more erratic. She'd disappear for days at a time, and when she did come home, she'd bring a stray cat or two with her or an expensive dog that she'd bought on her dad's credit card. I love animals as much as the next guy, but the flat was beginning to look and smell a bit like Pets R Us. One day, Midge would eat anything that wasn't moving, and the next day she'd refuse to drink anything wet. Her bedroom started filling up with dirty clothes because she'd stopped doing the laundry. Eventually, the pile would get so high that she'd run out of clean underwear or T-shirts. Rather than get some detergent, she'd go out and buy new knickers. When she wasn't wandering the streets, she'd stay in bed for days on end, lost in her hopelessness and despair.

Hindsight may be twenty-twenty, but foresight is worth so much more. When I look back on that time with Midge, I realize her actions were not just personality quirks. Sadly, those who'd known Midge for years, and witnessed these same patterns again and again, appeared to demonstrate no foresight in trying to get Midge any meaningful help to stop her descent into full psychosis.

I was twenty years old and just beginning to figure out who I was, yet even I could eventually see that Midge was heading for trouble. I watched her self-destruct before my eyes. In my young mind, I thought I was helping when I physically dragged her out of bed and gave her personal ultimatums, but all I was really doing was putting plasters on deep wounds. I'd yell, 'You may not go into your room until you've cleaned up the mess you made in the kitchen,' and then I'd block her bedroom door. She'd glare at me, but she'd clear up her clutter. I did my best to drag her from her slumps and restrain her during her highs, but what she really needed was intervention from a parent, not pity from a peer.

At times, when Midge was at her most manic, I resented the fact that I was the one taking care of her. Despite knowing about her deteriorating mental health, her family never insisted she be brought home. I think they were paralyzed by their perception that Midge's psychological state was somehow a reflection on their parenting, when, in fact, it was their neglect of her mental condition that was the real mark of it. I mean, this was the 1980s, not the Middle Ages. Midge could and should have been saved.

A few days before I was due to head to England to spend the semester abroad with USIU's theatre programme, Midge returned from a three-day bender insisting that a cult had kidnapped her. Her highs were getting higher and her lows were scraping rock bottom by now. The night before I left California for London, we laughed, drank champagne, and toasted each other's futures. Sadly, Midge didn't have a very long one ahead of her, and our evening together turned out to be the last time I ever saw her.

After I got the part in *Anything Goes*, I moved to London permanently. Since I'd only packed for a semester away from the States when I'd originally left, my parents had to drive out to California and, with my brother Andrew's help, pack up my belongings and haul them back to storage in Illinois.

They reported back to Midge's parents that Midge was a wreck and they didn't think she could continue living by herself. The flat was a mess and so was she. But instead of bringing her home immediately, her parents opted to send one of her brothers to take care of her. When her brother got there, the condo was a zoo. Literally. There were strays crawling on the furniture, filth and faeces everywhere. Midge had even thrown stuff over the balcony and just left it where it landed in the woods behind the building.

When Midge was finally brought home, she was diagnosed as a bipolar schizophrenic with multiple personalities. I'd met all of them. Seriously, I had, and so through all of this, the diagnosis, treatment and care, Midge kept calling me. I'd come out of a matinee and Midge would call. I'd finish an evening performance, and Midge would call. I'd remind her that she needed to stay on her meds, and that maybe in the future she could be the old Midge again.

Time passed, and I moved on to other performances. Only days after I'd had a long talk with Midge, I heard from my mum that she'd been hospitalized in a serious condition and diagnosed with leukaemia. Not a mental illness, but a physical one. Where had that come from?

Just a few weeks later, my mum called to tell me that Midge had died. I was devastated. For ages, I struggled to come to terms with how someone so young with so much life left to live could be gone, and in such a tragic way. To this day, I believe Midge committed suicide.

Her funeral was private and happened quickly. There was no obituary and no service of any kind. As far as I was concerned, this was Midge's final indignity. Her parents appeared to me to treat Midge in death the way they'd treated her in life, with as little fuss as possible. Friends and neighbours who were close to Midge's family and who had known her well – like my mum and dad, like me – wanted to remember her and grieve for her with some kind of public ceremony. It wasn't to be. At the very least, I wanted to send flowers, but I was discouraged from doing so. I was not alone in this. Close friends, even members of Midge's family, were shut down and shut out.

Not too long after Midge's death, my parents gathered with her parents and some other friends from Joliet for a weekend party at Midge's parents' lake house. The conversation in the room suddenly took a turn that set Midge's father off on a vitriolic rant about minorities and gays. After a couple of minutes, my parents put their glasses on the table, stood up and said to him: 'You're a bigot and a homophobe. You know John is gay and yet you can stand there and spout that poison. We're leaving. We'll not stay under the same roof as you anymore.'

Midge's mum tried to stop them, pleading that her husband hadn't meant what he'd said, but he had, and my parents knew it immediately, because sometimes the true measure of a person is revealed in their most unguarded moments.

My mum and dad went up to their bedroom, packed their suitcase, and within a half-hour they were driving through the unknown countryside in the middle of the night, in search of a hotel room. They called Carole to tell her what had happened.

Kevin went on his computer in Milwaukee and quickly directed them to a nearby motel. Then my parents called me in London. I stayed on the line with them until I knew they weren't going to go careening off the road into a ditch, given their emotional state.

Since that night, my parents have had nothing to do with Midge's family. When I think of Midge, which I do often, I can't help wondering how different her life might have been if she'd had the kind of parents who were willing to storm off into the dark night in her defence. Midge was generous and gorgeous, and we had lots of good laughs together. She was twenty-nine when she died and I still really miss her.

Top: On stage in my first ever musical, Joliet West High School's *Hello Dolly!* I'm on the far left.

Above: With Elaine Paige and Bernard Cribbins, my theatre mentors.

Right: My professional debut in 1989.

Right: With Stefanie Powers and Paco, after a performance of *Matador*.

Left: On stage with Martin Marquez in Trevor Nunn's production of *Anything Goes*.

Right: On holiday with Claudia Schiffer on Valentino's yacht.

Opposite page: Leading a company for the first time in *Matador*.

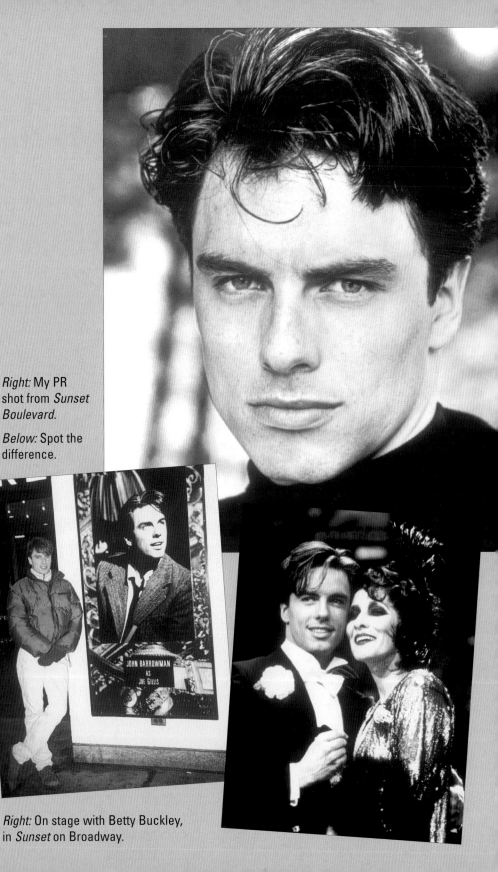

Right: My PR shot from *Sunset Boulevard.*

Below: Spot the difference.

JOHN BARROWMAN
AS
JOE GILLIS

Right: On stage with Betty Buckley, in *Sunset* on Broadway.

Above: On the plane with the legendary Shirley Bassey – notice the caviar.

Left: Backstage with Robert De Niro, after he watched my performance in *Hair*.

Some things never change.

Always the joker: backstage at *Putting It Together (above left)*; in drag as Belle in *Beauty and the Beast (above right)*; role reversal with my leading lady in *Evita (below left)*; backstage at *The Phantom of the Opera (below right),* with my brother-in-law Kevin.

Above: The *Putting It Together* crew *(from left to right)*: Ruthie Henshall, Carol Burnett, Bronson Pinchot and George Hearn.

Right: A few good friends: me and Suranne Jones.

Below: In costume for the Beast in *Beauty and the Beast*, backstage with Bev Holt and my mum.

Chapter Ten

'High Flying Adored'

Following my brief summer fling at Opryland, my first serious gay relationship was with a Spanish flamenco dancer from Cordoba called Paco Perez-Arevelo. When I met him, Paco was a dancer and the assistant to the dance captain in *Matador*, a musical that tells the fictionalized tale of a real-life bullfighter, Manuel Benitez, whom I portrayed in the same production. Rafael Aguilar, one of the world's most famous flamenco choreographers, composed the dancing in the show, using six flamenco dancers to dramatize the bull.[1] Paco danced as the head of the bull (and that is not a metaphor – I'm so not going there).

Matador originally opened in 1991 at the Queens Theatre on Shaftesbury Avenue. Unfortunately, it wasn't a runaway success in terms of ticket sales, despite receiving critical acclaim. It's my contention that the musical fell victim to a serious slump in tourism that occurred that year due, in part, to the war in the Gulf. As a result, it ran for only three months, regardless of the good reviews (that's the show, not the war).

My relationship with Paco began as a clandestine one, at least in

---

[1] Aguilar was awarded the 1992 Olivier Theatre Award for Best Choreographer for his work on *Matador*.

my mind, because technically I still had a girlfriend (remember Marilyn?). However, my dresser John Fahey – whom I worked with for the first time during *Matador* and have always requested thereafter whenever I work in the West End – Stefanie Powers, my co-star in the show, most of the rest of the company and, frankly, a good deal of the West End knew I was having an affair with Paco, so I guess it wasn't that secret after all.

When my peers from USIU had returned to finish their university year in San Diego in 1989, Marilyn and I had continued to talk to each other regularly. Somehow, though, we'd managed never to confront the realities of our relationship, until one afternoon when she paid an unexpected visit to the theatre.

At about noon on that fateful day, Paco and I drove into central London from my flat in Bow for a matinee performance. I'd just turned on to Wardour Street when John Fahey came bounding out the stage door and stopped my car on the corner.

'Marilyn just landed at Heathrow,' John announced breathlessly. 'She's on her way to surprise you.'

I was stunned and suddenly flustered: a sight to behold since it doesn't happen very often. Paco slammed the car door, saying, 'I can't fucking believe this,' or something along those lines. He spoke in Spanish. It sounded much more emphatic and dramatic.

I dashed upstairs to Stefanie's dressing room, told her what was happening and begged for help. Ever the trooper, she said, 'John, you've got two options. If you need me to, I'll pretend you're having a fling with me. I'll come into your dressing room and throw my weight around a bit. Or you can be a man and tell her the truth.'

I knew the second option was the right one, but knowing that didn't make what I had to do any easier. Marilyn was a close friend and the last thing I wanted was to hurt her or damage our friendship. When she arrived, I greeted her in mock surprise, and then she watched the show from the house seats. Afterwards, we went out to dinner, followed by a walk along the Thames. We sat on a bench and I sucked it up and spilled my guts.

When I was finished with my confession of sorts, she replied, 'That's why I came over, John. I figured you were gay and I knew we had to deal with this face to face.'

I grabbed her and hugged her and thanked her, because it was probably one of the hardest trips she'd had to make. While I was blissfully ignoring the entire situation in Paco's arms, and had only begun to anguish over seeing Marilyn when my dresser had leapt in front of my car earlier that day, she, on the other hand, had been stewing about this for months. We left the bench overlooking the Thames and met Paco at my flat, where the three of us had a big slumber party, watching movies, telling stories, laughing and singing.

It was not long after I'd resolved my relationship matters with Marilyn and Paco that a whole other bull raised its horns – and this one was not so easy to control.

When a personal phone call comes into a theatre for a performer, it's usually answered at the stage door, where it's either immediately forwarded to the actor's dressing room, or it's screened and then put through or dismissed. My success in *Anything Goes* had resulted in my attracting a few, let's say, exceptionally adoring fans, so I needed to vet my calls. I've never had anyone stalk me in any serious way, but even twenty years ago I had one or two female fans who, if they could catch me on my way to my car, would follow me home.

John, my dresser, answered the phone one day while I was changing into my street clothes. He covered the mouthpiece with his hand.

'Someone's calling on behalf of a Mr Garavani, John. Do you want the call put through?'

I'd no clue who that was, but he'd been insistent and convincing to the manager at the stage door, so I accepted the phone call.

An Italian-accented voice said, 'Mr Garavani saw the show last night and he loved it. He would like a meeting to discuss some possible business with you.'

'I'm flattered, but I'm sorry,' I said, 'who is Mr Garavani?'

'Mr Garavani is a designer. You may know him by his first name, Valentino.'

Describing Valentino as a 'designer' is a bit like saying Sondheim is a songwriter or Shakespeare just dabbled with words. Of course I knew him by his first name, and yes, I said, oh, yes, I'd be happy to meet with him. Over the next couple of weeks, Valentino himself regularly called my dressing room and, finally, he broached the subject of a meeting. He said he thought I'd be perfect to model for a new line of men's clothing he was designing called 'Oliver'. Might we meet to discuss this?

Valentino has dressed the rich and famous since the 1960s, including Elizabeth Taylor, Jackie Kennedy Onassis, Julia Roberts and Gwyneth Paltrow. His name was and still is synonymous with fashion royalty, and he travels in the same circles as the princes and princesses he regularly clothes. In the early 1990s, Valentino was the king of couture, the sovereign of the cognoscenti. I was twenty-four and the 'boy from nowhere',[2] more than a little in awe of the man and his work.

Paco was not happy about the calls and he wasn't thrilled about a meeting, but I agreed regardless. I made arrangements to go to Valentino's house in central London, a palatial estate in Knightsbridge. I was greeted by his butler and guided to a sitting room that I can only describe as a cross between a room at the Palace of Versailles

---

[2] Still a favourite song of mine from *Matador*.

and a museum gallery. The whole place was far from my taste, which leans more to the modern with clean lines and comfortable textures, but Valentino's overt lavishness was stunning nonetheless.

When Valentino eventually entered the room, he was immaculately dressed, his light brown hair perfectly coiffed, and his entire affect old world and refined. I was surprised at how much shorter he was in person than in magazine pictures, but his stature defied this first impression. His manner was impeccable, and his poise was suave and debonair. Throughout our conversation I felt as if someone's father was interviewing me before a prom date or, more accurately, as if an old-fashioned gentleman was vetting me before letting me near his daughter or son. While I sipped water from a crystal glass, he asked me about my life, my future plans and what I hoped to achieve as a performer. Although he took no notes, in time I discovered that he had listened very, very carefully to all my answers.

A few weeks later, after a number of lavish gifts had been sent to my dressing room at the Queens Theatre, Valentino contacted my agent at the time, Jeremy Conway, asking to hire me to model for his new 'Oliver' line. Valentino's representative explained to Jeremy that I would be needed as soon as possible for the photo shoot, which was to be set up on Valentino's personal yacht, the *TM Blue One*, while it toured the Mediterranean for two weeks. Did I need to think about this? Jeremy asked me. Oh, maybe for about an entire minute and a half.

Matador was in its final performances, and I'd planned a trip home to the States to visit my family after the show closed, but I agreed to travel to Rome directly after that. I could barely believe what was happening. To be a Valentino model would be no small accomplishment at that point in my career. I was incredibly flattered.

The trip to Rome was the first time I'd ever travelled first class on an international flight; Valentino was covering all my expenses. However, from the moment the plane banked out over the Atlantic, I knew this trip was going to be a rough one. In fact, to this day, that flight remains one of the worst of my life, and unlike flying in the Hawk, I had no easy eject system or the comfort of a personable pilot chatting with me on a comms system. Instead, the turbulence became so bad that the attendants stopped serving, after one of them smacked against the roof of the plane as we dipped and rolled through a serious storm. It was so bad I could hear wind hammering on the outside of the aircraft. When one of the crew needed to move down the aisle, he or she hooked on to the seats as they lurched past.

I truly thought my time had come. I even started to draft a note to my family because, of course, paper always survives a plane crash. I was absolutely fucking crapping myself. I later found out that the plane's flight path was following the edge of Hurricane Andrew, one of the most violent storms in US history. By the time I landed in Rome, I was exhausted and all I wanted to do was go home, cuddle up in bed and sob like a baby for a few hours. Instead, I had to get on another fucking plane! This one carried me to Sardinia, and from there I boarded Valentino's yacht.

After seeing the lavish luxury of his London home, I should have been better prepared for the *TM Blue One*, which Valentino had named after his parents, Teresa and Mauro. In my head, I'd imagined a gin cruiser, the kind of yacht you might see at Cowes during a regatta. The reality was a sleek one-hundred-and-fifty-foot luxury liner, which looked like the Love Boat on steroids. When I stepped on board, handsome and polished uniformed staff greeted me, and one of Valentino's stewards handed me a beautiful Bvlgari watch with the *TM Blue* insignia engraved on it, explaining that anyone who's a guest on the *TM Blue* receives such a watch.

Valentino himself then appeared on deck and politely welcomed me. He escorted me down to my stateroom, one of many on the yacht, where he introduced me to my personal cabin boy – I kid you not – of whose name I have no memory because he was so gorgeous. Let's call him Pierre. Pierre opened the stateroom's wardrobe and it was bursting with suits and shirts and sportswear all in my size and in all the colours and styles that I love. I told you Valentino was listening carefully at that first meeting at his house in London.

And so the trip of a lifetime began. I was relieved to find I was not his only guest. The supermodel Claudia Schiffer was also on board with her boyfriend du jour, as was Giancarlo Giammatti, Valentino's long-time friend, business partner and ex-lover, and a couple of exiled princes and princesses. I think they were from Bulgaria. There were also a few young male companions who appeared to be travelling with one or two of the other older men on board.

The yacht cruised the Mediterranean from Sardinia to Crete, and then turned north along the Amalfi coast. Every morning, I'd get out of bed early and eat breakfast with Giancarlo (for whom, in all honesty, I'd developed a bit of a fancy). I'd then spend the day sunbathing on the top deck with Claudia, diving off the yacht's swim deck, parasailing, snorkelling and generally having a ball … with not a photographer, camera, make-up artist or shoot director in sight. I also made calls to my family on the satellite phone, not being able to resist taunting Carole, the swimmer in our family, about playing in the Mediterranean, or letting my dad chat with Claudia as we sunbathed on deck.

In the evening, the group would gather to eat dinner together. A wealthy friend of Valentino's who, among other things, owned a number of art galleries in Paris and Rome also joined us every night for dinner. He was following the *TM Blue* in his own luxury yacht, where he lived with his sister and his lovely young male companion Tomas.

On some days, dinner would be the only time I'd have any extended contact with Valentino. Private cars would be lined up on the dock waiting with doors ajar if his posse came into port for a meal. If not, the yacht would dock at the best berth available and we'd eat up on deck, sprawling on luxurious white sofas as we dined. At many of our ports of call, we were not unlike zoo animals on display, because locals and tourists alike would recognize the *TM Blue* and stroll the piers, staring at us while we ate. No one was looking at me, of course, I was unknown, but everyone knew Valentino and he'd wave to all who greeted him. Claudia was also recognized and she was equally as gracious between bites.

During the day, Valentino kept his distance, sometimes sending Giancarlo with a message for me from 'Val', or sending a steward with a drink or a treat from 'Val'. We were well into the second week of the trip and there was still no sign of a photographer, other than Claudia and myself snapping shots the way any holidaymakers might. I felt like I'd time-travelled back to the court of a medieval king and intermediaries were the protocol of the state, making sure I was comfortable and enjoying myself on behalf of the king. Valentino did, though, insist that I sit next to him at dinner, and that's when he started to drive me a bit mental. While we were eating, he'd adjust my collar or he'd lean over and fluff my hair, but the worst was when he'd touch my neck.

Aaargh! You already know how I feel about that.

Extravagant gifts started to appear in my stateroom. First, it was a pair of beautiful silver cufflinks. Then one day, he came up to the sundeck after we'd all been swimming and presented me with a large cross encrusted with diamonds and sapphires because, he said, 'I watch you swim and your eyes shine like sapphires against the blue of the sea.'

If you know anything about Valentino, you know that his signature couture colour is red, and his personal colour is blue. The yacht was filled with blue in every hue: the pillows, upholstery, towels and bedding, and it also adorned the man himself.

By the end of the holiday, of course, it was obvious even to me that I was not on the yacht to model for any Valentino line: no mention of a photo shoot had occurred since we'd signed the contract back in England. I'm convinced Valentino brought me on board because he liked to travel surrounded by beautiful things. Perhaps he hoped I'd be one more lovely accoutrement to ornament his life. He treated me well, had a dry sense of humour, a terrific sense of irony, and style by the boatload, and I certainly enjoyed the trip of a lifetime. Nevertheless, I was twenty-four and I had a life to live. Valentino had given me a taste of high living – but all the things he'd shown me, I wanted to get on my own. I was determined to achieve my success on my terms.

And, today, I'm proud to say that I have. I own a Porsche, for which I worked hard to save and to buy; I have a Mercedes with my own driver, Sean Evans, a prince of a man; and I own a house in the States, a home in London and one in Cardiff. I don't own a yacht yet, but the day is young. Touch wood.

When I returned to my flat in London after the trip, there were already packages filled with designer clothes waiting for me, and a series of messages on my answering machine. The gifts continued over the next few weeks and became even more extravagant – a 1959 limited-edition Rolex, for example, as well as other expensive jewellery. I tried to return all of them, but he wouldn't accept.

Later that year, Valentino gave me something else for which I will always be grateful, something more precious than the most valuable gems in the world. The final gift he sent me was Penny, my golden cocker spaniel, who, until her death in 2007, was one of the loves of my life. Penny brought me more joy and companionship than Valentino could ever imagine, and for that I sincerely thank him.

I also have to admit that to this day, if I'm wearing a blue suit, I wear brown shoes with it – because it's classic Valentino.

However, the story doesn't end there. A couple of years ago, my partner Scott Gill – a successful architect and the other love of my life – and I were at a dinner party at a friend's house in Holland Park. A gorgeous tanned man in his late thirties was seated across from us. It quickly became clear that he recognized me from somewhere other than showbiz, and I knew I'd seen him somewhere before too.

Finally, as our host was serving coffee, the man remembered.

'Were you not a guest of Valentino one summer on his yacht?'

'Oh my God, yes! Were you there?'

'I'm Tomas,' he said. 'I was with my companion who was following the *TM Blue* in his own yacht.'

'What are you doing now?' I asked.

'My dear friend died a few years ago and we had an arrangement. He left me almost everything. His art galleries, his yachts, his homes on three continents.'

Scott leaned close and with a sly grin whispered, 'Christ, John, you should have fucked him.'

Chapter Eleven

'Love Changes Everything'

The Donner Party was a wagon train of pioneer families that travelled west from Illinois to California in the 1840s. Winter trapped them in the Sierra Nevada mountains. Eventually, out of eighty or so emigrants who began the trek, only about half survived. The circumstances in the camps where they holed up for shelter became so desperate during that winter that a few in the group succumbed to cannibalism, eating their dead friends and family to survive.

The Donner Party story fascinates Scott and me. We are both really interested in this period of nineteenth-century American history. We love nothing more than carrying our dinner on trays into the living room at our Kensington–Chelsea home, pouring a vodka tonic, and watching a historical documentary like Ric Burns's *The Donner Party* on the flat screen mounted above the fireplace.[1]

The tale of the Donner Party has become almost mythical in American history. A group of people venturing into the unknown, travelling a road not previously travelled in order to achieve a better life, and because of bad navigation and stupid risks most of them never made it to their destination. In 2000, Scott and I took a road

[1] Yup, we're party animals.

trip through the American West that included tracing the Donner Party's path. That journey has become just as legendary in our relationship as the trail itself in history. For me, in particular, it cemented in my head and engraved on my heart what I already knew. I wanted to be with this Englishman for the rest of my life.

We took lots of crisps and sandwiches with us just in case.

The trip started with skiing at Lake Tahoe. It was my first time skiing, but after only one or two times down the beginners' slope, I was a pro. Ask Scott. He'll tell you I was gliding down the most difficult runs and actually skiing better than him by the end of the day. Well, maybe he won't tell you that.

While we could still move the most important muscles in our bodies – our legs, our legs – we packed up the rented SUV and headed out of South Lake Tahoe to take the mountain route across the state. When Scott examined the map, this looked like a much shorter way than going down into the valley and then back up again. Our plan was to head south to Yosemite and then work our way northeast to Utah to see the Mormon Trail and visit Salt Lake City.[2]

Before we left Lake Tahoe, I noticed our petrol gauge was edging close to a quarter tank. No worries. We both assumed there would be a filling station before we left the Tahoe area. We secured Penny and Lewis[3] in the back of the SUV and went south. We quickly realized how wrong we were. For some reason, all the petrol stations we drove past were closed. We kept driving into the mountains towards Mono Lake, expecting at any time to come to an open garage. There were none.

We drove on and on in the direction of Yosemite, thinking there

[2] I told you we were party animals.
[3] Our second cocker spaniel and one of Penny's litter.

had to be somewhere to fill up soon. This was America, home of the Cadillac and land of the Ford, but as we got deeper and deeper into the mountains, and it got later and later, and darker and darker, the road became more and more deserted. The petrol gauge was now down to an eighth of a tank.

Scott and I first met in 1993 at the Chichester Festival Theatre. I was playing Wyndham Brandon in Patrick Hamilton's tale of death and desire, *Rope*, at the Minerva Theatre (one of the performance spaces within the CFT). For over forty years, the Chichester Festival Theatre has been one of the most highly acclaimed theatres in the world. Its first artistic director was Sir Laurence Olivier in the 1960s. For an actor as new to the stage as I was in 1993, to perform there was a real coup.

In the play, I co-starred with Anthony Head, of *Buffy* fame among other accomplishments, and Alexis Denisof, also of *Buffy* and its spin-off *Angel*. Keith Baxter was the director. One reviewer wrote of the play, '[S]uperlatives seem inadequate for Keith Baxter's splendid, electrifying production. John Barrowman (Brandon) and Alexis Denisof (Granillo) as the murderers have every changing mood tightly controlled. Both give hypnotically intense performances.'

How could Scott not fall in love with me?

The play opened with me alone on the stage after having committed a heinous crime. I was completely naked and not just metaphorically – literally, too. The full monty. The stage was in darkness and I was the only thing in illumination. Scott had come to see the play at the request of a friend of mine, who wanted Scott to meet me.

When they walked into my dressing room after the show, I was once again butt naked, about to pull on my jeans. I straightened up and looked at Scott directly. As clichéd as it may sound, I knew he was the one.

Some of the initial connection was lust, I can't deny that, but there was something else too, and Scott, thankfully, felt the same something else, the same charge of electricity, the same prophetic jolt. I was still dating Paco at that time, so the four of us went to dinner that night. Then months passed before I saw Scott again. When I did, he was trying to hail a taxi in Soho. I cruised past him in my car and I really checked him out. Scott remembers the drive-by, in part because he thought my Jaguar was an old man's car and he couldn't understand why someone so hot would drive a car like that.

When we finally had our first official date, Cher was with us. I was accompanying her to a function and I invited Scott along too. It was an odd threesome. Although I kissed Cher goodnight, an event that made the American tabloids, I went home with Scott.

That first date seemed a long time ago and very far away as we drove into the Sierra Nevada mountains, following in the Donner Party's wagon ruts. Around midnight, a weather front moved in and it began to snow heavily. Our visibility was becoming severely limited. When Scott and I take road trips, I generally drive and Scott navigates. He was worried we'd missed our turn, which would mean we were climbing higher into the mountains and heading for a pass that at this time of year was likely closed. Finally, after about an hour of white knuckles and chewed nails and a few harsh words, Scott spotted a lit filling station on the brow of the hill. We looked at each other and started to laugh from relief. It was short-lived. We pulled into the gas station, where a large tin sign flapped in the wind: 'Closed for the winter.'

Time to panic.

I looked at the petrol gauge, which was grazing empty. We had no clue where we were, but we needed to make a decision. Either stop and take a chance we wouldn't freeze to death, or keep moving and take a chance we might make it to Yosemite on fumes. Either way, we were probably screwed.

We drove on for another hour, turning off the engine on the downhill slopes and letting the SUV cruise in neutral. This seemed like a good idea until I hit a patch of ice on a sharp curve and couldn't use the engine to break. The SUV careened round the bend, our rear still fishtailing long after I'd straightened the wheel. The road was desolate and dark, and we were terrified because if we crashed, we knew no one would find us until we'd turned into ice lollies.

I was the first man Scott took home to meet his parents, Stirling and Sheelagh Gill. After a lovely Sunday lunch, Stirling set a jar of instant coffee on the table and asked if I'd like a cup. Without really thinking, I blurted out, 'You're not going to give company instant coffee, are you?'

Without missing a beat, Stirling replied, 'Of course not. I can brew you a pot, John.' This has become a bit of a joke between us, and to this day, when I go for dinner, everyone else at the table gets instant coffee while Stirling makes me my own pot.

A cup of coffee might have helped that night in the mountains if we could have poured it into the tank and used it for fuel. As it was, Scott and I were wired, but the SUV was slowing down, and it was then that it hit me like a hard punch to the gut. What if something happened to Scott? I knew I loved him, he knew I loved him, and we both already knew that we were together for the long road, but in that terrible moment of panic, I realized that as soon as I could, I wanted to make that commitment legal and public and truly forever.

In 1997, Scott's parents came to see me perform as Che in *Evita* in Norway at the 6,000-seat Oslo Spektrum. They stayed at the Oslo Hilton, where Scott and I also had a room. At breakfast one morning, the three Gills decided to eat from the breakfast buffet. In Norway, breakfast usually consists of a variety of meats and fish – no snap, crackle and pop for the Norwegians. That morning, the Gills chose to have the gravlax, fresh salmon cured with a mixture of salt, sugar and herbs. The three of them sat down to a platter full of fish. When I finally made it down to breakfast and reached for the plate, the three of them grinned at me like Cheshire cats.

'Sorry, John, we've eaten it all.'

The next morning, I came down to breakfast ahead of the Gills, but once again there was no salmon. I called the waiter over.

'Is there any salmon this morning?'

'No, sir,' he said, but he leaned in conspiratorially. 'We're not putting out the salmon until later, because someone ate the whole platter yesterday and there was none left for anyone else.'

Some couples have in-laws who drink or smoke too much. I have to keep mine away from the salmon.

By about 2 a.m. on that snowy winter night in the mountains, Scott and I were about a second away from full-blown panic when we saw lights off to the side of the road a few hundred yards ahead. Hallelujah! The lights belonged to a breakdown truck. One of us wouldn't need to make a fricassee with the other after all.

The tow-truck driver had an extra gas container and along with the petrol, he gave us a lecture. He informed us tersely that we were about twenty miles from our destination, but we'd never have made it on fumes. What had we been thinking, driving into the mountains without a full tank?

'Haven't you heard of the Donner Party?' he chided, walking back to his truck.

Apparently, not nearly enough.

On 27 December 2006, Scott and I became civil partners at a late-morning ceremony at the St David's Hotel and Spa overlooking Cardiff Bay. It was a glorious day, even if the weather was overcast and cold. I wore my kilt and Scott wore a black Neil Morengo suit with thin red piping on the cuffs and collar. I hired Claire Pritchard-Jones and another artist from *Torchwood* to do hair and make-up for the women in the family, and our three beloved dogs at the time, Penny, Lewis and Tiger, were accessorized with tartan ribbons and sprigs of heather. Scott and I adopted Tiger from Dogs Trust, one of the charities I support, and he was our present to each other in honour of the day.[4]

During the ceremony, my dad read the Robert Burns poem 'My Love is Like a Red, Red Rose' and my mum sang (as she had done at Carole and Kevin's and Andrew and Dot's weddings). Just as Gavin Barker, my close friend and manager, and his civil partner Stuart Macdonald stood up to be our witnesses, the sun burst out from behind the clouds and three white swans glided across the Bay and into view behind us.

After the ceremony, Scott and my immediate families and our close friends joined the happy couple upstairs at the St David's for a New York-style champagne brunch. Our guests included my *Torchwood* team, Eve Myles, Burn Gorman, Naoko Mori and Gareth David-Lloyd;[5] *Torchwood* executive producer Russell T. Davies and his partner Andrew; and my friend Martin Marquez, who plays Gino in *Hotel Babylon*,[6] and his wife and children.

Whenever Scott and I travel back to the States, the first morning after our arrival we love to pig out on a huge artery-slamming American breakfast. We order the works: pancakes, waffles, fruit,

---

[4] Sadly, Tiger, who was thirteen when we adopted him, died the following October.

[5] Aka Gwen, Owen, Toshiko and Ianto respectively.

[6] Martin and I first became friends when we both performed in Trevor Nunn's 2002–3 production of *Anything Goes*, of which there's more to tell later in the book.

bacon, muffins, hash browns, scrambled eggs and sausages. The brunch table at the St David's on our civil partnership day had all of this and more. The room was decorated with arrangements of green and purple heather, and each place setting had a traditional, individually wrapped Scottish cake for guests. The main cake was also a traditional Scottish fruitcake, with frosted icing sculpted into figures of Scott and me on top. Scott's back rested against three skyscrapers and he held a set of architectural plans in his hand, while I leaned against a curtained stage and held sheet music in mine. Later that day, as a gift to our families, Scott and I gave each guest a treatment at the spa. After eating my fill and receiving lots of toasts and good cheer, I dashed away to do two shows of *Jack and the Beanstalk* at the New Theatre in Cardiff to pay for it all.

Since that day, I've received hundreds of emails and letters of congratulations and goodwill regarding Scott and my commitment to one another. We were especially overwhelmed by the best wishes from the Welsh public. Cardiff is one of the most cosmopolitan cities in Europe – and I've travelled to a lot of European cities. I love Cardiff, and its sincere response to Scott and me has only strengthened my good feelings about the city by the Bay. Elderly people, young people, couples of all sorts regularly stop me in the shops or in the city centre to congratulate and thank Scott and me for choosing Cardiff as the setting for our public statement about our relationship. We chose Wales because we wanted to celebrate Cardiff the way Cardiff has celebrated us.

I've also had many people, gay and straight, ask me if the civil ceremony has changed our relationship. And I have to say it has. First of all, we both eat more cakes and ice cream. Seriously, we do. Secondly, even though before the ceremony we'd been together for over fifteen years, publicly acknowledging our commitment to each other has strengthened our partnership. We talk even more about 'we' and 'us' and even less about 'I' and 'me'. And we're less worried that in our future, when we are both tottering old men, someone else will make the important decisions in our lives for us.

Most gay couples I know have lots in common with their non-gay counterparts. They are devoted to each other, concerned for their families and their futures, and are active contributing members to their neighbourhoods and communities. When I stepped across the threshold of the St David's Hotel that December afternoon to greet the press and well-wishers, the rush of sheer joy I felt was one I wished all gay couples could experience.

In April 2004, my parents celebrated their fiftieth wedding anniversary. Carole, Andrew and I threw a surprise party for them at a hotel in Milwaukee. Close friends and family gathered from all over the States, and a few travelled thousands of miles from Scotland and Europe to celebrate my mum and dad and their marriage. Watching my parents wander the tables together, smiling at their friends, laughing with each other, dancing and holding each other with the same passion they'd had fifty years before, made my heart swell. Scott and I want to be able to mark our union with family and friends in a similar celebration when we reach our fiftieth, and in December 2006, we formalized that desire.

In our relationship, I'm a bit like a sailboat. I'm always moving, riding the crest of the waves, letting the wind carry me in lots of directions. Scott's my keel. He slows me down and gives me stability. He can guide me when I need to be redirected, and when I do on occasion, shall we say, 'cut loose', Scott gets me home, gives me two paracetamol and a glass of water, and puts me to bed.

In February 2005, Scott's sister Sandie died of glioblastoma – a form of brain cancer – at the Royal Marsden Hospital in London. One of the terrible ironies of Sandie's death was that Scott's brother Steven, one of the foremost brain surgeons in the world, could do very little to help her. The other was that Sandie's two oldest children, Iris and Gabriel, had already lost their dad to cancer when they were young. Sandie fought heroically to stay alive because she wanted to make sure her children, including her youngest daughter Eden, were prepared for her death. Steven was able to remove the tumoured section of her brain and this gave her a little more time.

Through those long, achingly sad months, I watched Scott help take care of Sandie. He never treated her as if she was sick. He never saw her as a burden. He took time away from his work and sat with her during her stays at the hospital. When she came home, he took her to movies and out on short day trips to visit family and friends. He spent a week with her at the seaside on the Norfolk coast, reading, talking, watching films, living.

The night before Sandie died, she rang everyone in the family. After she talked to Scott, she spoke to me.

'John,' she said quietly, 'remember to look after my brother.'

'I will,' I promised.

Chapter Twelve

'Anything Goes'

In many cultures, the magpie is considered to be a harbinger of good fortune, and magpies are everywhere in Cardiff. On any given morning on my way to the *Torchwood* set, I find myself saluting like crazy and saying, 'Hello, Mr Magpie. How are your wife and kids?' over and over again, which, in case you didn't know, is how you greet a magpie in order to benefit from the aforementioned good fortune. If you ever pass me on the motorway or on a city street, don't panic about all this manic gesticulation. Remember I have a driver, Sean. All my saluting is not the least bit distracting, although he may think otherwise.

Why all this tip o' the hat stuff, you may ask. Well, it's because, as I mentioned in an earlier chapter, I have a few teensy weensy phobias and superstitions. On a scale of one to five – one being slightly superstitious to five being obsessive–compulsive about superstitions – theatre people in general are a six. I'm about an eight and a half.

As the song title from *The Producers* says, 'It is bad luck to say good luck' in a theatre – and that's probably the most rational of all the superstitions I've acquired over the years. Theatre folks prefer 'break a leg' to 'good luck' because during Shakespeare's day, or thereabouts,[1] actors went down on one knee when taking their bows. Lots of bows meant a risk of falling or wrenching your knee; therefore, 'break a leg' implies a performance worthy of many bows.

A theatre is 'dark'. It is never 'closed'. Why? Because a closed theatre sounds terribly terminal, while darkness implies that at some point the lights will be turned back on.

Never whistle in a theatre. To purse your lips and blow is bad luck because stage managers didn't always call 'thirty minutes, ladies and gentlemen' over comms systems. Years ago they used real whistles to give cues to the company instead. You can imagine the chaos it might cause if someone whistling for the hell of it sent an over-enthusiastic actor into a scene before his or her cue.

Dark-coloured roses before a performance are bad; red roses after a performance are good. Yellow roses are really bad at any time. A poor dress rehearsal is considered a good omen. Peacock feathers are an ominous sign (which is why real ones are never used in costumes). If you leave something belonging to you, like a bar of soap, somewhere in your dressing room, you'll be invited back to that theatre in the future.

The mother of all superstitions, of course, is that 'the Scottish play' should never ever be mentioned anywhere in a theatre.

Do I really believe all this stuff? I'm the idiot sitting in his car saluting birds, for God's sake. What do you think?

During my run as Billy Crocker in *Anything Goes* at the National Theatre in 2002–3, a stagehand's foot was run over by a scenery truck and the show had to stop. You guessed it. Some asshole said, 'Macbeth.'

Ssshhh!

Another time – same show, different night – a light fell from its

---

[1] Looking for exact historical accuracy? Not that kind of book either.

rigging and just missed hitting a gaffer.[2] You got it. Someone mentioned the M-word. You may be thinking, 'A load of bollocks, just coincidences,' but you'll never convince those of us in theatre that's all it is. Sometimes people think it's funny when they find out I really believe these superstitions, and they deliberately mention you-know-what just to be a prick. I once held a curtain[3] in *Sunset Boulevard* and refused to go on until the person who'd mentioned 'the Scottish play' was sent outside the stage door, made to spit twice, turn round three times, and come back inside only once he'd been invited. This is standard procedure in such circumstances. I've been told it's something to do with the fact that 'the Scottish play' opens with three witches cursing, 'Fair is foul and foul is fair.' The fates of the theatre are fickle and even those of us who are not particularly religious bow down to them before every performance in one way or another.

Most of my family is superstitious, too. My mum never puts shoes on the table, always throws salt over her shoulder if any spills, and if she were to drop a glove, she'd stand around for hours waiting for someone else to pick it up for her, because it's bad luck to pick up your own dropped glove.

Hang out backstage with me and you'll see that superstitions are only one small part of what keeps a company on its toes, actors fresh and at their creative best. Audiences attending the theatre may enjoy the performance of a lifetime, but there's always another show going on behind the scenes, one that never interferes with the quality of the one they're watching, but that can be just as entertaining.

A theatre company backstage is a lot like a big family getting ready for a visit from the Queen. Lighting folks, stage crew, stage management, wardrobe artists, wig designers, hair and make-up

---

[2] The official theatre name for an electrician. Now you're in the know.
[3] Strong though I may be, this is just a figure of speech for not letting the show begin.

people, musicians, dressers for all the performers, and then the performers themselves are all running around frantically, all with a mission: put on a great show. Behind the scenes in a theatre there's a complex network of people all supporting each other.

After the preview performances, the director of the show makes only an occasional visit to the theatre, and he rarely has anything to do with the show going on behind the scenes that he never blocked or rehearsed. Once the production opens, it's down to the rest of the cast and crew to keep the energy up and the standard high. Performing in live theatre, on average actors have eight or nine shows a week, depending on the matinee schedule. If they're lucky, and the show runs into years, that's eight shows multiplied by fifty-two weeks, minus one day off for Christmas. That's 415 shows in a year. When you, the audience, come to see the show, it may be our 365th performance, but it's your first and may be your only one. In order to keep ourselves fresh and to keep our creative adrenalin running at the level it was during show number ten, we shake things up on stage for each other. Sitting in the stalls, you perhaps had no idea – did you? Until now.

During a scene in *Matador*, for example, we had to recreate convincingly a dinner party as a backdrop. Many of the characters were seated around a table, being served a meal, while the main action was taking place at the centre front of the stage. The audience could see us enjoying a meal, and they had to believe we were having a dinner party, but they could not hear a word we were saying.

Oh my God, some of the things we said. The actress playing my character's sister, Caroline O'Connor, who later went on to appear as Ethel Merman in *De-Lovely*, would begin the conversation by introducing Stefanie Powers as Ginger Dungbucket. That's all it took. We were off. One of the boys, dressed as a waiter for the scene, would serve us stupid notes with dirty jokes on them or he'd bring us someone's panties on a silver tray. Through the whole scene, no one could hear or see what we were really doing around that table, which was just as well, on reflection.

In 1994, I played Joe Gillis to Betty Buckley's Norma Desmond in Andrew Lloyd Webber's *Sunset Boulevard* at the Adelphi Theatre in London. *Sunset* has one of the best opening scenes in musical theatre. When the curtain rises, the audience is looking at Norma's swimming pool where my character, Joe, is floating dead on the shimmering surface. The musical is told in flashback from that moment.

The show is set in 1949 and is about an ageing Hollywood diva, Norma Desmond, who is clinging pathetically to her past glory in silent movies twenty years before, and hoping once again to find fame. Joe Gillis is a poor, disaffected writer who accidentally meets Norma late one night when he is trying to flee his creditors. Norma sees in Joe the chance to perfect her comeback script, *Salome*, at long last. Joe views Norma as a meal ticket. Their relationship eventually collapses under the weight of Norma's delusions and ends with Joe's watery demise. His death is hastened by his developing relationship with Betty Schaefer, whom he meets in Artie's Bar, and who helps Joe to write his own movie script.

The set for *Sunset* was one of the most complex and massive stages ever created. It was constructed to look like the inside of Norma's decaying Sunset Boulevard mansion – spiral staircase, chandeliers and all. The entire set shifted at various times during the show with two levels that moved up and down using powerful hydraulics. During one scene, Norma Desmond's house 'flies' into the upper area of the theatre, leaving the set underneath visible for a scene we affectionately called the 'Artie's Party' scene because it took place in Artie's Bar. The room was furnished for a sing-along party with a table and chairs, a piano, a bar and a small toilet off to the side. The toilet's interior wall was cut away so that Joe and Betty Schaefer, played by Anita Louise Combe, can have a private moment to which the audience is privy (pun intended).

The final matinee of an actor's run in a production is usually the one in which the most pranks are pulled. During my last matinee of *Sunset*, Anita and I moved into Artie's small toilet as usual for the scene where we flirted in song using the towel rail as a dance bar. The song started and Anita promptly hiked up her skirt, dropped her knickers and proceeded to sit on the loo as if she was having a pee.

I couldn't lose my composure, because it's impossible to stretch or stop one of Andrew's duets once it's begun. Between my lyrics, I was biting my cheeks so hard to keep myself from laughing that I could taste blood. I still don't know how I made it through the number with my romantic interest taking a leak in front of me. To make matters worse, for the entire duet we were full front to the audience, who I can only imagine thought such an intimate moment was part of the script. When Anita was finished, she wiped – she really did – and then she flushed all before the song ended. By then, I could barely hold it together, though I managed to make it into the wings before completely losing it and peeing my own pants.

Unfortunately for me, Anita was just getting warmed up with her stunt in the toilet. Later, in the same performance, during one of the final scenes, Anita's character stormed into Norma's mansion to tackle Joe about his infidelity. The moment was dramatic and very 'in your face'. When Joe – me, that is – saw his girlfriend charge down the huge spiral staircase, he turned in anger and confronted her.

'What are you doing here?' I said angrily to Anita as Betty.

'I'm here with my twin sister,' she replied, and then Anita pulled her understudy on to the set behind her. The understudy was dressed in the same outfit as Anita. This was so not in the script.

'Your sister?' I sputtered, choking back laughter and turning my back to the audience in an attempt to regain my composure.

We proceeded to play the scene with two Betty Schaefers and probably most of the audience had no idea how wrong the whole scene really was. The understudy said nothing. She just stood there grinning while I desperately tried to avoid making a fool of myself and wrap up the scene as quickly as possible. After all the jokes I'd played during our long run of *Sunset*, I was the first to admit that payback was in order, and Anita's were gems.

Earlier in the week, during another performance, I'd made a mistake during a scene with Betty Buckley and I think Anita had taken her cue to pull a prank or two from my screw-up. In the scene before Joe and Betty Schaefer have their confrontation on the stairs, Norma Desmond rushes to the phone, picks it up and out of pure spite calls Betty to tell her what Joe has really been doing in the mansion for all these months.

Into the phone, Norma says, 'Miss Schaefer, why don't you come over and see what Mr Gillis is really doing at my house?' or something like that.

My character, Joe, then marches into the room, catches Norma on the phone betraying him and, in a two-can-play-at-that-game routine, he's then supposed to pull the phone from her, give Betty the address of their house on Sunset Boulevard and slam the phone down. My character's intention is to explain everything when Betty arrives and then both of us will abandon Norma to her pathetic lonely existence.

Instead, I entered from the left, marched over to Betty Buckley as Norma, grabbed the phone from her hand and my mind went blank. Nothing. No lines came into my head and I slammed the phone down without saying anything. No address. No cue.

Betty looked at me as if I was insane and then she covered and said, 'I have to call her back,' and began dialling again. She really did have to call her back because if she didn't, there was no way to explain how Betty Schaefer, the girlfriend, could get to the mansion to confront Joe and Norma, which had to happen in the next scene.

As if I needed to prove I was really insane, I then did it again – in the very same scene. I took the phone and, once again, drew a complete blank, another major brain fart. I slammed it down without the required '10,086 Sunset Boulevard'. I don't know what came over me. By the third try, Betty Buckley couldn't decide whether to sob or sucker-punch me. To the audience, she and I must have looked like we were wrestling back and forth with the phone. She was yelling, 'Joe, don't hang up the phone,' then whispering under her breath, 'John, we're running out of music. Give me the fucking phone.' Finally, I let her snatch the phone from me before I could get near it for a fourth time. She gave the address and the cue herself.

As Cole Porter wrote, 'in olden days, a glimpse of stocking' may have thrown an audience into a swoon, but if you were in the audience of *Sunset Boulevard* on occasion, if you were really paying careful attention, you may have seen something even more scandalous. Some actors are known for their quirky dressing-room requests, some for their temper tantrums, and some for their weird rehearsal rituals. Me? I'm notorious for flashing my bum or bringing my Willie[4] out to play.

On the *Torchwood* set, my co-star Eve's breasts are known as 'the girls' and my naughty bits are 'the boys'. Whenever we've had too many night shifts in a row or when morale needs a bit of a boost,

---

[4] A moniker from my Glasgow childhood.

the boys and girls come out to play. This kind of exposure is often a bit of a shock to non-theatrical folks, but modesty is not something that you can have much time for when you have about thirty-four seconds to change costume in the wings or if you have to pee in a bucket offstage because you'll never make it back to your dressing room before your cue. There is not a pause button in live theatre.

Well, maybe I've used it once. Let me pause here to explain.

Over the years, I've developed a shellfish allergy.[5] Like turning thirty, the whole thing kind of crept up on me.[6] One evening, I'd eaten dinner at a noodle bar in Guildford before a preview performance of *The Beautiful and Damned,* or *The Beautiful and Doomed* as the cast not so fondly referred to the F. Scott Fitzgerald story because we knew the production was never going to make it beyond previews. I hadn't known the bar used fish oils in their cooking. I got dressed for the show, as my stomach started to make rumbling noises and then began to cramp. The stage manager gave the curtain call. My character had to be kneeling on stage as the curtain came up.

'Everyone in place,' the stage manager announced.

By this time, the cramps were almost unbearable, so I thought I'd release a bit of the pressure – you know, Rabbie Burns, free wind and all that. Not a good idea. I completely shat myself. For the twenty seconds that I knelt there, in my mind I played out the entire show, every scene and every song, thinking, 'How far will I have to go through Act One before I can change?' I knew I couldn't make it. The curtain had already gone up an inch. I yelled, 'Stop the curtain!' By now, the audience could see my feet, but I dared not tell anyone what I'd just done. I'd never have heard the last of it.

[5] I blame Stephen Sondheim. I'll tell you why later.
[6] I'm not into birthday parties and usually celebrate quietly. My thirtieth was the exception: Scott threw a surprise party for me.

I raced off the stage and ran upstairs, with my dresser flying behind me.

'I'm sorry to have to tell you this,' I said as I stripped off my costume, 'but I've shit in my suit pants.'

'Get them off,' she ordered,[7] 'and I'll scrub them.'

She cleaned my trousers while I had the fastest shower in theatre history. I was a little damp, but I was back on stage within four minutes.

Now, that's talent. The dresser's and mine.

Rewind to *Sunset Boulevard*. During the 'Artie's Party' scene, before Anita and I moved into the bathroom for the flirtatious section of the scene, I had to play the piano for a few minutes to establish some party ambience. Except on some nights, I'd play the piano perfectly with my penis.[8] I kept this up, so to speak, for a number of shows, until I received a letter from Andrew Lloyd Webber's Really Useful Group insisting I stop. Andrew wrote, 'Your penis may not upstage my music.'

I went back to playing the piano with my hands. In reality, the audience couldn't really see what I was doing, but I have to admit I was quite proud that some folks thought my 'boys' might be seen from the centre stalls.

That wasn't the only time I received a wry reprimand from producers. There was another during my run in *Miss Saigon* in 1993, when I played the character of Chris. Ruthie Henshall, a terrific actor and singer with as wicked a sense of humour as mine, portrayed my American wife. We had a scene together where we were raised above the stage in a double bed, in which Ruthie would sing to me. One day, we were called into the company manager's office to be informed

---

[7] My fave dresser John Fahey was not available for this show.

[8] Don't you love alliteration?

that we were making too much noise in the bed.[9] I blamed it on Ruthie who, every time the bed rose above the set, would try to flick my jockstrap. My retaliation of pinging her bra was clearly the only appropriate response. Ruthie and I have worked together a number of times now, and she and I always seem to pick up where we left off.

In 2000, Ruthie and I both starred in Stephen Sondheim's *Putting It Together*, along with Carol Burnett – the queen of physical comedy and a brilliant performer. Carol and I had a ritual before going on stage where we'd hug each other and then say we'd be 'back in bidness', using an odd pseudo-southern American accent. Carol would then start the 'Back in Business' number. One night, she was looking at me funny through the whole first part of the song. She kept touching her skirt and playing with her waistband. Suddenly, she shouted, 'Stop!' and threw her hands into the air. When she did, her skirt dropped right to the floor because the waistband had snapped. I laughed so hard, I actually fell down myself. Hilariously, the entire sequence was caught in the extras of the DVD that was being made of that particular live show.

Later on in *Putting It Together*, Ruthie and I had to do a complex *pas de deux*. Even after all my years of performing, my dancing is still what I worry about most in a show. Nevertheless, while working with the choreographer Bob Avian during this production, I'd asked him to push my dancing abilities, to stretch me into new territory (no pun intended). He did as I asked. During one performance, I gracefully picked Ruthie up … and split my expensive Gucci pants. For the rest of the sequence, everyone could see my white Calvins.

The National Theatre production of *Anything Goes* in 2002–3 had more than its fair share of mishaps, what with the falling rigging

[9] Obviously, they weren't complaining about the volume of the singing.

and the crashing cart. In more than one performance, I unwittingly added to the list of calamities when, during the 'You're the Top' dance routine with Sally Ann Triplett, who was playing Reno Sweeney, I'd throw myself into my deckchair – and the chair would shatter beneath me. This happened multiple times. Clearly, they don't make deckchairs like they used to.

The slapstick chaos didn't stop when the production transferred to the Theatre Royal Drury Lane later in the year, either. One night, Susan Tracy, who was playing Evangeline Harcourt, Hope Harcourt's mother, was late for her cue.[10] A bit panicked, she came bounding around the set of the liner, carrying her character's dog Cheeky, a real perky little pup. Susan was moving a little faster than usual to catch up to her mark and she tripped, chucking the poor dog far into the audience and herself into the sixth row of the stalls.

The ensemble was dancing, stalling a little, waiting for her entrance – and then, all of a sudden, Mrs Harcourt wasn't there anymore. I was backstage waiting for my next number when one of the sailors came running off stage, shouting, 'Susan's just thrown herself overboard!' A quick-thinking sailor on the upper deck grabbed a fake life preserver and actually tossed it into the audience. With great aplomb, Susan carefully climbed back up on to the stage, acting as if she was getting out of the water, which itself was truly hilarious. She was ashen, but ever the professional, she shook herself off. While she was composing herself, a man ran up the aisle from the audience and handed her the dog.

'Oh, Cheeky!' she exclaimed, and went right on as if nothing had happened.[11]

---

[10] I don't care how many years you've been in theatre, there isn't an actor among us who hasn't once or twice missed a cue.

[11] At the interval, I poured her a stiff whisky from the bar in my dressing room.

In many ways, it was during the 1989 production of *Anything Goes* that I was fully initiated into this glorious thespian[12] world of pranks, pitfalls and unplanned calamities. My co-stars Elaine Paige and Bernard Cribbins introduced me to the rituals, the rules, the drama, the decorum and the general silliness of theatre life, and for that I'll be forever grateful. I could not have had a more professional, more talented, or more compassionate pair of mentors. I was young and inexperienced when I got my big break, and although I never felt overwhelmed by any of it, I knew I had a lot to learn.

Elaine has the most expressive eyes in theatre and, sometimes, she'd look at me a certain way and I'd crack up – inside my head, of course. Bernard, meanwhile, is credited with the inspiration that became known as the 'Dick of the Week' award. Bernard hired an artist friend to sculpt a trophy in the shape of a very large life-like phallus, which, in a grand ceremony backstage at the end of each week, he'd award to the person who had been the biggest 'Dick of the Week'. We were all presented with it at some point in the show's run for some blooper, goof, or generally stupid thing we'd done on stage. Directly after our final performance, Bernard could not find the 'Dick of the Week' award anywhere. I've absolutely no idea who would have had the, erm, balls to have kept such a revered symbol after the close of the show.

Sometimes before the curtain went up for the second act, Bernard or I would run out to a sweet shop not far from the theatre and buy pounds of chewy toffee, which we'd then shove in our mouths just before the brig scene in Act Two. We'd have contests to see who could keep the toffee in his mouth the longest before our cue. Bernard was the master at masticating toffee into submission. No doubt about it.

[12] I said thespian!

During the brig scene in *Anything Goes*, Billy Crocker and Moonface Martin are locked up together until the ship's captain can figure out their true identities. Given how much fun Bernard and I used to have playing this scene, it was inevitable that in the 2002–3 National Theatre revival of *Anything Goes*, the scene would invite some kind of competition again. In the NT production, my good friend Martin Marquez played Moonface Martin, and he and I used to have farting contests during this scene. We're both pros – at acting and farting – so it was always a fight (or a fart) to the finish. During the scene, when Billy Crocker sings 'All Through the Night' and Moonface sings 'Be Like the Bluebird', Martin and I would try to get in as many farts as possible during the other's number. Some nights, we made terrible enemies of the rest of the cast because of the deadly blue cloud that would emanate from the brig.

Enemies and company rifts, I'm proud to say, have never really played a part in my career. I've also not thrown many strops – that is, out-and-out tantrums where I could have brought the house down on my own from the upstairs dressing room – but I do remember a vivid one I threw during the run of *Matador* in 1993.[13]

In *Matador*, the kind of dance moves I had to do with a thirty-pound cape had demanded that I fly to a real bullfighting school in Madrid to receive tutoring from the experts before the show opened. During one of the dance numbers, I had to swing this heavy cape around my legs, around my waist, up and down and across my sides for what felt like an eternity, while the six dancers playing the bull dodged, weaved and generally avoided being slapped by the huge cape.

Now, there was a dance assistant on this production who one night took it upon herself to make a few changes to the show. She

[13] Incidentally, this is the only show that my parents never saw, because I thought it would make it to the West End and they delayed coming over from the US.

instructed the dancers to up the tempo on this particular flamenco number. By the end of the number as it stood, I was knackered – and yet she decided to speed up the bloody routine without telling me. Let me repeat, without fucking telling me!

When I left the stage that night, after the bull had quickened its pace, I walked past her and screamed, 'You! My dressing room. *Now!*'

John Fahey followed directly behind me as I stormed upstairs. I crashed into my dressing room, absolutely livid, practically snorting, steam coming out of my ears like the bull I'd just been pretending to fight.

'John, calm down. Take some deep breaths. She's not here yet.'

'Why the hell not?'

'Because she's waiting till you're calmer and then you won't have the upper hand.'

'What should I do?'

John had been a dresser for years and this was my first time as a company leading man. I went to school on his advice.

'I'll go get her right now,' he said. 'You need to have one of these tantrums now and again. Otherwise, they'll pull that shit with you all the time.'

The dance assistant stood sheepishly while I yelled at her, and her only defence was that she'd thought she was helping the show by speeding up the number.

'Helping the show?' I roared. 'How does it help the show to make the leading man look like a stupid twat who can't spin a fucking cape? This show's not about the bloody bull. It's about me!'

The changes she made to the choreography were really very dangerous. I could have broken a nail spinning that cape faster and faster. Or, even worse, I could have torn a testicle, and then I'd never have been able to play the piano again.

Chapter Thirteen

'There's Nothing Wrong With Us'

O n Clare and Turner's first trip to the UK in 1998, they travelled with my mum and dad from Milwaukee to London. One weekend during that visit, I took all of them on the Eurostar to Paris. When the train went into the tunnel, Turner was glued to the window for the first ten minutes because I'd told him to watch for fish. Don't tell me you've never seen them either?

While we were in Paris, we ate lunch at a cafe on the Boulevard St Germain, a place where Oscar Wilde and Ernest Hemingway[1] are said to have enjoyed a patisserie or two. Well, Wilde may have enjoyed one or two, but I'm thinking Hemingway was more about watching the women strolling down the boulevard. Strolling musicians headed our way that day.

'Turner, five bucks if you get up and dance.' He was about eight at the time.

'Ten.'

'Done.'

Turner started out with a few easy bobs of the head, some funny

---

[1] God, not at the same time. They'd have killed each other.

sliding moves and then he broke into a full breakdance routine, much to the delight of the people at surrounding tables. When the musicians finally wandered to the next cafe, Turner had my ten plus a handful of coins from other diners in his pocket. This event established a significant pattern in my relationship with Turner.

'Turner, twenty bucks if you eat this dog food.' He was about nine at the time. We were at my parents' house in Orlando, Florida for Christmas.[2] He looked at the bowl. Picked it up. Waved it slowly under his nose.

'Just a mouthful?'

'A mouthful, but you can't spit it out.'

'A hundred bucks.'

'Deal.'

He used a fork and ate dog food.

During a different December in Florida, the heater broke down in my parents' swimming pool. God, life was tough that year. The air temperature was in the sixties.[3] The water temp was about the same. I know that seems balmy to us in the UK, but it was frickin' frigid for Florida.[4]

'Turner, ten bucks if you jump into the pool in your underwear.' He was about eleven at the time. He eased over to the edge, keeping his back to the pool in case Scott or I tried to shove him in without paying for the pleasure. He stuck his toe into the water.

'It's freezing!'

'Twenty bucks, then.'

He jumped for thirty.

---

[2] Shortly after my dad retired from Caterpillar Inc., my parents began a seasonal lifestyle of living in Florida in the winter and Brookfield, Wisconsin in the summer.

[3] That's about 15–20°C.

[4] I'm enjoying these moments of alliteration.

When I think about our deals, Turner wasn't as daft as the incidents themselves might suggest. For a few seconds of freezing his balls off or barfing up Pedigree Chum, over the years Turner has won a fortune from me. Once, when he had gone about two years without a haircut, he accepted a video camera from me just to get his hair sheared. I even sent him to my salon in London to have it done and he still took the bloody camera. Young people today have no shame. I think I've primed Turner for a career in arbitrage or at the very least to be a hell of a grifter.

Since they were babies, I've been close to all my nieces and nephews, adoring every one of them, but Clare holds a particularly special place in my heart. Clare was born in 1987, just as I was getting ready to leave for San Diego and my first term at USIU. Clare was, and I guess still is, a twin. Her sister Anne was stillborn. Both babies experienced what's known as a twin-to-twin transfusion, a rare condition that means they share a placenta and many of the same blood vessels, but something goes wrong in the symbiosis of the relationship and one of the twins, in this case Anne, draws more blood than she really needs, putting her twin in jeopardy of not getting enough.

In 1987, the result of a twin-to-twin transfusion was usually the death of both babies, one from anaemia and the other from an enlarged heart. However, due to the work of a superb team of neonatologists, Clare survived the trauma of her birth with no permanent side effects from the condition. Well, maybe one or two little quirks, but we really can't blame them on her being a preemie.

When I first met Clare, she was in her 'womb with a view', an incubator in the neonatal intensive-care ward at St Joseph's Hospital in Milwaukee, Wisconsin. Because she had developed jaundice, she was wearing baby eye-shades, like the kind you get on a plane to block out the light, to protect her eyes. She was the teeniest tiniest baby I'd ever seen, and as I've mentioned earlier in these pages, she is still pretty small.

It broke my heart to see her so tiny and so helpless and yet, on that day in August, she was also the most beautiful baby I'd ever seen. From that day forward, Clare and I have always had a special bond with each other. Given what she went through in the first weeks of her life, I knew she was going to be a little fighter, and she still is. Even at three or four, if Clare didn't want to do something I'd asked her to do, she'd scrunch up her nose and snort through it. It became a secret signal between us when she was growing up, and we still snort to each other on occasion. Clare's more than capable of starting an argument in an empty house – add that to my, shall we say, slightly controlling nature, and the two of us can go at it like siblings sometimes.

I was twenty when Clare was born and in a way we've grown up together. As a result, she's as much a younger sister as she is my niece. Over the years, she's also been my personal Barbie doll, willingly allowing me to send her all the cute girly stuff I see when I'm shopping. She admits this is a chore, but someone has to do it. When I need to talk to someone about something other than work, Clare is always game for a chat about trashy television shows – we both love programmes like *Desperate Housewives* – and we share a passion for shoes, bargains of any kind, TK Maxx and luggage.

Over the years, I've taught all my nieces and nephews lots of important things: as many words as I know for 'excrement', a rich repertoire of cheeky songs, and an occasional mild obscenity. I mean, what else are uncles for? My nephew Andrew, my brother Andrew's son, has even had the experience of hearing the wild scratching and snarling of the werewolf who wanders my street in London. The werewolf's haunting of our Kensington–Chelsea neighbourhood began in 1981, when the flat a few doors down from ours became the set for the film *An American Werewolf in London*. When my brother and his family were over for a visit one time, we watched part of the movie. Guess what happened next? The werewolf began haunting the street, that very evening, right outside our door. My nephew Andrew, who was about four or five at the time, and I had to don some super-protective gear and march into the street in search of it.

I've also tried to keep up the Barrowman family traditions, teaching my nieces and nephews how to pull pranks with a degree of seriousness, how to be silly even when you're a grown-up and – probably my most important legacy – how to put on a damn good show.

When I began to do pantos at Christmas, and returning to the US during the holiday season became impossible with my schedule, I flew the clan to Cardiff to celebrate. In the years before that, however, we always gathered at my parents' house in Florida for a family Christmas and New Year celebration. There are lots of traditions surrounding this family event and one of them is that everyone has to come prepared to do a party piece.

Carole can't hold a tune in a Tupperware box, and although Kevin can, they will usually perform an 'air band' number to start the evening off. Over the years, they've produced an awesome Springsteen routine with Kevin on the best imaginary sax ever, a rousing version of the Dave Matthews Band's 'Ants Marching', and I remember a year when they did the David Bowie/Bing Crosby version of 'Little Drummer Boy' that would have brought tears to Bob Hope's eyes. Seriously. Tears. They were awful that year.

My brother Andrew's children, who are considerably younger than Carole's kids, naturally have limited experience of these parties, but when they have participated, they've often done dance numbers.

Frankly, Andrew and Dot's daughters, Yvonne and Bridgett, currently aged six and three respectively, are adorable doing just about anything they want.

For many years, Scott always opted to be the designated photographer or the enthusiastic audience member during these events. But a few years ago, he was bitten by the Barrowman vaudeville bug and gave a performance worthy of the Royal Variety Show. Scott rehearsed for weeks before the holiday. On Hogmanay, usually the night we all perform, he belted out his interpretation of Glen Campbell's 'Rhinestone Cowboy' in an outfit comprising chaps, a sequinned shirt, a holster and a six-shooter.[5] On any given night, Scott is only slightly better at holding a tune than Carole, but what he lacked in pitch he more than made up for in his choreography.

After the opening acts, we always play a few rounds of charades, where my dad will get red in the face from trying to hold his tongue as he acts out a film title without reciting any of the dialogue, and my mum will stutter her way through sixty seconds of repeating the same gesture over and over and over again, and then get into a fit of giggles so that none of us have any clue what she was supposed to be doing in the first place. But who cares? My nephew Andrew can hold his own in these games, especially if he picks a footballer or a baseball player from the 'sorting hat'. However, no matter how good they all are, I am most definitely the 'king of charades'.

Even if I say so myself – and, of course, I am saying so myself – I'm an amazing charades player. On the other hand, if we play Trivial Pursuit, Carole, Kevin and Scott must never be on the same team. If we have a game of Scrabble, we just don't let Carole or Dot take part at all, and if we play cards, Kevin needs to be watched very carefully.

---

[5] He has a fine 'six-shooter'.

He's a shark. Kevin's parents Bud and Lois Casey, who live in Minnesota, are the king and queen of cards. One summer evening, when Scott and I and Scott's nephew Gabriel spent a few days at Bud and Lois's lake home in northern Wisconsin, Lois, who's a feisty broad, almost karate-chopped my fingers when I tried to take back a card I'd already played during an intense game of 'Nickel Nickel'. It's a game that can turn even mild-mannered individuals, like myself, into raving lunatics. It was worth it, though: I won 85 cents that night.

At a certain point during the Barrowman New Year's Eve celebrations, when our creative juices are pumping, to say nothing of the vodka tonics, it's time for the main event. Clare, Turner and I disappear to wardrobe (when we're in Florida, it's my mum and dad's walk-in closet), where the three of us begin our transformation. Usually, Turner and I get in drag and Clare dresses as a man. If we're lucky, we talk my dad into dragging it up too. Once, he dressed as a bodacious blonde thing, scooted out the back patio doors, re-entered through the front door, and burst into the party. A couple of neighbours at the bash, who did not know my dad very well at that time, thought he was a loose woman friend of the Barrowmans who'd crashed the celebration. A couple of the men flirted shamelessly with her/him.

Another year, when Turner was about six, Clare and I found a plastic mould of boobs and a big belly at a costume store. We dressed Turner up as a slutty-looking Dolly Parton.

Was that adjective redundant?

Turner then recited a dirty ditty as he pointed to his fake boobs and his plastic booty. The poem he recited went something like this: 'Milk, milk, lemonade. Turn the corner, fudge is made.'

Turner was the highlight of that year's performances. In fact, over the years, Turner has been primped, painted and puffed more times than I can remember, and he's worn more wigs than Marie

Antoinette. Because Turner was the youngest in the family for a long time, and because he had a bit of the performer in his genes, too, he was often the one whom Clare and I most 'dolled up'.

Other than me, that is, and I still love to drag it up; I have done all my life. In 1997, I was performing as Che in the Oslo concert production of *Evita*. Between performances one evening, my co-star Jacqui Stewart dressed up as Che, I slipped into Eva Perón's clothes, and we put on a terrific performance for the cast and crew.

In the summer of 2007, during Turner's annual visit to the UK, he and I were driving back to Cardiff one night after recording *The Friday Night Project*, where I'd dressed in drag as Davina McCall, and then as the *Big Brother* housemate Ziggy, for a parody of the Channel 4 reality show. Turner and I were reminiscing about all the years we'd spent with red lips, stuffed boobs, big hair and big heels at Hogmanay, when he said, with all the wisdom of a seventeen-year-old, 'You know, Uncle John, I'm straight, and if you think about all the times when I was a kid that I've been dressed up in women's clothing and made to sing and dance, I've got to be proof that you can't turn someone gay.'

I laughed so hard I almost drove right through the toll barrier at the Welsh border.

At another New Year celebration, Clare dressed up as Sonny to my Cher and we did a fabulous rendition of 'I've Got You, Babe'. A special favourite of mine is the year Clare, Turner and I did a kind of manic version of the Pointer Sisters song, 'I'm So Excited'. The three of us made theirs look like a geriatric version. The year before that, Clare dressed up as Tony Orlando, and Turner and I were the backing singers, the lovely Dawn. We performed 'Knock Three Times' and had the family in stitches. I think that may have been the year the performing bug bit Scott.

Half the fun of these performances was in the process, which always began with a shopping spree to find the perfect shoes and accessories. Clare, Turner and I didn't always have to hit the high street to find these. Over the years, I've accumulated wigs and other sundry costumes from my professional life, and bits and pieces that I've bought from my TV shows usually end up in our acts. Clare once performed with a purse and shoes worn by Victoria Principal in *Titans*, while Turner once donned a sparkling halter dress that Mariel Hemingway wore in *Central Park West*. He looked fabulous, dahling.

In fact, in a life-imitates-art-imitates-life kind of moment,[6] I gave my mum an evening dress that Victoria wore in *Titans* while playing my screen mum, and my mum – real one, that is – wore it one Christmas Eve. She looked fabulous too, dahling.

My mum and dad have shared in my success in other ways, too. They've both chatted with Bob Hope and Kirk Douglas at a concert I gave in LA, *Red, Red, Rose*; they've had dinner with Dame Diana Rigg in London after a show; and they consider Elaine Paige a special friend.

Performing may be one of the dominant passions that's shaped my life, but the importance of my family and the ability to share my success with all of them is an equally strong drive. I want to give them the world – and so when I can, I do. Over the years, Scott and I have taken our nieces and nephews on trips that they might not normally have had a chance to take. For example, soon after Gabriel's dad died of Hodgkin's lymphoma in 1997, we took Gabriel, who was then seven years old, on an American road trip with us.[7]

The holiday included some time in Las Vegas. While there, we stayed at the hotel New York, New York, but they wouldn't let our

---

[6] Head hurt from that?

[7] Gabriel's mum was Sandie, who also died of cancer in 2005.

dogs into the room, so we rented a room next door in the LaQuinta Inn just for our canines, Penny and Lewis.[8] One morning, we told Gabriel we were going there to walk the dogs and he could order whatever he wanted for breakfast. When we came back, what we saw was like a vision from a Tim Burton movie.

Gabriel was sitting in front of this huge hotel window, which looked out on to an amazing roller coaster. Two trays piled high with food sat on the table in front of him. He'd ordered everything on the menu from steak and eggs to pancakes with cream, as well as sausages, bacon and a rich sticky selection of buns and doughnuts. He was having the time of his life and he finished everything on the trays. As you might have guessed, he was ill for the rest of the day.

When Scott and I came back from walking the dogs, we stood at the hotel-room door for the longest time, quietly observing Gabriel. We got such a rush of pleasure as we did, because there was something very poignant about this wee boy, who had just lost his dad, watching the roller coaster as if it was his childhood whizzing around in front of him while he enjoyed every last mouthful of food.

On this same cross-country road trip, the three of us visited what I think was one of the best off-road stops I've ever made. In a small town called Alliance in the plains of Nebraska, an artist, Jim Reinders, has recreated Stonehenge using rusting American cars. This Carhenge, as it's called, is not the only car sculpture on the site, but it's the most impressive. Over thirty cars are arranged in a wide circle, with the pillar stones formed by vehicles stood on end in pits, with other cars welded across the top. The dimensions and placement of the cars are exactly the same as the real Stonehenge. The keystone at Carhenge is a classic Cadillac.

---

[8] As you may recall, Tiger didn't become part of our family until our civil partnership ceremony in 2006.

I'd have to think a bit on which one is the more interesting – the real one or the kitsch?

On that same trip, Gabriel, Scott and I travelled along part of the Oregon Trail, which pioneers from the 1840s and 1850s followed up into the northwest of the United States. At Guernsey, Wyoming, the place known as the 'hub of the Oregon Trail', we were able to examine the deep ruts made by hundreds of Conestoga wagons. But that wasn't the coolest part of the day. (I know it's hard to believe it gets cooler than staring at ruts in the rocks, but hold on, it did.) As the pioneers lumbered past a limestone cliff on their route west, many stopped and carved their names into the limestone. The three of us were able to read their imprints after almost two hundred years.[9]

In the classic 1952 western *High Noon*, Gary Cooper walks up a hill to a white picket-fenced graveyard. During this trip, we visited a graveyard that could have been the set for *High Noon* and hundreds of other westerns. I even had to dart away from a huge rattlesnake slithering its way across the parched ground. Get the picture, pilgrims?

The best part of having lots of nieces and nephews is that there will always be children in the family for Scott and me to spoil. We can't wait until Andrew's children are old enough to go on adventures with us too.

A year after our trip with Gabriel, Scott and I took Clare and Turner on a holiday to the Sequoia National Park in California, at the southern foothills of the Sierra Nevada mountains. I think the park is a natural wonder of the world. Amazingly, until a law was passed in 2006, it was under threat from the Bush administration, which wanted to make it legal to farm the ancient, gorgeous giant trees. But I digress. Never happen again.[10]

---

[9] That's really old in America.
[10] I lie, because I'm sure it will.

In 1998, Scott and I took Clare, then almost ten, seven-year-old Turner, and the dogs, Penny and Lewis, and travelled through the Sequoia National Park. On the way, we stopped at Kaweah Lake and Three Rivers, where we shot the rapids – and almost lost Turner in the current. Almost, mind, because like me when I was a child, he has a habit of coming back. Later, the four of us climbed to the top of the mountain at the Giant Sequoia National Monument to see the view, which was spectacular.

Both Clare and Turner had taken smaller road trips with Scott and me before, so they were prepared for lots of silliness. For example, on a different trip, while we were driving back from Disneyworld in Florida, I suddenly realized we were driving on petrol fumes. It was Scott, of course, who'd forgotten to fill the tank. I dropped the car into neutral. I could see the gas station calling to us in the distance and it was all downhill. Nevertheless, we were still yards away when the car began to slow.

'Emergency flapping!' I yelled, and, as if we had all practised the manoeuvre, each of us opened a door and began flapping it back and forth.[11] We made it into the petrol station on our own wing power.

One of the reasons Turner was especially excited about this trip to Sequoia was because I'd told him that we might be staying at a couple of fancy hotels – and fancy hotels often leave chocolate on your pillow at night. On our first evening, Turner came rushing into his room, only to find a wee pile of poo on his pillow. I've no idea how it got there, but as the song from the musical episode of *Scrubs* suggests, 'everything comes down to poo.'[12] Until he leaned in close, Turner thought it was his chocolate treat.

[11] Do not try this with your own car. 'Flapping' should only be done by a trained professional.
[12] For the record, I've made it my mission to pester Russell T. Davies regularly about writing a musical episode of *Doctor Who* or *Torchwood*.

When we reached the Sequoia National Park, we left the van near a campsite and decided to hike for a while. Signs were posted everywhere warning of black bears, telling tourists how to protect themselves against an attack, and alerting people about the dangers of exposed food and neglected garbage. Bears, you know, are smarter than the average campers and can recognize coolers and backpacks bearing jam rolls. Four or five German students had pitched tents just off the hiking trail and we watched as they finished up their picnic lunch and bundled their packs into very high-tech-looking metal containers. We chatted to them for a few minutes, and that was how we knew they were German, in case you were wondering.

Afterwards, we took a few pictures of each of us standing under the General Sherman Tree, one of the oldest and biggest in the park. Five bucks if you know who General Sherman was. Kidding – only Turner gets to guess.

We were heading back towards our van when I saw a shadow off to my right.

'Don't move,' I whispered urgently, grabbing Turner's arm. 'I saw a bear.'

Clare looked up at me, terrified. 'Where?'

'Near the tree, directly behind Scott.'

'What should we do?' said Turner, edging behind me.

'Is it in its bluff stance?' asked Scott.

Now, let me pause here to point out one of the differences between Scott and me. I see a bear and want to run like hell. Scott sees a bear and wants to know if it's in its 'bluff stance'.

'What does that mean?' Clare asked.

'It means he may not attack us,' Scott replied.

'Who are you?' I yelled. 'Doctor fucking Doolittle?'

'He's moving,' said Scott, suddenly grabbing Clare's arm and shoving her back on to the trail.

'Run!'

Clare and Turner shot down the trail towards the van so fast they left cartoon speed lines in the air. Scott and I sprinted behind them. When we passed the Germans in their tents, I screamed maniacally, and in my biggest West End voice, 'Bear!'

They scrambled from their tents as if the bear was inside the space with them, abandoned their camp and ran off, flapping wildly, into the trees. Clare got to the van first, threw the door open, and she and Turner hurled themselves inside. Seconds later, Scott and I reached the van and climbed breathlessly on to the front seats.

Clare looked at the red button blinking on the video camera. After a beat, she said, 'There was no bear, was there, Uncle John?'

No bear, only a couple of loony uncles.

Chapter Fourteen

'Nice Work If You Can Get It'

When visitors first walk on to the site in Cardiff where *Torchwood, Doctor Who* and *The Sarah Jane Adventures* are filmed,[1] the first thing they notice is how crowded the lot is. Each of us on *Torchwood* has our own trailer and each one is lined up side by side with the names of our characters taped to the door. There's a catering trailer, a production trailer, a hair and make-up trailer, a wardrobe trailer, and then a host of trailers for men and women working on things like lighting, special effects and set design, who occasionally bustle in and out of said trailers when they're not leaning up against them drinking tea and smoking. Oh, I'm going to pay for that remark.

My trailer has a bedroom, a fully kitted-out kitchen – supplied with bottled water every day[2] – a bathroom, a shower, and a living area with a couch (where I spend most of my time), and a recliner (which is Eve's favourite spot in her trailer). When we move to a

---

[1] The shows are not usually filmed on the lot at the same time. When they are, shooting is staggered: one programme films at night, the others during the day.

[2] You thought I was going to say champagne, didn't you?

location, the transportation crew haul the entire lot full of trailers to that remote site. It's not an exaggeration to describe these moves as similar to shifting a small city from place to place.

In the hair and make-up trailer, a bulletin board located directly inside the door is covered with pictures of the main cast of *Torchwood*, and also any supporting actors who'll be in the episode that's on the filming schedule for the day. The snaps display each of the cast in samples of the make-up that's needed for the episode, as well as the way our characters look on a regular basis. If Captain Jack needs to have blood on his cheek or a cut on his lip, days before the episode will actually be filmed, Claire or Marie Doris create the scar or mix the blood that will be used for the wound, and an image of it is put on the board for reference. Eve, Burn, Gareth, Naoko and I are listed on this board as numbers one through five. I'm number one, Eve is two, Burn is three, Naoko is four and Gareth is five. When I sit in my make-up chair at the beginning of each day, I still get a rush when I read that number under my name.

My first job in television was on *Live and Kicking*, a BBC variety show for children broadcast live on Saturday mornings in the early nineties. The programme was successful because of its format and the variety of guests that were booked. In 1993, my agent at the time, Janet Glass, who helped steer my early career, heard that the show was hiring presenters. So one afternoon, I took my video camera and walked around Oxford Street with a friend. We taped a segment of 'What's Hot and What's Not'. I hung out at Hamleys toy store for an afternoon, where I chatted with children, played with toys and generally entertained shoppers until the store manager kicked me out, politely but firmly. I sent the tape to the BBC and within days of receiving it, they called me in for a screen test with Andi Peters and Emma Forbes, who were already signed up as the show's main anchors.

The *Live and Kicking* producers offered me the role right away, but as is often the case in these situations, I was not allowed to tell anyone I had the job. Over the years, I've gotten much better at keeping a lock on my lips in those circumstances. My cheeks, all four of them, ached from keeping the *Live and Kicking* news to myself.

Hours after accepting the position as a presenter of the show, I was in a production studio recording an album of the musical *Godspell*. The album's producer, John Yap, had brought together a number of musical theatre performers to make the record. Yap heard from someone that one of the other artists involved in the project, Darren Day, had been offered a job on *Live and Kicking*. To cash in on this news, John asked Darren to sing the part of Jesus, an irony of casting that was not lost on any who knew of Darren's personal proclivities.[3]

My old friend Ruthie Henshall was also on the record, and we were both present in the studio when John Yap brought in a photographer to shoot the album's cover and its publicity photos. The poor guy thought putting Darren on the sleeve would boost his sales. While the photographer was snapping pics of Darren, I sat at the back of the studio with Ruthie, eating chocolate and having a cuppa.

Finally, I couldn't take John Yap's fawning over Darren anymore. I leaned over to Ruthie and whispered, 'Darren's not going to be on *Live and Kicking.*'

'How do you know?'

'Because it's going to be me,' I grinned, with a piece of warm chocolate smooched across my front teeth as if I'd been eating dirt … or worse.

---

[3] Love this word. Sounds so much more refined than what the tabloids claimed were 'addictions to sex and drugs'.

'You're evil,' she laughed.

My introduction to live television quickly became a classic blooper clip. I jumped enthusiastically on to the back of the golf-cart-like vehicle behind Andi and Emma to introduce myself – and my momentum carried me right off the cart and on to the ground.

As a presenter of *Live and Kicking*, the experience I gained in front of the cameras was fantastic, but not so much from behind them. Emma and Andi were terrific and they have remained good friends, but this was my first foray into television – not just live television, but television in general – and given my, erm, slight stubborn streak, my sense of humour, and my love of improvisation and creating characters, working with the producers of *Live and Kicking* was a bit like working for a bunch of Captain von Trapps before Maria came into their lives. There was little room for any creative deviation and I had to do exactly as I was told exactly when I was told, whether or not it made any artistic sense.

Despite all this, I had a great time on the programme. It was my introduction to British TV and gave me an opportunity to extend my visibility beyond the world of the West End. I also interviewed some great guests. My first one was Lulu, whose family lived in Mount Vernon, not far from my mum and dad's old haunts. In fact, back in the day, my dad drew the plans for an extension to their bungalow, and my brother Andrew was a mate of her brother. This was one of the first public interviews where I used my Scottish accent. Funnily enough, another early interview was with Jayne Torvill and Christopher Dean, who later coached my ice dancing for *Dancing on Ice*.

My work on *Live and Kicking* was one of the reasons Cameron Mackintosh put me back into *Miss Saigon* for another short run in 1993 – my second time playing Chris after I'd first taken on the role in 1990. As I'd now become more recognizable, my increased profile brought a younger audience to the theatre to see the show.

The experience also led to some 'pin-up boy' work for me because *Live and Kicking* had its own teen magazine.[4] As a result of this adulation, I was invited to lip-sync – I know, gasp, the horror – a song called 'Bare Naked' at a *Smash Hits* concert. I was wearing a Nicole Farhi scarf I'd been given on loan. In the middle of the song, I leaned into the audience to shake some of the outstretched hands. Suddenly, four girls in the front row grabbed my scarf. I knew if these ladies succeeded in yanking it from my neck it would cost me about £600 to replace. Plus, they were trying to separate a gay man from his accessories.[5]

There I was: hanging off the stage, no longer in sync with the song, fighting with four teenage girls for the fucking scarf. Of course, I got it back, but I think that was the moment when I realized I didn't want to be a pop idol. My album *Another Side*, which SonyBMG released in November 2007, was my chance to embrace that side of me again – only this time I personally picked all the songs and I've bought extra scarves for the tour.

Live and Kicking whet my appetite for children's television, for which I have a real fondness. Not only because I'm a big kid at heart, but also because I love acting and interacting with children, and I hope that my career continues to present me with opportunities to do this.

My exposure on *Live and Kicking* also led to me securing another kids' TV programme to present, *The Movie Game*. Although the show had been on the air with two other hosts before me, this was a coup given my limited experience on television. I loved doing this

---

[4] Little-known fact: Penny had her own cartoon in the magazine.
[5] Never ever attempt this at home.

programme. It was mostly a game show, with three teams of children competing. The game was very active for the kids and for me, involving lots of costumes, props and opportunities for skits and slapstick here and there. Signing up to present *The Movie Game*, though, meant my schedule was now packed to the rafters. A typical weekend meant rolling out of bed at 5.30 a.m. on Saturday to be driven to the BBC studios in Shepherd's Bush for 6 a.m. We'd rehearse *Live and Kicking* until the show went on the air at 9ish and ran live until noon. I'd then head back into the West End to perform two shows as Chris in *Miss Saigon*. On Sundays, I'd get up before dawn. Viv Rosenbaum, the wife of my driver at the time, Dave, would make sandwiches for us to eat on our drive north to Birmingham, where I'd tape two shows of *The Movie Game*, and then return to London in time for a Monday production meeting for *Live and Kicking*. All week, of course, I'd perform a daily production of the musical, too.

In the spring of 2007, my schedule looked a lot like this one from 1994, only substitute filming *Torchwood* in Cardiff for *Miss Saigon*, and replace my drive back and forth to Birmingham to shoot *The Movie Game* with motoring to London for the live TV finals of *Any Dream Will Do*.

Don't take this litany of commitments as a complaint, however. I've always been busy and I always want to be busy. I like to keep my schedule packed because, honestly, I'm a nightmare to be around when I'm doing nothing or when I don't get to do all the things I want to. Just ask a certain bear with a cracked jaw from Oswego, Illinois.[6]

Unbeknownst to me, though, something was about to happen to ease some of the pressure on my schedule. Over the course of my two years on *Live and Kicking*, my role grew smaller and smaller. I

---

[6] Surely you've not forgotten the bearskin rug that crossed my path when I was a toddler?

was more and more the roving reporter, and less and less involved in developed segments on the set. The proverbial last straw for me was when we were in a production team meeting for about three hours, and by the end of the meeting I'd been assigned three small segments. I pushed my chair away from the table and stood up to address the team.

'Listen, there's no point me being here anymore if all I'm getting is one or two segments. But you could at least have had the balls to tell me you don't want to use me anymore. I'm an adult and a professional. Treat me like one.' The following season, I was gone.

I later heard from a friend on the production staff that the show's producers essentially had no clue what to do with me. They didn't know what I was able to give and no one took the time to take me under their wing to give me any kind of training or help. I thought I did okay under the circumstances, but the producers were certainly not much help in that area.

What I disliked most about the experience was that the producers didn't respect me enough to be honest with me. Thankfully, on *The Movie Game*, which I continued presenting after I left *Live and Kicking*, the production team recognized my potential and gave me more artistic freedom.

The Movie Game treated its audience as smart, interesting and funny individuals without condescension or pandering. Once, though, we almost credited the teams of children with just a bit too much maturity. A skit we were about to shoot required me, dressed as a shepherd, to herd the children, dressed as sheep, into a pen. What the folks in the wardrobe department didn't realize was that the sheep costumes had been ordered from an adult costume shop – and the 'sheep' all had anatomically correct arseholes and vaginas. Needless to say, those all had to be taped up completely before we could film.

The Movie Game ran right before *Blue Peter* and, like *Live and Kicking*, got great viewing figures. Even today, I get a kick from their popularity as grown-ups regularly stop me in the street because they remember me from one or other of the shows. In 1995, I left *The Movie Game* to film the drama *Central Park West* for American television.

Both *Central Park West* and *Titans*, my two US TV shows, were dramas about rich and powerful families, and I played a son in each family. Both programmes were clones of the *Dallas* prototype, by which I mean they centred on beautiful people conniving, manipulating and back-stabbing their friends, family and, well, pretty much everyone else. The variations on the theme were that *Titans* was about a fabulously rich and incredibly dysfunctional family in the aviation business in California, while *Central Park West* was about a fabulously rich and incredibly dysfunctional family in the publishing business in New York City.

Another element both of these shows had in common was that in each one I had a terrific TV mother. In *Central Park West*, my mother was played by Lauren Hutton, and in *Titans*, as I've mentioned, it was Victoria Principal. Lauren was a bit of a loony[7] and she confirmed a conclusion that I was already formulating at that point in my career, which was that all leading ladies are mildly off-kilter.[8] From Elaine Paige to Betty Buckley, Lauren to Victoria, they were all tough, quirky broads and I think that's why I've always got along with my leading ladies so well.

I did have one weird experience while working on the set of *Central Park West*, though, and that was the producers kept telling me not to smile on camera. You've seen me on television. Why

---

[7] I mean this in the nicest possible way, since I'm a bit of one myself.
[8] I mean this in the nicest possible way too.

would you not want me to smile? I thought about this edict a lot and could never figure out the reason, until one day when I was called into the production office for a chat.

I must add here that producers rarely ask you into their office for something good. In fact, it's one of the most irritating things about producers because, as my mum always told me, you get so much more out of people when you praise rather than disparage. However, no matter how many things an actor may do well on set, or out in public with fans, or even schmoozing with network execs, a producer only ever invites an actor into his or her office to chide or berate.

So there I was sitting in the production office of *Central Park West*. Although the producers didn't say it quite this bluntly, the message was loud and clear: do not let the public know that you're gay and stop being seen in public with your partner.

I suddenly thought, 'Was that why they didn't want me to smile? Because only gay men smile and look happy, and since my character was straight, he couldn't smile?'

Who knew? Regardless, the request was outrageous and pissed me off.

As it turned out, it wasn't something I had to worry about for very long, which was just as well. The series was cancelled after a brief half-season run, by which time my character had already been shipped off to South America for reconstructive surgery after a terrible accident.[9] As you can probably judge from that plot twist alone, the scripts had gone from okay to pretty weak to utter shite: thus the cancellation.

And speaking of shite, as I've told you once before, 'everything comes down to poo.' In television in particular and in show business

---

[9] I should say here that I'm quite sure the accident to my character had nothing to do with my smile.

in general, sometimes a performance is reduced to the most base of our human instincts. Think about this. A scene in *Doctor Who* opens with Captain Jack, Martha and the Doctor stepping out of the TARDIS. To achieve this, all three actors are crammed inside a prop box like sardines for what can be some of the longest minutes of the day, because I have to tell you, between David Tennant and I, we can create an enormous amount of methane from our arses. Freema Agyeman,[10] like Naoko on *Torchwood*, never farts. Naoko claims that folks of Japanese heritage take pills so they don't fart.[11] I've never asked Freema her excuse.

After *Central Park West*, my next series television show was Aaron Spelling's night-time soap *Titans*. As much as I adored working with Victoria and the rest of the *Titans'* cast, Yasmine Bleeth's drug addiction marred the entire experience. Yasmine played my character's stepmother Heather, who was secretly in love with my character's brother Chandler, played by Casper Van Dien, and if I remember correctly, she was pregnant with Chandler's baby: you know, typical family dynamics.

In the end, the family dynamics weren't enough to save the show: *Titans* was cancelled in early 2001 after eleven episodes had aired.

It has been a pattern in my life, one for which I'm always thankful, that new friends arrive with each new stage of my life and they stay with me for the long road. As I adjusted to a schedule without a regular gig, my West Hollywood friends Javier Ramos and Bret Vinovich took care of me while I got back on my feet.

I'd met Bret and Javier the day I moved into my West Hollywood condo. They lived in the apartment next door. After I'd tired of unpacking boxes on that first night, I'd knocked on their door and

---

[10] She plays Martha Jones on *Doctor Who*.

[11] She may be pulling my leg, or my finger, depending on your perspective.

introduced myself. Although they thought their new neighbour was good-looking (and when they realized he was the 'hot one' from *Titans*, one of their favourite shows, they were thrilled), they also thought he might be a bit of a nutcase, because no one in California introduces themselves directly to their neighbours in such an upfront way. They were right, of course, I was a nutcase. Regardless, Bret, Javier and I spent many a night in each other's company, eating Mexican food, drinking margaritas and becoming fast friends while admiring the West Hollywood view from our balcony.[12]

After the cancellation of *Titans*, I admit my professional ego was wounded. Now two TV shows I'd been in had been shelved. But closings, cancellations and rejection are part of this business. You just have to move on. However, at that time, in 2001, my professional horizon seemed a bit too vast and empty for my bank account, so I began working with Bev to create my own cabaret show. Since 2002, I've performed that cabaret at Arci's Place in New York; the Kennedy Center in Washington, DC; Stackner Cabaret in Milwaukee, Wisconsin; the Lincoln Center, New York; the Feestzaal Stadhuis in Aalst, Belgium; and Pizza on the Park in London.

Sometimes, when life hands you lemons, you put a few in a vodka tonic.

---

[12] When I say view, I don't mean the landscape.

Chapter Fifteen

'Putting It Together'

Ernest Hemingway wrote that '[I]f you are lucky enough to have lived in Paris as a young man, then wherever you go for the rest of your life, it stays with you, for Paris is a moveable feast.' In 1995, when I was playing Peter Fairchild in Darren Starr's *Central Park West*, Hemingway's granddaughter Mariel was my co-star, so I picked up a few of her grandfather's books to read. If I remember correctly, Hemingway's memories and tales from Paris in the 1920s were tinged with cynicism, regret, a great deal of homophobia and a lot of booze, but at the heart of Hemingway's *Moveable Feast* was a memoir about friendships, good and bad, and inspirations for his writing. From the moment I debuted on the West End stage in *Anything Goes* in 1989, London became my 'moveable feast' and since then, no matter where I've performed, I carry with me all that I've learned from the directors and producers I've worked with in London over the years.

Sir Trevor Nunn is one of the best directors in the world for interpreting musicals because he always gets the relationships right and he pays attention to the nuances of the characters in those relationships. When I worked opposite Betty Buckley in Trevor's *Sunset Boulevard*, Trevor wanted my character Joe to be a bit harder, a bit colder and more obviously a lover to Norma Desmond than had been portrayed in the Broadway production. During a preview performance before opening night, I entered on cue for the scene where Joe meets Norma for the first time. As I opened my mouth, I realized I'd not spat out my chewing gum, so I worked it into the character.

'Great touch, John. It was just what the character needed,' Trevor told me afterwards.

I admitted it had been an oversight on my part and had nothing to do with my portrayal of Joe.

'Don't care. Leave it in.'

In those situations when Trevor appreciated something you'd done, he'd grab you by the head and squeeze you under his armpit while giving a 'Nunn noogie'. It was a playful and affirming gesture, but by the middle of a show's rehearsal period, it could be a bit of a whiffy one. Trevor's superstitious quirk is that he wears the same shirt and the same jeans and doesn't cut his hair until after his show opens. By the end of the rehearsals for *Anything Goes* at the National in 2002, his shirt and jeans were hanging off him. When he stripped at night, I'd not have been surprised if they could have stood on their own.

An opening-night tradition in a company is to exchange gifts, with the leads buying presents for each other and sending a bottle of champagne or flowers or food to the dressing rooms of the ensemble players. On the opening night of *Anything Goes*, the company presented Trevor with a new polo shirt and jeans to replace the ones he'd been wearing for weeks. When the show transferred venues in 2003, and the company went into rehearsal at the Theatre Royal Drury Lane, Trevor wore those same jeans and polo shirt every day until we opened.

Another of Trevor's quirks on this particular production was that

Top: Posing with my co-hosts Andi Peters and Emma Forbes for my first job in television, presenting kids' show *Live and Kicking*.

Above: As part of my role, I interviewed Kylie.

Right: Dressed as Widow Twanky for my second TV venture, *The Movie Game*.

At the Cannes Film
Festival in 2003, with
De-Lovely co-stars
Ashley Judd *(right)* and
Kevin Kline *(below left)*.

Above right: Singing with Alanis Morissette to promote *De-Lovely*.

Above: As a blond for the 'Springtime for Hitler' number in the 2005 film *The Producers*.

Left: With Mel Brooks.

Above: On the set of *Any Dream Will Do* with my fellow judges Denise Van Outen *(far right)* and Zoe Tyler.

Right: Torvill and Dean trainees: on the ice with my *Dancing on Ice* partner, Olga Sharutenko.

Above: On the *Doctor Who* set, during my first week of filming in December 2004. Little did I know it then, but the building in the background would become a key part of my own show, *Torchwood*.

Left: Posing with the Dalek that killed Captain Jack.

Above: On set with the Doctor, David Tennant, and his assistant, Freema Agyeman.

Right: Me with *Doctor Who* guru Russell T. Davies and executive producer Julie Gardner.

Left: Me watching ... me! The first ever broadcast of *Torchwood*.

Below: Joining me for that first viewing were *(from left to right)* Naoko Mori, Burn Gorman, Eve Myles and David Tennant.

Left: Scott and me messing about with Eve.

Over page: The name's Jack ... Captain Jack.

he refused to let either theatre make any kind of announcement about the prohibition of cameras or recording devices. He believed it would break the illusion of the audience being on a cruise ship.

They paid forty pounds for a ticket. They know they're not on a goddamn boat.

Now, when I go into Marks and Spencer's, TK Maxx or even Tesco, I do not put bits and bobs into my pocket or shove a few sweeties in my mouth and leave without paying. That, we all know, would be considered stealing. However, there are still folks who attend the theatre who think it's perfectly acceptable to slip the performing company's artistic property into their pockets via their cameras or phones. Even in the years before YouTube, pirated versions of performances from *Anything Goes* were showing up on the Internet.

People weren't shy about it either, and of course with no announcement from the theatres before each show began, they saw no reason to be. Let me explain. At one performance at the National, Sally Ann Triplett as Reno Sweeney was singing 'Blow Gabriel Blow'. It was the big number in Act Two, in which a chorus of sequinned dancers tap-danced its way to the front of the stage. In fact, the whole cast was on set, gathered in the nightclub of the *SS American*. The stage was crowded and every movement precisely timed and choreographed. The slightest change could throw everyone off. One wrong step could sink the ship. Sally Ann was belting out the song in fine Ethel Merman fashion when, all of a sudden, there was a burst of flash photography from the theatre.

I'd like to make an important aside here. When an actor's on a stage, he or she's generally well lit,[1] whereas the audience, of course, is in the dark. When a flash goes off in said audience, the actor's eyes

---

[1] Especially if you're from the Dean Martin school of acting.

are instinctively drawn to the light and, for a few seconds, the flash is blinding. In the case of 'Blow, Gabriel Blow', to be blinded was bloody dangerous. The flash goes off and thirty sequinned dancers are coming at you doing kick ball change … and you're on your back with your feet in the air.

After the second or third flash, cast members were complaining, whispering during the number, 'John, there's a camera out there.' When I was finally able to look without another burst of blinding light, I could not believe what I saw. A huge video camera was resting on some woman's shoulder in the front stalls. Seriously, this camera was big enough to film the BBC's evening news. It even had a fucking spotlight and every time she turned the camera from side to side, the light created a strobe effect like a flash in our eyes.

We were moving into the next part of the number when the flash exploded again. In these situations of camera or mobile-phone use, someone from the front-of-house staff should immediately move down the aisle and remove the device, but that was not happening at this performance. Would you like to know the reason why? Trevor had insisted that the house staff stay out in the lobby, so most of them were sitting there playing cards! Years ago, the ushers had to remain at the end of the aisles or at the very least stand near the curtained exits and scan the audience, but not during this run. The curtain went up and they left to have a drink or a smoke.

Needless to say, with the last camera flash, I'd had enough.

The woman with the massive video camera was seated midway up the stalls. I started the extended dance routine in 'Blow Gabriel Blow'. I knew how many beats I had before the end of the song. One, two, three and I leapt off the stage, sprinted up the aisle and leaned right into the woman's face.

'Turn off that camera!'

She turned and directed the camera at me. I couldn't believe it.

She kept filming as if Billy Crocker in her face was part of the show. I must admit, I lost it a wee bit at that point.

'Turn off the fucking camera!' I screamed.

She set it down on her lap and looked up at me. '*Que?*'

I felt like I was in a musical episode of *Fawlty Towers*. The band played on. I grabbed the camera from her lap.

The rest of the audience, meanwhile, were all watching me, smiling happily, as if this was the best moment of the show so far. 'Oh, this is so wonderful, John Barrowman's involving the audience. He did say "fuck", but that's okay. We're having a grand time at the theatre.'

With only a few beats left before the song ended, I darted back up on to the stage, camera in hand, and hit my mark on cue. Instead of everyone looking at Sally Ann for the close of the number, they were all looking at me, stunned. After that night's performance, lots of dancers in the ensemble thanked me for what I'd done. Many of them, if they'd not been in the chorus and therefore at risk of being fired and replaced for taking such action, would have done the same thing.

Wyn Howard Thomas, our company manager, was naturally furious. In my dressing room after the show, he read me the riot act: 'John, you cannot do that. Never leave the stage during a performance again.'

I didn't … until two weeks later. On that night, the culprit was a woman up in the balcony with a video camera. Once again, no help was forthcoming from the house. The cast was enraged. This time, there was no easy way for me to leap from the stage to the balcony.

Step, shuffle, step, off stage right.

I sprinted down the wing, darted through a pass door,[2] ran along the corridor and burst out into the lobby.

[2] A door in a theatre that connects the backstage area to the auditorium.

The card game was in full swing. I yelled as I ran past the ushers, 'What the fuck are you all doing out here? There's a camera again and—'

They all gawked at me as I flew by. I heard one of them say, 'He's off his fucking head,' as I raced up the stairs to the balcony.

'Give me the camera!' I hissed at the woman, moments later. 'Do you realize this is illegal?'

Like the other woman days before, she had no clue. I snatched the camera away from her, and told her where she could pick it up after the show. The tape of *Anything Goes* would be erased and a lovely little message from the crew would replace what she'd filmed. I vaulted over the arm rail, took the stairs three at a time, sprinted back through the lobby, passed the card sharks, and made it back up on stage on cue to start my next number.

That's talent.

Sometimes, it's not only cameras that can throw a performance off. During my West End debut in *Anything Goes* in 1989, I remember two old women in the front row at one show loudly discussing the merits of cucumber-and-cheese sandwiches, while Elaine and I were on stage early in the first act.

'You all right, Janice?' one said to the other.

'Mmm! A lovely piece of lettuce that, wasn't it?'

'Do you want the cucumber or the salmon next?'

Oh, and don't get me started on sweetie wrappers. I don't mind eating in the theatre, but don't do it during the quiet moments, and don't open the packaging during the love songs. Believe it or not, we can hear you, and the super-slo-mo wrapper opening makes us want to yell, 'Just eat the fucking sweet!'

As well as directing me in musicals, in 2003 Trevor Nunn also directed me in his final production as Artistic Director of the National, in Shakespeare's *Love's Labour's Lost*. I played Dumaine, one of three noblemen to the King of Navarre, who was played by Simon Day. Joseph Fiennes took the part of one of the other noblemen, Berowne. The play is one of Shakespeare's least known comedies, but according to many critics, it's probably one of his smartest, with lots of puns, wordplay and odd plot twists.

Trevor really took a chance in casting me in such a show. I did give him the goods, but before we opened, I was nervous about playing this role. I might have come over to the UK sixteen years before in order to study the Bard, but this was my first opportunity to be in one of his plays. Funnily enough, *Love's Labour's Lost* ran in repertory with Trevor's revival of *Anything Goes*. There I was playing Billy Crocker again, as I'd done when I first came to England with my USIU class, but now I was also acting Shakespeare, not just studying him. In another of life's weird coincidences, during an episode in the third season of *Doctor Who*, 'The Shakespeare Code', Martha's first trip in the TARDIS takes her to Elizabethan England, where she and the Doctor cross paths with Shakespeare, who is writing *Love's Labour's Won*.

'Once you do Shakespeare, John,' said Trevor, 'your career will change.'

I've always been a good student of the profession and when people like Trevor give me advice, I pay attention. When I explained I was nervous about my performance, he pulled me aside at a rehearsal.

'You'll be fine, John, because musical theatre actors know about heightened reality. Shakespeare is a heightened reality and you have to play it that way. Usually, musical theatre folks who act in Shakespeare are very good at it for that reason.'

Later, in 2005, when I was offered a part in *A Few Good Men* with Rob Lowe at the Theatre Royal Haymarket, I remembered Trevor's advice. Although the script was not as stylized as Shakespeare, an Aaron Sorkin play can be as linguistically complicated for an actor. Anyone who's ever watched an episode of *The West Wing* can tell you Sorkin packs lots of words into every line. I took the role.

Two cool things came from my work with Rob and the company. The first was that he and I found we worked well with each other. When he returned to the States to join the cast of the TV show *Brothers and Sisters*, and found out the producers were looking for someone to play the part of his brother on the show, he recommended me. They offered me the role, but because of my *Torchwood* schedule, I was not able to do it. I was flattered at the request, though, and sorry I wasn't going to be able to work with Rob on that particular project.

The second thing that came out of the play was that I found a surrogate mother for my future children. Ah, so you're still paying attention!

With many of my shows, along with the professional lessons I've learned, I've been lucky enough to leave each production with a new friend to join me on the long road. I know this may be starting to remind you of primary school, but it's the part of this business that I love the most. Actors spend long and intense hours together when working on a show, whether it's in the theatre or on TV. The friendships forged are, in fact, necessary and important to a show's success.

From the play *A Few Good Men*, I gained a good friend in the actress Suranne Jones, or Sara as she's known to her mates. Among other things, we shared a fondness for 'bin chicken'. Sara and I would dash out between the matinee and the evening performance and buy lots of takeout, shovel it in before our dress call, and then toss what was left into the bin in my dressing room. But when we came off stage at the end of the show, we'd be starving again. We'd dive into the garbage and eat what remained of our earlier meal.

After a couple of nights of this, the gastronomical delicacy 'bin chicken' was born.

After a performance, Sara and I could spend hours talking about everything and anything over a drink or two or three. One night, she told me that if Scott and I ever did decide we wanted to have a child of our own, she'd be happy to accommodate us.[3] Perhaps one day I might become a dad; we have a lot of love to give and I adore kids.

In the spring of 1997, I couldn't believe my professional luck when I was cast in Cameron Mackintosh's production of *The Fix*, which ran at the Donmar Warehouse in the early summer of the same year, with Sam Mendes at the helm as director. Sam was then the Artistic Director of the Donmar, and his Academy Award for *American Beauty* was still to come.

Sam was the kind of director who let his actors work through the script on their own first, and then he'd watch for a while before he'd step in to refine and develop the performances. This process allowed many of us in the cast to push ourselves close to the edge with our characters before Sam jumped in and pulled us back.

In *The Fix*, I played a character named Cal Chandler, a man from fictional political royalty, but not unlike the Kennedys or the Rockefellers in America. Chandler was a man being groomed for the American presidency after the death of his father, who gets caught up in organized crime until his world eventually collapses around him. I was later nominated for the 1998 Olivier Award for Best Actor in a Musical for this role.

One night, the cast and Sam went to dinner after a long day of rehearsal and we all had a few too many cocktails. During the meal, Sam decided that he wanted one more run-through before he

[3] Okay, so it's a tacky pun.

released us for the night. Despite our slightly inebriated state, he insisted we go and rehearse. It turned out to be one of our best because we were all relaxed and less inhibited – not that that's usually an issue for me, but that night I tried some things I'd never done before and Sam kept a few of them in my eventual performance.

Sam, like the rest of us in the theatre world, had his own personal rituals during the production. He loved chocolate and before a day of rehearsals began, he would line up seven or eight chocolate bars to sustain him over the course of the day.

Of all the directors and producers I've worked with over the years, Cameron Mackintosh has been my Obi Wan. Cameron has given me lots of opportunities, a great deal of guidance, and has become a close friend. His name is legend in the musical theatre world for producing such hit shows as *Miss Saigon*, *Les Misérables*, *Cats* and *Mary Poppins*.

Larry Oaks, my mentor and the resident director from *Anything Goes* in 1989, first introduced me to Cameron and we became immediate friends. In 1990, Cameron cast me as Chris in *Miss Saigon*. Cameron also had a Scottish upbringing and because he worked his own way up in the business, he has a fondness for others doing the same. That's not to say that he doesn't offer support when it's needed, though. Since I first met him, I've lost count over the years of the number of times a friend or colleague has needed help, financial or otherwise, and Cameron has stepped in.

During the run of *The Fix*, Scott and I were invited to spend a weekend at Cameron's twelfth-century priory home in Somerset. The stone priory sits on over 600 acres of land, which includes an ancient Norman chapel, a swimming pool and pool house, working farms and acres of gardens: all of it lit as if set for an outdoor theatrical show.

At the time, Cameron's beloved dog Hugo, a Rhodesian Ridgeback, was still alive, so Scott and I took Penny, then our only dog, along as well. Now, as you may know, when dogs walk into an environment where they can smell another dog, they often feel the need to mark their territory. Scott and I had barely settled into one of Cameron's beautiful oversized couches when Penny squatted and crapped in the middle of a rug that was probably worth hundreds of thousands of pounds. Michael, Cameron's partner of many years, freaked out a little bit, but Cameron waved away our embarrassment.

'Don't worry about it. A dog's a dog. We can clean it up.'

That's Cameron in a nutshell. He's generous, self-assured, talented, and really, like many of us in the business, he's the kind of guy you could bring home to meet your mother. In fact, Cameron and I have this long-running joke that he keeps employing me because he's never had me. He has, though, watched.

Scott and I once spent a weekend in the South of France at Cameron's vineyard. During our visit, Cameron arranged some wine tasting one afternoon. We sipped the liquid going into the vats and we sipped it coming out. At the end of the session, Scott and I were thoroughly pickled. It was the height of summer, the weather was warm, and the scent of wildflowers and wine filled the air. Scott and I thought we'd lie down by the swimming pool. As can sometimes happen when the wine, the weather and the surroundings conspire, Scott and I felt a bit amorous and – oh, to be this young again – we had sex hanging from one of the huge ancient trees. When Scott and I headed back into the house, we thought our gymnastic performance was our little secret – until we caught up with Cameron, who was standing grinning in front of a picture window that had a clear view of the tree on which Scott and I had been enjoying ourselves. Ever since, I've figured that Cameron has always expected more of me as a dancer in his shows because he knows exactly how flexible I can be.

Cameron and I have more than just our Scottish backgrounds in common. Like me, he can be a wee bit of a control freak, and at a dinner party he held at the priory one weekend, I shamelessly used this trait against him in a prank.

Cameron is a gourmet and he was cooking dinner that evening, so everyone else was assigned a job to help in the process. My role was to pick the vegetables for the salad; Cameron grows his own produce on his farm. As a joke, one of the other guests at the dinner party handed me two baskets. One I filled with good stuff from the vegetable garden, and the other with rotting veg from the nearby compost heap.

It's important at this point in this story for you to know that early in my career Cameron had given me advice that went something like this. If you want to be a leading man, John, you need to do things leading men do, because if you do otherwise, producers will treat you otherwise.

That afternoon, I walked back into the fully kitted-out kitchen and set the basket filled with wilted lettuce and shrivelled carrots on Cameron's counter. Now, Cameron has a great sense of humour, but if you don't get something right that he's asked you to do, he can really throw a fit. That day, his shouting could easily be heard in the other room.

'What the fuck is all of this? Haven't you seen a piece of lettuce before, Barrowman?'

I interrupted him. 'Cameron, I'm a leading man. I do not know vegetables, and I don't want to know vegetables,[4] and besides, it is beneath me, as a leading man, to pick my own vegetables.'

Laughing, he lobbed the lettuce at me.

---

[4] Actually, I know lots about veggies. I can pick a parsnip from a turnip any day.

Later, at dinner, he sent me into the kitchen to open another bottle of wine.

'Taste it before you bring it back,' he called after me.

At that time in my life, I knew nothing about wine, but I could open the bottle, which I did, and then I tasted the wine as he'd asked. The flavour was a bit woody, I thought, so I was in the middle of pouring it down the sink before going for another one, when Cameron came into the room.

'Jesus Christ, Barrowman! What the fuck are you doing? That wine is about £400 a bottle!'

I'm surprised he ever invited me back.

From the beginning, Cameron – like my family; Bev and Jim; Alex and Ian; Bret and Javier; Gavin and Stewart; and Sara – was on the long road with me. As well as playing a significant role in shaping my career, Cameron also introduced me to the man who, if I'd not fallen in love with Scott, I could easily have fallen for. David Caddick was the musical director for *Miss Saigon* and later for *Sunset Boulevard*, and has supervised the music for scores of other musicals and films, including the soundtrack for the film *Evita*, starring Madonna. When I first met David, it was during an initial sing-through for *Miss Saigon*. Claude-Michel Schönberg, one of the brilliant composers of *Miss Saigon*, was at the piano with David.

'John,' Claude-Michel said to me. 'I want you to put passion into it.'

He sang the first few lines of 'Why, God, Why?' in his thick French accent.

I repeated the lines, singing with an equally thick French accent, and had David cracking up at the piano.

'Yes, Meester Barrowman, you are veree fuckeen funny. Now seeng it correctly.'

After *Miss Saigon*, David went on to become important in both

Cameron's and Andrew Lloyd Webber's organizations. He has a very good ear and is brilliant at what he does. David's demeanour with people is so calming and so wonderful that he gets more out of his performers than anyone else I've ever worked with.

Along with Cameron, I've known Andrew Lloyd Webber since my early days in theatre, although Andrew and I didn't see each other very much when I played Raoul in *The Phantom of the Opera* in 1992. Over the years, I've come to appreciate even more his talents as a composer and a man who truly has music in his veins. Simply entering one of Andrew's homes is an experience to savour. His walls are covered in superb works of art, particularly paintings from the nineteenth century and the Pre-Raphaelites. Andrew's hospitality is equal to his art.

During the initial stages of auditions for *Any Dream Will Do*, Andrew invited my fellow judges, Zoe Tyler and Denise Van Outen, their partners, and Scott and I to his castle in Ireland for a weekend stay. After a long day, Scott, Zoe, Denise and I all went skinny-dipping in Andrew's swimming pool. When we climbed out and dried off, we sat with Andrew in one of his living rooms while he regaled us with many fascinating theatre stories. These are the moments when Andrew is at his best and we listened into the wee small hours.

While I sat with Andrew and the others that night in Ireland, I remembered an evening in the States the year after high school, when my friend Laura Sales and I spent several hours in her bedroom listening to the cast album of *The Phantom of the Opera*. She and I imagined what it would be like to be in a musical as grand as that. I looked over at Andrew, who smiled as he finished up a story, and I smiled back. It's at times like that when I'm reminded that I'm truly living my dream.

Chapter Sixteen

'There's No Cure Like Travel'

Whenever Scott and I travel, we have certain rules. Clearly, one of them isn't about remembering to fill the petrol tank. One of the more important ones is that there are limits to how much historical rubble I'll look at in any one day. I don't mind going to places of historic interest, but staring for days on end at a pile o' rocks left by one group or another is not my idea of a vacation; however, relationships are all about compromise and commitment. Scott compromises and I commit him to sticking to the compromise. Kidding.

At some point during a holiday, I'll get bored and there will have to be shopping. I don't care if it's a bead stall in a market on the Greek island of Santorini – where Clare and Scott's brother's daughter Mary and I found some lovely trinkets while Scott lounged by the pool and read his fourth book of the trip – or an outlet mall in Palm Springs, there must be time to shop.

I have to admit, though, while we were on the Santorini trip in 2004, Scott, Clare, Mary and I did visit some awesome rubble. We went to a 3,500-year-old Bronze Age town. The settlement was perfectly preserved under ash and petrified lava, and the four of us were able to walk down the streets as if the whole event had happened only days ago.

Our accommodation for this trip was fabulous. We stayed in a private villa overlooking a volcanic crater with our own swimming pool, where, every afternoon, we'd perform our own improvised air-band dance routines before the cocktail hour. You haven't lived until you've seen Clare, Mary and Scott perform Bon Jovi under the Grecian sun.

During many of the hot sultry days, we all tried to do something cultural and then something outrageously fun. I know cultural can be fun, but go along with my distinction anyway. I know you know what I mean. One day we paired up – Clare with me, Scott with Mary – and we paraglided above the Aegean Sea. I peed from the sky and hit the speedboat.

Now, that's talent.

The four of us also kayaked around the smaller volcanic Cyclades islands. Because Clare and I were a teeny wee bit competitive with Scott and Mary, we challenged them to a race to one of the private coves. Clare and I were kayaking so fast and furious that we lost sight of Scott and Mary. A boat horn blasted us out of our celebratory reverie.

'Uncle John, that boat's heading right for us.'

'No, it's not, Clare, but row faster anyway or we're gonna fucking die!'

Clare and I did make it to the cove first, but only after a few tense minutes of squabbling as the two of us tried to row in unison in order to kayak quickly to safety. In our haste to get ahead, we'd raced into the cruise-ship lanes.

Over the years, Scott and I have taken many memorable trips, and although not all of them were life-threatening or life-changing, they were most certainly life-affirming. The American poet Langston Hughes once wrote a poem, 'City', in tribute to his beloved Harlem. I read it in high school. In its vitality and grace, the poem always reminds me of Rome, one of my favourite places to visit.

Rome, of course, is the ultimate city of rubble, but, oh my, what wonderful rubble. It is bursting with 'stone that sings', as Hughes wrote. Audrey Hepburn, Gregory Peck and romance notwithstanding, Rome is also one of the best shopping cities in the world.

When Scott and I arrived there, a trip we took in the mid 1990s, we rented scooters and travelled around the city as if we belonged there. The ease of movement those scooters gave us on the crowded, chaotic Italian streets really turned us on to scooter travel, so much so that when we returned to London after this particular vacation, we bought our first and not our last scooters. For Christmas one year, I bought Scott a Kawasaki Versys 650. I currently own a Piaggio 125.

While in Rome, we rode our Vespas along the Appian Way, the ancient road that once connected Rome to its conquered cities in the southeast, and although the cobblestone road was a bit hard on 'the boys' at times, I did feel like Spartacus in my chariot nonetheless. We visited the Trevi Fountain, into which I made Scott throw three coins (tossed over his shoulder with his left hand) to ensure we'd both return to Rome some day. Considering the thousands of superstitions I hold dear, he's lucky that's all I made him do.

On our last day in the city, I shopped. My biggest challenge was how many Armani bags I could fit in and on the scooter. Let me tell you, I was able to carry quite a few, with two hanging off the handlebars, three in the scooter's pack, and two slung around my neck. Given that you've read about how much I hate anything or anyone touching my neck, you'll appreciate the sacrifice I made.

Scott and I have taken a number of holidays during the course of our relationship in order to satiate our love of scuba-diving. We are both certified PADI open-water divers. On one diving expedition, we went to the Yucatán Peninsula, the isthmus of land that juts out on the east coast of Mexico and separates the Caribbean Sea from the Gulf of Mexico. During this trip, Scott and I went on a night dive. The amazing thing about diving at night was that everything in the sea appeared to be luminous. It was like watching an animated film. I expected Nemo to greet me at any minute.

The night was warm and the water was like black glass. When I rose to the surface, before flashing my light so the dive boat could see me, I floated on my back and admired the night sky twinkling above me. It was a profoundly humbling moment and one that I try to remember whenever I find myself giving in to some of the glitzy trappings of fame and success. Oh, it happens. It's easy when you're an actor to think that you're the centre of your own universe, and so it doesn't hurt to remember that we are none of us the centre of the real one.

As I floated in the darkness, the fact that Scott and I had spent the day visiting the ruins of the Mayan pyramids at Chichén Itzá magnified the feeling of insignificance. The ruins are all that's left of a once-vibrant ancient culture, a civilization that before any on the European continent had a sophisticated understanding of mathematics and the cosmos.

Since Scott and I travel whenever my schedule and his allows, we are both adept at planning and reserving all that we need for a holiday. On this particular trip to Mexico, I'd rented what I hoped would be luxury accommodation on the white sand of the Mayan Riviera on the island of Cozumel. The first night in our 'beach bungalow' (and I use the term loosely because it was basically a thatched hut), we huddled together the whole night – and not for any romantic reasons. The tropical temperature drop, coupled with the close location of the sea, which was literally touching the door of our hut, I mean bungalow, made it so bloody cold that we were freezing our asses off. By the second night, we'd moved into a beautiful beach resort hotel instead.

The funny thing about the hotel was that it was filled with couples from Minnesota. Don't get me wrong, I love Minnesota – the Mall of America, home to all of Carole's in-laws and 10,000 lakes or thereabouts – but throw into this hotel scenario two good-looking, very tanned gay guys dressed in skimpy Speedos, while everyone else was incredibly pale and wearing considerably more clothing … well, we did stand out. However, after only a few days, Scott and I had all the wives playing on our beach volleyball team and we were killing the husbands' team. After the volleyball games, I organized sexy dance contests and beach fashion shows for the women, and the men kept buying Scott and me drinks because we were loosening up their wives for them.

On another trip, this time to Israel, we not only went diving in the Red Sea, but we also visited a number of sacred sites. We spent time at the Dome of the Rock, an Islamic temple in Jerusalem, where it's believed Muhammad appeared before he ascended to heaven. We stood silently in front of the Wailing Wall, and watched holy men in their traditional Jewish garb touch the bricks and pray at the tables lined with Torahs and ancient scrolls that populate the courtyard area.

Afterwards, we moved from the spiritual to the sublime, spending a few nights at Masada on the Dead Sea at a great spa hotel, where we had incredible mud baths and hydrotherapy treatments. Masada is actually an ancient fort and was the place where, during the height of the Roman Empire, a small band of Jewish fighters held off legions of Roman soldiers. According to a guide at the fort, the battle didn't end well for the Jews, who killed themselves rather than be captured and forced into slavery in Rome.

We concluded this trip with a visit south to the Mediterranean port of Caesarea, where we explored King Herod's palace. The view from the edge of the palace across the desert was awe-inspiring, and from there we headed to Bethlehem to see the Nativity Church.

On another diving holiday, in Egypt, Scott and I once dived one of the most famous wrecks in the world: the *Thistlegorm*, a Second World War carrier that was sunk off the coast of Egypt by a German bomb in 1941. Not only was the dive one of my favourites of all time, it was also one of the spookiest because the remains of aircraft, trucks and motorbikes filled the submerged wreck. Side by side, Scott and I swam through the passageways and cabins as if we were time travellers bearing witness to this terrible loss.

I've organized a number of vacations so that Scott and I can put in some quality diving time. I even once accepted an acting job in part because of the scuba-diving possibilities. As it turned out, my diving skills actually saved my life. Seriously.

In the autumn of 2001, the producers of the *Shark Attack* DVD film series made me an offer that, frankly, at the time was hard to refuse. *Titans* had been cancelled and my first cabaret booking in New York was a few mortgage payments away, so I accepted the male lead in the movie *Shark Attack 3: Megalodon*, which was set to film in Sofia, Bulgaria. The film has since become a cult classic in this fishy genre because, among other things, it has one of the most famous awful lines of movie dialogue ever.

When I left to film *Shark Attack 3: Megalodon*, from LAX on a 747 bound for Munich, it was the first day that planes in the United States were cleared to fly again after the tragedy of 9/11. I thought about not flying, but, along with lots of other folks that year, I made a decision that I wasn't going to live in fear. Fly in fear, maybe, but not live in it. When I boarded the aircraft, the attendant checked my ticket and directed me to the back of the plane.

Normally, a 747 seats close to 200 passengers; there were five of us on board. I looked at the huge expanse of empty seats and turned back to the attendant.

'Listen,' I said, 'given everything that's happened this month, I'm not sitting in the back by myself. I'm sitting here in business class.' She didn't argue.

I'm a nervous flyer at the best of times. This flight was taking off during one of the worst of times. I had everything that could be tightly clenched, clenched. I was having my own wee panic attack. As the plane began barrelling down the runway, the woman sitting in front of me turned and asked, 'Have you found Jesus?'

Jesus! I could have punched her. She's saying this to me, Mr Superstition. We're taking off after the most horrific terrorist attack in history, and she wanted to know if I'd found Jesus. If I said 'no', I'd panic even more.

'Jesus isn't lost,' I shouted at her. 'Mind your own fucking business!'

From Munich, I boarded a plane to Sofia, a resort in the Black Sea. This second plane was like a prop from the cartoon *The Flintstones*. All it was missing was the space for our feet to stick through the floor so we could assist the take-off. Inside, the seating was cramped and oppressive. Although an attendant was present, she didn't seem to be paying too much attention to the fact that there were oxygen canisters hanging exposed from the overhead compartments and that all the passengers, except me, were smoking like chimneys.

The plane looked as if it was held together with pipe cleaners – and everyone inside was puffing away on the bloody pipes. I was a basket case once again. I did not want to sit in an aircraft filled with smoke, and despite signs designating this as a no-smoking flight, nobody gave a shit.

Eventually, I sucked it up and the plane took off safely. But as we were levelling off, I suddenly collapsed to the floor, gasping, wheezing and tearing at my chest. The flight attendant rushed down the aisle to help me. She immediately insisted everyone put out their cigarettes. She opened one of the canisters of oxygen, flipped the face mask over my mouth and nose, and after my body stopped wrenching from the apparent asthma attack, she helped me back to my seat. The plane soon cleared of smoke and I got a little high from the oxygen. My performance was Academy Award calibre. Norma Desmond would have been proud.

Sofia is one of the oldest capitals in Europe and it's a beautiful city – but in 2001, it was still reeling from the last vestiges of Communist rule, plus it was fucking freezing. In fact, if you look carefully at the movie's opening scene of sunbathers frolicking in the so-called Californian surf, you'll see that all the slapping of arms and bobbing in the water was from the frigid sea and not the pleasure of the setting.

The majority of the movie was filmed at a holiday resort in a huge swimming pool, which was made to look like the ocean. This setting made it easier to manipulate the special effects, the model shark and the underwater camerawork, all of which would have been far too dangerous to execute in the sea. For one of the crucial action sequences, I needed to get into a kind of submarine-like shell, close the top panel, open the other side, and swim out. The camera would capture me in close-up swimming out, and later the shark would be superimposed on the scene so it would look like I was swimming through the shark.

Before any actor performs a scene that has any degree of danger, the stunt crew must clear it as safe. Stunts cleared the equipment above and under the water. I couldn't take my big oxygen caddy, so I had a small handheld canister with about two minutes of air, which under good circumstances should have been adequate.

I swam down into the submarine and, once inside, I let the top close. I now had no choice but to swim forward to the other exit. Seconds later, I heard 'Action' on my comms unit. I let go of the air canister and swam to the other opening. It was locked. I couldn't get out the way I came in anymore and because the entire crew was watching from the pool deck, I couldn't be heard banging from this far underwater.

One of the first and most important lessons taught in scuba-diving is not to panic. I swam back and retrieved my air canister. I figured I'd sit down, breathe lightly, and hope the director would eventually see nothing was happening on the shot, and the stunt crew would come down and open the door.

Those were the longest and the shortest two minutes of my life. I was slowly running out of air when the stunt crew finally realized something was wrong. They dived down to release me. I gave the hand signal that I was okay and swam back up to the pool deck. When I got back on dry land, I completely lost it with the crew and reamed all of them new ones.

The actress playing my love interest in *Megalodon* wasn't the most expressive woman I'd ever met. In fact, she gave new meaning to the term 'cold fish'. In every scene, she had two shades of the same expression – deadpan, and deadpan with a thin smile. Even in our sex scene in the bathtub, there was more life in the bar of soap. The director kept asking me to do things to get her to react to the camera with some passion. As a result, in many of our scenes together, I improvised a lot.

One day, after we'd finished shooting the scene where I'd been stalking the shark, I was supposed to come up to my love interest and say, 'I'm wired. Let's go home and make love.' Since I'd already been ad-libbing in other scenes, the director egged me on and told me to say something, anything, to try to provoke a reaction from her.

She stepped towards me and instead of my scripted line, I said, wait for it, 'God, I'm so wired. What do you say I take you home and eat your pussy?'

Her reaction was priceless. Her face turned every shade of red, but she took the line and went forward, and the director got his reaction and his scene. Meanwhile, the crew was in hysterics. I'm surprised you can't hear them howling on the DVD. The director agreed the line would be cut during ADR, which is the acronym for 'automatic dialogue replacement' – the process of going into a studio and doing voice-overs for dialogue that the mics have not picked up clearly, as well as adding any necessary sound effects.

Months later, I went into a studio to do the ADR for the film, and the sound was so crappy that I basically had to redo the whole script. I got to the line, wait for it again, 'God, I'm so wired. What do you say I take you home and eat your pussy?' and discovered they'd kept it in for the DVD after all.

However, I had to dub the line for television because in most markets you can't say 'pussy' unless it's meowing. What they'd written for me to say was priceless. Keep in mind, my character has been chasing Megalodon, the biggest motherfucking badass shark you've ever seen, and my character's looking for some serious action. This was the line I had to say to dub for TV.

'God, I'm so wired. What do you say I take you home and watch *I Love Lucy*?'

Over the years, like many of us, I've made decisions that didn't work out the way I'd hoped, and I've listened to people I probably shouldn't have, but I've never regretted anything I've done. I take responsibility for all my choices, even the not so great ones. *Shark Attack 3: Megalodon* may be one of those dubious decisions, but in America it continues to be one of Blockbuster's more popular B-movie rentals, which is a good thing for, well, Blockbuster.

During a family gathering after the release of *Megalodon*, someone was giving me grief about the film. Turner butted into the conversation and said to them, 'Hey, how many movies have you made?' I gave him fifty bucks.

Chapter Seventeen

'Being Alive'

On the afternoon of my first rehearsal for *Anything Goes* in 1989, as I walked down Wardour Street in London towards the Prince Edward Theatre, I was shitting myself. I knew the cast had already settled into their rhythms and not only was I arriving as the new American kid, but I was also the somewhat inexperienced American kid. I was ready for the challenge, but at that moment it did not escape me that as soon as I stepped through the door, my life would become very much like the musicals I loved so much.

Relative unknown, handsome and amiable,[1] travels to England to study Shakespeare. Gets job offer within forty-eight hours, performs well on opening night, becomes established leading man, gets the girl – oops, not that part – gets the handsome man, never returns to the schoolroom. Applause. Curtain. Lights.

When I stopped outside the stage door of the Prince Edward Theatre, that plot was still to unfold. The notice above the door read, 'The World's Greatest Artistes Have Passed and Will Pass Through These Doors.' My throat went dry and I had to take a deep

---

[1] My book, remember?

breath to stop myself shaking visibly. The sign's implications were slightly overwhelming, but at the same time incredibly exciting. I imagined a host of twentieth-century performers crossing this same threshold: Noël Coward, Ivor Novello, Josephine Baker, Elaine Paige, Bernard Cribbins, Arthur Askey … I'm serious. Askey was an entertainment genius in his day, a terrific comedian and the king of pantomime dames. He appeared at the Prince Edward off and on for many years, and during the time when it was known as the London Casino, Askey and performers like him kept London laughing through the Second World War.

I was about to head on in when I spotted another historic plaque on the brick wall directly above the stage door. This one read, 'In a house on this site in 1764–5, Wolfgang Amadeus Mozart, 1756–91, lived, played and composed.' Now I was thoroughly intimidated. Talk about music legends. Given his amazing productivity and his enduring melodies, I've always thought that if Mozart were alive today, he'd be competing with Andrew Lloyd Webber for the musical theatre composer crown. I'd watch that talent show, wouldn't you?

I backed up into Wardour Street, just missed getting swiped by a messenger bike, and looked to my right in the direction of Old Compton Street. I walked a few paces towards the clusters of men and women, okay, mostly men, to loosen my tense muscles a little and stopped again when another blue sign caught my eye: 'In 1926 in this house, John Logie Baird, 1888–1946, first demonstrated television.' This had to be fate. Two doors away from where I was about to make my West End debut was the place where a fellow Scotsman, Baird, had successfully transmitted the first television images, a medium I knew I wanted to be part of, even in the early days of my career.

It's easy now to look back on those few awe-inspiring minutes outside the Prince Edward Theatre and interpret those historic signs as being prophetic in some way. It gets even weirder. As I turned back to the theatre, a black cat crossed my path, which in my family is a sign of good luck.

I passed through the stage door, my hands no longer clammy, my head clear and my determination to succeed in this business utterly stoked. The rush of adrenalin I felt when I read those inscriptions and prepared myself to cross the theatre threshold has repeated itself a few times in my career. Moments when I've said to myself, 'If this is as good as it gets, and it's pretty fucking good, I could leave all of this and be happy.'

Over the years, I've developed a theory about the path my musical theatre career has taken and it's a little like what happens on TV talent shows such as *Any Dream Will Do* and *How Do You Solve a Problem Like Maria?* My theory is that from the beginning of my West End career, Cameron Mackintosh has been supporting and training me to be a leading man. I think he's done the same for other performers, like my friend Ruthie Henshall, for example. Early in my career, Cameron encouraged, mentored and auditioned me in different roles in a variety of musicals – *Miss Saigon*, *The Phantom of the Opera*, *The Fix* – until he felt that I was ready to handle the master, Sondheim.

For those of us in musical theatre, the pinnacle of the game is to perform in a Stephen Sondheim show, especially one in which Stephen himself is directly involved. I've done two Sondheim productions, *Putting It Together* (first in Los Angeles in 1998, and then at the Barrymore Theater on Broadway in 2000) and *Company* (at the Kennedy Center in Washington, DC in 2002). Both of these shows were particular favourites of Stephen's and with each one he was personally involved.

Putting It Together is a revue of many of Sondheim's songs from other musicals, organized around a loose plot about two couples, one at the beginning of their relationship, 'The Younger Man' (whom I played) and 'The Younger Woman', and an older couple, 'The Husband' and 'The Wife', who've been together for decades.

I met Stephen for the first time during the one of the early rehearsals for *Putting It Together*, which had its initial run in 1998 at the Mark Taper Forum in LA. The theatre world is a lot like an extended family, but despite me already knowing many of the players on the team, including Cameron, who was producing the show, I was still in jaw-dropping awe of Sondheim. For me, those first few rehearsals were like being back at Opryland as a student again, asking to be pushed, to be stretched, to be taught by someone who was *the* 'master of the house'. When we began the run of *Putting It Together*, I believed that my career still remained in London in the West End, but all of us had an inkling Broadway was a possibility for this production.

The cast for the LA run included Susan Egan, Bronson Pinchot and Carol Burnett, the latter of whom I'd adored as a performer since I was a kid. When my family had settled in Joliet, Illinois, back in the early eighties, sometimes on Friday nights my mum and dad would go out to dinner or to a party with friends, and they'd ask if I'd stay home with Murn. Every time, I said I would. She always thought she was babysitting me on those nights. Even though by that time in her life she was in a diminished state following a series of strokes, Murn and I would have a blast together. After Murn went to bed, which was usually pretty early in the evening, my friends and I, with my parents' full knowledge, would gather in the basement rec room and we'd have our own shindig.

On nights like this, Murn and I would eat loads of sweeties, drink lots of cider, and watch reruns of *The Carol Burnett Show*. Murn would laugh at anything Carol did, while I loved watching the moments in the show when one of the other performers was clearly about to crack up, but couldn't and was trying desperately to hang on to his or her dignity in front of the live audience. *The Carol Burnett Show* was sketch comedy at its best. Some day, I plan to produce and perform in a similar format, a desire I've had since my youth.

The other cool thing about working with Carol was that I was able to meet the designer Bob Mackie, who has dressed Carol and a load of other glamorous performers, including Cher, for years. One afternoon, I dragged two boxes of my collectible Barbie dolls into my dressing room and asked Bob to sign them for me, which he did, and then we spent an hour or so talking dolls, clothes, fabulous dresses and the women who wear them.

The night we opened *Putting It Together* at the Mark Taper Forum in LA was one of the first times I experienced the Hollywood red-carpet treatment for a show in which I was one of the leads – and let me tell you, I could learn to love that glamorous sort of occasion. For the opening night, I flew my parents out to California. The show was a terrific success, and at the premiere party my mum and dad swapped family stories with *The Golden Girls* star Betty White and had a good laugh with Doris Roberts from *Everybody Loves Raymond*.

I've since enjoyed a few other opening nights of this style. One of my particular favourites was the New York premiere of the film *De-Lovely* with Kevin Kline and Ashley Judd, which took place in 2003. Scott was not able to join me for that event and so I invited Clare instead.

We flew first class to the Big Apple and walked the red carpet together. Who knew all those years of dressing up my niece at Barrowman holiday parties would pay off? She was a pro at walking in stiletto heels down the carpet and into the cinema. At the party after the premiere, I performed a couple of Cole Porter songs for all in attendance, while Clare and Ashley Judd compared stories about

Milwaukee, where Ashley's husband, the racing-car driver Dario Franchitti, has spent many hours speeding round the track at the Milwaukee Mile.

In the hiatus between *Putting It Together* finishing its run in LA and its subsequent move to Broadway in 2000, I finally accepted a job with Disney, in the West End production of *Beauty and the Beast*. The show itself was a treat to be in, and Clare and Turner (Andrew's children weren't old enough) flew over to see the production and hang out for a while with their Beast of an uncle.

When the Broadway production of *Putting It Together* eventually went into rehearsals in New York, because most of the cast and crew knew each other, it was like a family reunion. There were a couple of cast changes for the transfer. The legendary Broadway actor of Sondheim's *Sweeney Todd* and Jerry Herman's *La Cage aux Folles* fame, George Hearn, came in to play the husband of Carol Burnett's character, and because Susan Egan had other commitments, Cameron recommended Ruthie Henshall for the part of 'The Younger Woman'. Together again, Ruthie and I had a blast. We called ourselves the 'Two Brits on Broadway'. In fact, many of us involved in the show had worked together before.

The theatre world is small. Loyalty and family are important. If you play well with others, they ask you to come back and play again. For example, Eric Schaeffer, who made his Broadway directorial debut with this production of *Putting It Together*, and I later worked together. Eric went on to be the Artistic Director of the Sondheim Celebration at the Kennedy Center in 2002, of which I was also a part with my role in *Company*, and which was the first retrospective of Sondheim's work at the Kennedy Center and a singular event.

During *Putting It Together*'s run on Broadway, I lived in a brownstone owned by Cameron Mackintosh in the centre of

Manhattan, about three blocks from the Ethel Barrymore Theater, where the show was running, and next door to the Actor's Studio.[2] If London was my 'moveable feast', New York was a delicious dessert: decadent, not always good for you, but filled with everything I love about a city: theatres, good restaurants, and loads of fabulous shops.

For my second time[3] working with Sondheim, in *Company*, many of the same crew were putting it together again. However, the director of this show was Sean Mathias, a talented playwright and actor, who also happens to be Ian McKellen's ex. I tell you, play well together …

Company, unlike *Putting It Together*, is a fully realized musical, but the two shows share similar themes. *Company* depicts five couples at various stages of love and lust, as seen through the eyes of their single man-about-town friend Robert or 'Bobby', whom I played. The relationships are complicated and cynical, and the show can leave audiences not only with a melody or two in their heads, but also an idea or a question that merrily rolls around for days.

After the opening performance of *Company*, Stephen Sondheim came down to my dressing room. What he said to me that evening I consider to be one of the seminal moments of my entire career. Another such occasion was seeing my name in the opening credits of the third series of *Doctor Who* for the first time; my name spins on screen just after the spiralling TARDIS appears.

---

[2] A private organization for actors, directors and playwrights that was founded by the director Elia Kazan and that supports its own drama school, which has trained Julia Roberts, Robert De Niro, Steve McQueen, Edward Albee, Marlon Brando, James Dean, Al Pacino and Paul Newman, among others.

[3] Third, really, if you count the LA *Putting It Together* separately from the Broadway production.

'John,' Stephen said to me, on the *Company* opening night, 'of all the years I've seen this show, you've shown me who Bobby really is. You brought tears to my eyes.'

In this business, you don't often get compliments like this from inside the house and I was appropriately stunned. Man, this was Stephen Sondheim speaking these words to me. His assessment of how I'd performed Bobby was incredibly affirming and I like to think that my success was partly the result of a little of my own tenacity. I'd pushed Stephen at lunch one day to talk to me about Bobby. Normally, I'm not the kind of actor who requires a lot of subtext. I don't need to know what a character is like beyond the page when I'm acting. This is my profession, and if I'm good and the writing is strong then I don't need anything else. Having a genius like Stephen on hand is not to be sniffed at, though, so I took every chance I could to learn from him.

During rehearsals for the show, he and I used to head to a local restaurant and eat oysters, platters and platters of fresh raw oysters. Although I loved them, we ate so many at each sitting that I think my greed triggered the shellfish allergy I mentioned earlier. To this day, I can't so much as look at a prawn without going into cold sweats and my throat swelling shut.

On this particular day, we were taking a rest before hoovering up the next plate when I asked Stephen directly about Bobby's character.

'Is Bobby gay?'

'Definitely not,' he adamantly replied.

I took this answer to heart and I played Bobby as a kind of Peter Pan, a man refusing to grow up, afraid to embrace the responsibilities of being an adult, of being alive.

Company happened to be the first show that my nephew Andrew saw me perform on stage. At four years old, he sat through the entire performance – didn't move a muscle, didn't blink, and didn't open a sweetie wrapper once.

During our run in Washington, DC, I lived in an extended-stay hotel overlooking the famous Second World War monument to Iwo Jima. Working on *Company*, which was part of the Sondheim Celebration, felt like being at a summer camp. The atmosphere in and around the Kennedy Center was electric because nothing of this magnitude, a run of Sondheim's most renowned musicals showing in repertory, had ever been done before. I loved being on stage with my co-star Alice Ripley, who played Amy, and whose version of 'I'm Not Getting Married Today' still makes me breathless. I can't compliment Alice enough for her sheer talent. Matt Bogart played David and was one of the sexiest guys I've shared a stage with. His real girlfriend let me flirt shamelessly with him. Working with this company of talented men and women proved something to me that I'd learned years ago at Opryland: if your company gets along, your show will too.

As it turned out, working on *Company* was a remarkable achievement in my career not just because of the wonderful cast, nor even because it was another opportunity to work with Stephen, but because playing Bobby was a role that adjusted my outlook on life. After seventeen performances, I realized that I was a lot like Bobby. Despite my self-confidence, my professional successes, my outspokenness and my sense of humour, at that time I still relied too much on people and on the opinions of others. Sometimes, this stopped me from taking more public risks in particular areas of my life. Playing the character of Bobby made me realize my responsibility to those beyond my immediate orbit.

Bobby is morally frozen, and this coolness affects his personal happiness. At that time in my life, I was politically frozen. I realized that my reticence to speak out about issues that concerned me might be affecting someone else's personal happiness. I had to be more confident and clear in who I was as a gay man, and I needed to become more of an activist in areas where I could make a difference.

Sir Ian McKellen also played a role in helping me foster this side of myself. Ian has been unflinchingly loud and proud about this aspect of his own life, and he has had a brilliant career in theatre and film. Ian's smart and sure of himself, and over the years I've watched and admired how his support and activism for gay rights has made a difference.

Ian and I have been friends for a number of years, and he would often come up to my dressing room for a visit if he was in the West End and I was in a show. In fact, one of my favourite visits of his took place one night during the Christmas holidays of 2004, when I was performing in *Anything Goes*. Ian was the invited guest judge for the company's Dressing Room Holiday Decorating Contest. A Christmas tradition in many theatres, everyone decorates their dressing room and puts on a tableaux. John Fahey and I dressed up from a scene in *What Ever Happened to Baby Jane?* I was Joan Crawford in a wheelchair strung with holiday lights and other festive frivolities; John was a pretty scary Bette Davis. Ian wandered round all the dressing rooms, taking notes, and probably a few bribes – kidding – until he came to the Bullpen, the dressing room belonging to many of the show's sailors. Those boys had designed an old-fashioned peep show, where Santa was doing all sorts of very naughty things to a reindeer. They charged a pound to get in, and from Ian and my parents that night they made a bunch of money for the charity West End Cares.

Later that evening, I'm proud to say we also helped Ian make history. Despite all the shows and plays he'd performed in over the years, he had never been in a West End musical. During the 'Blow

Gabriel Blow' number, we got him into a costume and snuck him on stage for his West End musical debut.

In 2006, Ian, who is one of Stonewall's founders, accepted their Entertainer of the Year Award on my behalf, which I won for being a positive cultural role model, an honour I was incredibly proud to receive. I was delighted to be acknowledged by my community, and I believe I can trace that achievement back to the epiphany I experienced while playing Bobby.

I remember a conversation I had with Ian once, in which he suggested that he and I should plan a dinner party and invite all the actors who are gay and afraid to come out. We'd make them stay at the table until they realized that they *can* be successful and gay at the same time.

Who would be at this dinner party? Sadly, too many.

When I was eighteen, I found myself in a compromising position on a bed in a New York loft with a man whom I would consider to be one of the finest actors of my generation. Nothing ended up happening, but over the years our paths have crossed at a distance, and I think this man would be a prime candidate for an invite to Ian's imagined dinner party.

One of the many lessons I've carried with me over the years from S. E. Hinton's novel *The Outsiders* is that our identities are complex and changing. With the help of a number of real friends, and a couple of fictional ones such as Bobby and Ponyboy, I've come to terms with all aspects of mine.

Chapter Eighteen

'Together Wherever We Go'

Guns drawn, torches on, Eve, Burn, Naoko and I stand in *Torchwood* team formation outside an empty industrial building in early July 2007. No. Stop. That's not quite right. Let me start again. Guns drawn, torches on, Gwen, Owen, Toshiko and Captain Jack stand alert and poised to enter a suspicious warehouse, where, a few moments earlier, Rhys, Gwen's boyfriend, disappeared and Ianto followed him into the darkness.

'Quiet on the set.'

'Sound rolling.'

'And, action!'

One by one, the team enters the warehouse. Jack in first, followed by Gwen, then Owen, and Naoko brings up the rear. When they've all entered safely and stealthily, they fan out across the mouth of the building. Suddenly, one at a time, they stop moving as they look up into the vast expanse of the site. They're stunned by the implications of what they've discovered. A noise from the far corner of the industrial space distracts the team and, ignoring the horror of their discovery, they move cautiously towards the distant sounds.

All of a sudden, they hear wild fluttering above them. The team freezes again. A bloody big pigeon swoops down from the rafters, flies across their heads, and splatters thick white shite on Captain Jack's iconic blue coat.

'Cut!'

After we'd all stopped laughing, and I'd been cleaned up, we finished the scene, which was part of a sequence for a series-two episode. As far as I was concerned, the dramatically timed dropping meant the day's shoot would be a breeze – because it's good luck to have a bird shit on you. The problem was more with the mess it had made on my coat.

Wardrobe actually has a number of coats that Captain Kack, I mean Jack, uses, which vary according to the demands of the scene. If Jack needs to be digging around in one of the tunnels under the Hub, or climbing in and out of a crater, or shooting the hell out of cannibals in their cosy kitchen, Jack has a coat that's dirty and distressed to fit the occasion. If Jack's walking, or striding, across the Millennium Square, he wears what wardrobe refers to as the 'Hero Coat', which is immaculately tailored and longer than the others. Finally, if Jack needs to run across a desolate future landscape chasing his past, his coat is shorter, so that Jack's legs are less encumbered when he runs.

The Doctor, played by David Tennant, has a similar problem with his wardrobe. Like Jack's, the Doctor's coat is pretty long and can easily wrap around his legs and pull him down faster than a Slitheen's slippery tentacles. Next time you're watching *Doctor Who* or *Torchwood*, notice how the Doctor and I throw our coats behind us before we begin to run. The move has become second nature to our characters now. When we were filming the episode 'Utopia', however, which was written by Russell T. Davies and directed by Graeme Harper, and which formed the first of a three-part episode narrative that concluded the third series of *Doctor Who*, running with our coats was the least of the shoot's challenges.

The opening sequence of this episode, after the TARDIS has landed and Jack's been chucked unceremoniously to the ground, was filmed at an abandoned quarry in Cardiff, at night in the pissing rain. An interesting fact about filming in the rain is that unless it's pouring down in buckets, rain generally can't be seen on film. Therefore, as long as wardrobe can keep the actors dry, filming continues. But it's still bloody raining for us!

When Martha, followed by the Doctor, bursts from the TARDIS in this first scene, Jack lies dead on the ground. In reality, that meant I'd been lying on the cold damp ground for more than thirty minutes before Freema made her dramatic entrance because the crew had to set up the establishing shot. It was small consolation that there was a tarp spread across the gravel beneath me; the tarp was covered with more gravel so it wasn't seen on the shot. Whenever possible, someone from wardrobe would stand over me with a huge golf umbrella, which led to a wonderful moment on set when I burst into song – 'Singing in the Rain', of course, while lying prone on the cold wet ground.

On freezing night shoots like 'Utopia', wardrobe is more than up to the challenge of protecting 'the talent', as us actors are known on set. The three of us, Freema, David and I, were all wearing wetsuits under our clothes for extra warmth that night. Each of us on *Doctor Who* and on *Torchwood* has our own set of green wellies and our own heavy, ankle-length warming coat, which is immediately wrapped around us as soon as we step off camera.

And so, with his spectacular return in 'Utopia', Jack is finally back with the Doctor, after a wait of an entire season. One of the reasons that Jack's return on *Doctor Who* took so long was that Christopher Eccleston, the actor who launched the revamped *Doctor Who* in the title role in 2004, quit after only one season. The executive producers of the show, Julie Gardner and Russell T.

Davies, thought that their new Doctor, David Tennant, needed to establish himself with the audience and with his assistant without a more established iconic male character like Jack in the picture. Julie and Russell called me in for a meeting at the BBC, and told me they wouldn't be using Jack in the second series. Naturally, I was devastated.

When I got home after the meeting, I called my manager, Gavin, and told him what had happened. Even as I explained the gist of the meeting to him, I still couldn't believe that this might be the end for Captain Jack.

Fortunately, although I didn't know it at the time, all was not lost. The next day, Gavin called Andy Pryor, the casting director, and asked what the possibilities were of casting Captain Jack in his own show. There was a silence at the other end of the line. After a significant pause, Andy swore Gavin to secrecy before he explained the idea that Russell and Julie had for a show called *Torchwood*, in which Captain Jack would be the main character.

On 7 July 2005, I was in the middle of a week of performances of my cabaret show at Pizza on the Park in London. As my musical director, Bev had flown in from the States earlier for rehearsals, and the show debuted on 4 July and ran until 9 July. Unbeknownst to me, Gavin had invited Julie to come to the cabaret that night. After I'd performed, they planned to tell me the exciting news about Captain Jack.

Sadly, that morning all hell broke loose in London. Suicide bombers blew up a double-decker bus during the mid-morning rush, after exploding three other bombs on the London Underground. By late morning, it was clear that over fifty innocent people had been killed and hundreds of others were seriously injured. Central London looked like a war zone.

After the threat of more bombs subsided and I could get an

international line to let my family in the States know I was fine, Gavin and I talked about whether or not the show should go on. Public transportation was essentially shut down, and every theatre in the West End planned to be dark that night. I knew I could get through to the venue on my scooter and so, after a long debate, we decided to carry on with the show as planned. I guess I felt that to cancel would be another win for the bombers and, for what it was worth, all of us gathered together that night could be a small tribute to those who'd died.

Surprisingly, a sizable number of people did turn up. Gavin arranged for Scott to collect Julie from the BBC; he brought her to the venue on the back of his bike. Later, over drinks and dinner, Julie broke the news that while Jack was taking a hiatus from *Doctor Who*, his own show *Torchwood* would fill the rift in time. Despite the horrors of the day, to say I was thrilled with the news would be an understatement. I think I may have kissed the waiter.

Come the third series of *Doctor Who*, the programme was ready to welcome Captain Jack back on board. When David Tennant and I finally did begin filming together in early spring 2007, the hardest part of the experience for me was to resist speaking to him in a Scottish accent and remain as my American self, which, after a few days on set, ceased to be an issue. I found the set to be a lighter one with David as the Doctor than it had been with Christopher Eccleston in the lead role. I think David is a happier person, whereas I found Chris a bit angsty.

David and Freema[1] are tenants (sorry, couldn't resist) in the same apartment building on Cardiff Bay where Russell and I live, so by the time David, Freema and I were working together on the set, we'd already helped each other upstairs with shopping, had drinks

---

[1] I call her Freema Agyeagyemanman on set.

and dinner at the Bay, and chatted frequently in the elevator, which made establishing our working relationships a breeze.

Incidentally, our building has become a planned stop on the Cardiff Bay boat tour. The tour guide plays the *Doctor Who* theme tune as the boat idles in the water beneath the flats, and the guide announces that, 'This is *Doctor Who* tower.' It's not at all annoying to hear that sound effect at 10 a.m., after a night of filming and having gone to bed ten minutes before …

The atmosphere on *Doctor Who* is professional and fun and feels like family. The atmosphere on the *Torchwood* set is equally as professional and also feels like family, but the set is looser, and a bit wilder. *Doctor Who* is David's show and he leads the group. I'm number three in the cast. Whereas in *Torchwood*, as I've mentioned, I'm number one on the cast list. On the *Doctor Who* set, David's the brains, I'm the brawn and the assistant is the beauty. We have a good time working together.

In 'Utopia', a few on-screen minutes filled with some witty banter among the three characters have elapsed, but in reality, on the set, time had moved much more slowly. At last, the directors were ready to film the next sequence. Jack, the Doctor and Martha are supposed to sprint down the side of the quarry towards the protective cover of the hive-like city where Derek Jacobi's Professor Yana awaits with a plan to save humanity.

Racing in front of us as we pelted down the hill was an ATV quad bike manned by a crew member and the camera operator, who was armed with lights and his camera.

'Action!'

The quad bike took off, David and I flipped our coats back and ran like mad down the steep gravel hill. Freema was in full-tilt boogie behind us.

'Cut! Go again.'

And again, and again, and again. Finally, after the fourth or fifth take, I yelled down the hill to the director: 'This isn't a fucking marathon! If we're going to go again, tell him on the bloody bike to slow down.'

David turned to me and said, 'Having a bit of trouble, Captain?'

'That's all right for you to say,' I laughed, breathlessly, 'but I'm carrying a rucksack on my back with your fucking hand in a glass jar inside.'

While filming the final three episodes of season three of *Doctor Who*, I realized that I'm now the only actor who's been there since the beginning of the new incarnation of the series. I've celebrated two birthdays on *Doctor Who*, and each time the cast and crew have thrown a party. On one birthday, they gave me a remote-control Dalek, which I added to my growing toy collection, and a delicious cake, which I added to my waistline.

During the filming of one of the final episodes in the third series, David and I were starving and dinner seemed to be decades away. The prop department told us, 'No worries, the chips you're eating in the next scene are real and they're delicious.'

For health reasons, we're not always fed the real thing when filming. When we're drinking alcohol of any kind, it's usually iced tea, which looks a lot like whisky or beer; or ginger ale or sparkling water, which can mimic champagne nicely. David and I couldn't wait for the chips. When the steaming brown packages were finally set in front of us, and the director called, 'Action,' David and I could barely control our salivating. By the eighth take, though, the chips were cold and rank, and we both needed a packet of Rennies.

Once, during a scene in *Torchwood*, I had to shove an entire jammy doughnut into my mouth. Six takes later, I couldn't look at the fucking pastry anymore. My throat felt as if it was coated with thick cough syrup and my fillings ached. I've never touched a jammy doughnut since, and I used to love them.

On both sets, it's possible to perk up a grumpy, tired cast and crew with chocolate. Both productions love their sweeties, especially chocolate. I always bring bags of it on to the set and if anyone needs a sugar rush, they always know John is the candy man.

Days can be long ones when we're filming *Torchwood*, since the pace of a TV production involves so many more complicated set-ups and rehearsals than live theatre, where there is no 'cut' or 'do over'. The motto on a TV-show set is very much 'hurry up and wait'. The result of hours and hours of hanging about is that the cast has become great friends, and we all play well together. In my trailer, for example, I keep a generous supply of NERF toys, balls of all shapes and sizes,[2] hula hoops, skipping ropes, and a colourful variety of kites. When we have some down time between scenes, we play – and like any group of grown children, we have nicknames for each other too.

Eve's nickname is 'Evie – I don't like it', which I like to pronounce in a whiny Welsh accent. We refer to Burn as 'Binny Bots'. Naoko will answer to 'Coco Chanel' or 'Ping Pong Buckaroo', and Gareth responds to 'Gaz' or 'Gaza'. My nickname is 'Ginny Baza'. I could try to explain the etymology of all these names, but I'm not sure I remember anymore.

Filming a TV show may not be equal to mining coal, but it's hard work nonetheless. Our days are twelve hours long and every few weeks in our shooting schedule, we film at night. This means that the only family we see on a regular basis is each other. When we work together, we work hard, and when we play together, we play hard too.

[2] Puhleeze. Get a hold of yourself – the kind from Toys R Us.

When we were filming the 'Countrycide' episode in the Brecon Beacons National Park, northwest of Cardiff, life imitated art a little for me when we were put up for the night in creepy rooms and cottages, not far from the set where the villagers were eating their neighbours. The shoot for this episode was demanding and long. The Brecon Beacons may be one of the most stunning landscapes in Britain, but a bone-cutting wind blows constantly across the moors and, despite the layers from wardrobe, we could never stay warm while filming. We only managed to succeed in that department after we shut down for the night.

It didn't take long for that party gene to kick in. We headed back to our digs and the four of us – Eve, Burn, Gareth and I – had a blow-out night together. We drank too much, laughed too much and sang too loud. At one point, Gareth hit his head on an antique brass bell and we thought we'd killed him. The landlord complained about the noise[3] and then he accused Burn of moving the bathtub. Have you seen the size of Burn? The bathtub had to weigh 500 lb.

We told ghost stories and managed to scare the shit out of each other – so much so that in the middle of the night, I knocked on Evie's door in my Transformer PJs (she answered in a thong and a bra). We cuddled up in bed together and protected each other from the ghoulies like a couple of terrified siblings.

The next morning, we were all a bit worse for wear when we gathered in the make-up trailer, to say nothing of what we sounded like trying to explain the nasty gash on Gareth's forehead, which had to be covered up.

Sometimes, the crew joins us in our rambunctiousness. In one of the early episodes of the second series, Ianto has a meltdown in the Hub one night, for reasons far too complicated to go into here,

[3] More than once, if I remember correctly.

but if you've seen it, you'll know. I have to admit it's one of my favourite episodes to date. Anyway, while Jack comforts Ianto, he shifts from innocent consolation to a full-on, passionate embrace and kiss.

Gareth and I 'assumed the position' and went for it. The episode's director never called 'cut'. By the time Gareth and I were hitting the two-minute mark, my lips were getting numb and Gareth was getting twitchy.

'You fuckers!' we both yelled in unison, when we finally realized what was going on and pulled apart.

The delight of the crew was obvious and the joke carried them for hours through a tough shoot. Sometimes that's the whole point of having a laugh or pulling a prank or two or three: the residual benefit of the laughter and the release of stress helps you to deal with the long day or night ahead.

Since we began *Torchwood*, Burn and his wife Sara have had a son, Max; we've been trying to get Naoko a boyfriend; and we're teaching Gareth how to deal with newfound celebrity. Eve and her partner Brad, and Scott and I have both bought homes in the Cardiff area. The cast has bonded as a family, and we've also grown to love the important people in each other's lives.

Once, when my niece Clare was visiting Cardiff, she and I headed down to the Bay for dinner, where we met up with Eve and Brad. Clare and Eve hit it off immediately, and we all moved together from the restaurant to a bar in town, where two of my favourite girls proceeded to have a champagne-chugging contest[4] to see who could drink a bottle the fastest. Not as easy as you might imagine. I called the contest a draw when I noticed they were downing £60 bottles of the good stuff. Eve and Clare and I

4 They're both such classy lassies.

were singing so loudly that night, we eventually got kicked out of the bar.

I remember Elaine Paige telling me in the early days of my career that when your work family and your real family support you equally, you're on the right road. As Eve, Clare and I stumbled home that night, the road felt pretty steady under my feet.

Chapter Nineteen

'Live, Laugh, Love'

After school one afternoon in 1985, I had a conference with my high school's guidance counsellor. As part of her responsibilities, she was interviewing all the graduating seniors and chatting with them about their career goals. My interview went something like this.

'John, what are your plans?'

'I'm going to be an actor.'

'But what will you study in college?'

'Drama and theatre.'

'But what else are you going to do?'

'I don't want to do anything else.'

'John, you need a plan B.'

She kept insisting that I think about majoring in something like English or history or business or psychology or communication, anything, anything 'serious', so that I could be assured of having a job when 'the acting thing' didn't work out. She actually used the phrase, 'the acting thing'. I was getting angrier by the minute.

'Seriously, John, you need to have something to fall back on.'

'Listen,' I finally said, standing up to leave, 'if I fall back on anything, it'll be my ass. I'll get a plan B, if or when I actually need one.'

To date, I've never needed a plan B. I'd no idea that men, women and children would embrace me as a performer as much as they have, or that Captain Jack would be so popular, but I'm thankful for both. I certainly never set out to be a hero to gay men and women, although I've perhaps become one, as the piles of letters and emails I regularly receive attest. I'm just a regular guy, and I'm humbled and honoured by fans' recognition. Their sentiments touch me deeply.

In the prologue to the philosopher Bertrand Russell's *The Autobiography*, a piece I was once assigned to read in high school, Russell writes, 'Three passions, simple but overwhelmingly strong, have governed my life: the longing for love, the search for knowledge, and unbearable pity for the suffering of mankind.'

When I was an adolescent, I could understand and even appreciate the first two, but it wasn't until I was an adult that I recognized the existential nature of the third. Being a man of integrity and compassion in the twenty-first century is not always easy, but I do what I can and will continue to do what I can. My own passions are my family, including my dogs, my ability to entertain, and my love of life and all I can make of it.

As you've read, many people have shaped my passions and made me who I am at this, the midpoint (I hope) of my life. Pardon me while I spin three times again and touch all the wood I can reach. Any magpies nearby? Since I've known him, another Russell has taught me a similar message about living a life of integrity. With his nonchalance, his frankness, his brilliant skills as a writer, and his straightforward approach to life, love and laughter, Russell T. Davies's friendship has been an added bonus to playing Captain Jack.

At a press conference once, Russell and I were on a panel together to discuss *Torchwood*. A journalist for one of the baser tabloids asked Russell what the 'T' in his name stood for.

'Some other fucker in the business is called Russell Davies, and when he dies, I'll drop the "T",' Russell replied.

He then proceeded to berate the reporter for asking inane questions. The audience, full of other journalists I might add, was eating out of the palm of Russell's hand by the close of the session, because he responded to them with honesty, respect and good humour. Well, except for the guy he rebuked.

Two years before I left university in San Diego to study Shakespeare in England, I travelled alone to New York to visit my friend Anthony Rapp, and to see my first live Broadway shows. Anthony and I, you may remember, performed together in Joliet West High School's 1983 production of *Oliver!* Off and on through my early college experiences, Anthony, who was a few years behind me in school, and I kept in touch.

Anthony had been acting professionally since he was quite young. In 1986–7, he was playing Freddy, the youngest of two sons, in George Furth's family drama *Precious Sons*, at the Longacre Theater in New York. Anthony's co-stars in the play were Judith Ivey and Ed Harris. I was psyched to be heading to the Big Apple to see Anthony perform and to see some real Broadway shows for the first time in my life.

On that trip, Anthony and I went to see Eugene O'Neill's *Long Day's Journey Into Night*, starring Jack Lemmon, Peter Gallagher – whom I love as an actor and who was brilliant in Sam Mendes's *American Beauty* – and Kevin Spacey, who played Lemmon's character's youngest son in the play and who was also great in *American Beauty*. After this show, Anthony and I found our way backstage and I ended up having a whisky in Jack Lemmon's dressing room while we listened to him tell stories about Broadway and Hollywood, Marilyn Monroe and Tony Curtis, and about the 'good old days' of theatre. Kevin Spacey came down to say hello and ended up joining us for drinks.

Later that evening, Anthony, Kevin and I went for a bite to eat, and then Kevin took us to the Limelight Club, a dance club in Manhattan in a converted old church, where I drank vodka tonics with Phoebe Cates and a very young Drew Barrymore. A vodka tonic was the only mixed drink I knew back then because I'd ordered them all the time on my dad's tab.[1]

On my last afternoon in New York, before I had to fly home, I went to see Rupert Holmes's musical adaptation of Charles Dickens's unfinished novel *The Mystery of Edwin Drood*, which remains one of my favourite musicals. Despite the ominous tone of the title, the show was funny and poignant and, although I didn't understand this until much later, it owed a huge debt to the English pantomime tradition. Characters talked to the audience, the audience jeered at and taunted the characters, and a woman played the title character, the orphan Edwin Drood. Years before I came to know her as one of my leading ladies, I sat in the balcony of a theatre on Broadway and I watched Betty Buckley perform as Drood.

No matter how many shows I've seen or performed since that trip to New York, no matter how many scripts I've read or songs I've sung, I often return to those days and remember how I felt that afternoon watching Betty Buckley belt it out, or recall the excitement building up inside me while I lounged on a dressing-room couch, listening to a legend like Jack Lemmon tell stories. I knew then that I wanted to be an entertainer.

---

[1] A Grey Goose with tonic remains my drink of choice as a result.

Charles Dickens's *The Mystery of Edwin Drood* has no conclusion and neither does this autobiography. My ending isn't written yet, my show's not over. Stay in your seats. This is only the intermission.

Timeline

1989   Billy Crocker in *Anything Goes*, Prince Edward Theatre, London

1990–1   Chris in *Miss Saigon*, Theatre Royal Drury Lane, London

1991   Domingo Hernandez in *Matador,* Queens Theatre, London

1991   *Matador*, CD single

1992   Raoul in *The Phantom of the Opera*, Her Majesty's Theatre, London

1993   Claude in the Twenty-Fifth Anniversary Production of *Hair,* The Old Vic, London

1993   *Hair,* studio cast recording

1993   Wyndham Brandon in *Rope*, Minerva Theatre, Chichester Festival Theatre, Chichester

1993   *Godspell,* studio cast recording

1993–4   Presenter – *Live and Kicking* (BBC)

1993–4   Chris in *Miss Saigon*, Theatre Royal Drury Lane, London

1994   *Grease,* studio cast recording

1994   Joe Gillis in *Sunset Boulevard*, Adelphi Theatre, London

1994–5   Presenter – *The Movie Game* (BBC)

1995–6   Peter Fairchild in *Central Park West* (CBS)

1996   Joe Gillis in *Sunset Boulevard*, Minskoff Theater, New York

1996   Robert Burns in *Red Red Rose,* Concert Hall, Aarhus, Denmark

1997   *Aspects of Lloyd Webber*, solo album

1997	Alex in *Aspects of Love*, Olympia Theatre, Dublin (6 weeks); Cork Opera House, Cork (1 week)
1997	Cal Chandler in *The Fix,* Donmar Warehouse, London
1997	Che in *Evita,* Oslo Spektrum, Oslo, Norway
1998	Concert – *Hey! Mr Producer: A Celebration of Cameron Mackintosh*
1998	'The Younger Man' in *Putting It Together,* Mark Taper Forum, Los Angeles
1999	The Beast/The Prince in *Beauty and the Beast*, Dominion Theatre, London
1999–2000	'The Younger Man' in *Putting it Together,* Ethel Barrymore Theater, New York
2000	*Reflections From Broadway*, solo album
2000–1	Peter Williams in *Titans* (NBC)
2002	Cabaret – Arci's Place, New York
2002	Bobby in *Company,* Kennedy Center, Washington, DC
2002	Cabaret – Kennedy Center, Washington, DC
2002	Cabaret – Stackner Cabaret, Milwaukee, Wisconsin
2002	Cabaret – Lincoln Center, New York
2002	Concert – *Sondheim Celebration*, Lincoln Center, New York
2002	Ben Carpenter in *Shark Attack 3: Megalodon*
2002–3	Billy Crocker in *Anything Goes*, National Theatre, London
2003	Dumaine in *Love's Labour's Lost,* National Theatre, London
2003	Concert – *An Evening with the Boston Pops* (PBS)
2003	F. Scott Fizgerald in *The Beautiful and Damned,* Yvonne Arnaud Theatre, Guildford
2003–4	Billy Crocker in *Anything Goes,* Theatre Royal Drury Lane, London
2003	*Anything Goes*, studio cast recording
2003	Guest appearance – 'Children in Need' (BBC)
2004	Reporter in *Method*; titled *Dead Even* in the UK
2004	Jack and 'Night and Day' soloist in *De-Lovely* (premiere at Cannes Film Festival)

2004	*John Barrowman Swings Cole Porter*, solo album
2004	Billy Flynn in *Chicago,* Adelphi Theatre, London
2004	Presenter – *Friday Night Is Music Night* (BBC Radio 2)
2004	Concert – *Elegies: A Song Cycle*, Arts Theatre, London
2005	Captain Jack in *Doctor Who* season one (BBC); John's premiere episode 'The Empty Child'
2005	Guest singer – *Friday Night Is Music Night* (BBC Radio 2)
2005	Concert – *West Side Story Selections: A Tribute to Leonard Bernstein*, Feldherrnhalle, Munich
2005	Cabaret – Pizza on the Park, London
2005	Cabaret – Feestzaal Stadhuis, Aalst, Belgium
2005	Lt Jack Ross in *A Few Good Men,* Theatre Royal Haymarket, London
2005	Presenter/performer – *The Sound of Musicals* (BBC)
2005–6	Prince Charming in *Cinderella,* New Wimbledon Theatre, London
2005	Lead Tenor in *The Producers* (film)
2006	Competitor – *Dancing on Ice* (ITV)
2006	Judge – *How Do You Solve a Problem like Maria?* (BBC)
2006	Presenter – *Keys to the Castle* (HGTV)
2006	Captain Jack in *Torchwood* season one (BBC)
2006	Awarded Stonewall's Entertainer of the Year Award
2006	Opening and closing performer – Royal Variety Performance, London Coliseum, London
2006–7	Jack in *Jack and the Beanstalk*, New Theatre, Cardiff
2006	Concert – *A Musical Christmas: Friday Night is Music Night*, Queen Elizabeth Hall, London (BBC Radio 2)
2007	Co-presenter – *Live from the Red Carpet* BAFTAs (E! Entertainments)
2007	Presenter – *The National Lottery* (BBC)
2007	Subject – *A Taste of My Life* (BBC)
2007	Panellist – *The Weakest Link:* Doctor Who *Special* (BBC)
2007	Judge – *Any Dream Will Do* (BBC)
2007	Captain Jack in *Doctor Who* season three (BBC)

2007	Launched Royal Air Force Tattoo with the RAF
2007	Concert (host and performer) – *A Jerry Herman Tribute*, Prince Edward Theatre, London (BBC Radio 2)
2007	*Another Side*, solo album
2007	Guest appearance – 'Children in Need' (BBC)
2007–8	Aladdin in *Aladdin*, Hippodrome Theatre, Birmingham
2008	Captain Jack in *Torchwood* season two (BBC)
2008	Captain Jack in *Doctor Who* season four (BBC)
2008	Presenter – *The Kids Are All Right* (BBC)
2008	UK Concert Tour

With thanks to George Seylaz, webmaster for www.johnbarrowman.com.

Index

(The initials JB and SG denote John Barrowman and Scott Gill.)

Adelphi Theatre, London 153
Aguilar, Rafael 129
Agyeman, Freema 188, 231, 233, 234–5
Ahearne, Joe 18
All My Children 123
American Beauty 199, 243
American Cinema Awards 92
American Werewolf in London, An 169
Angel 141
Any Dream Will Do 41, 91, 111, 184, 204,
    219
Anything Goes:
    JB's first rehearsal for 217
    Joliet Drama Guild 79
    London 12, 14, 83, 111–14, 126, 131,
        145 *n*, 156, 159–62, 191, 192–6,
        197, 226
    pirated versions of 193
    plot of 112–13
    video-camera incidents during 194–6
Arci's Place, NY 189
Askey, Arthur 218
auditions 12–13
    for *Anything Goes* 111–13
    for commercials 59, 95
    for *Doctor Who* role 16–17
    for Opryland 93, 94–5
Aurora, IL 52, 59, 62
    JB starts school in 60
    Prestbury in 62, 66, 69, 74
Autobiography, The (Russell) 242
Avian, Bob 159
awards:
    Theatregoers' Choice Awards 83
    TV Quick 83
    Welsh BAFTA 83

Baker, Tom 16
Barker, Gavin 13, 15, 45, 145, 231–3
Barnicle, Andy 16, 94, 110
Barrowman, Alex (uncle) 30, 38–9
Barrowman, Andrew (brother) 15, 22–8, 31,
    33, 53, 54–7, 59, 70, 71–2, 126,
    168–9, 182
    accent of 60–1

arrival of, in USA 60
effect of emigration on 61
frisbee incident and 72
at high school 69
JB's HIV test and 76
JB's revenge on 71–4
university soccer team role of 61
wedding of 31, 145
Barrowman, Andrew (nephew) 61, 168–70,
    224–5
Barrowman, Bridgett (niece) 61, 169–70
Barrowman, Carole (sister) 8, 22–8, 31, 44,
    53, 54–7, 59, 70, 101, 127
    accent of 60–1
    arrival of, in USA 60
    Christmas/New Year celebrations and
        169, 170
    effect of emigration on 61
    JB's HIV test and 76–7
    teasing of 62–3
    university degree of 61
    wedding of 31, 64, 145
Barrowman, Charlie (uncle) 30, 38–9
Barrowman, Dorothy (sister-in-law) 61,
    170
Barrowman, Emily (paternal grandmother)
    31, 38–9
Barrowman, John:
    accent of 60–1, 233
    acting classes taken up by 95
    adventurous activities of 39
    AIDS charities and 77
    awards and 83
    bagpipes bought for 29–30
    birth of 21–3
    boyfriend to Marilyn 109, 130
    Captain Jack part offered to 13–14
    cars owned by 137
    childhood singing of 31
    civil union of 31
    Disneyland offer to 102–3
    Dreamers Workshop set up by 88–90
    dual nationality of 43
    early life of 23–38, 52–9, 69–75, 77
    emigrates to USA 16*n*, 58–9

first American home of 62
first car of 83
first gay kiss of 97
first serious gay relationship of 129–30, 142
first talent contest entered by 58
First Tenor award for 87
first university show of 106
flute played by 64
flying feared by 42, 62, 210–11
flying's effects on 42
Forensic Competition entered by 83–5, 86–7
frisbee incident and 72
graduation of 91
junior-high band joined by 64
HIV test on 76–7
houses owned by 137
matinee pranks played on 154–5
with Old Gold Singers 93–4, 121
Olivier nomination for 199
on-set nickname of 236
phobias of 62, 149–50
pranks played on 99–100
prankster nature of 98–99
Royal Air Force Tattoo and 42, 43–9
school drum major 66
school musical role for 80–1
schooling of 32, 33–4, 60, 64–6, 80–3, 121, 241
scuba-diving by 207–8, 210
sexuality of 75–8, 96–7, 109, 187
SG's civil partnership with 144–7
SG meets 141–2
shellfish allergy of 157
soap operas loved by 66, 168
Sondheim's praise of 224
sounded out for *Doctor Who* role 15
Stonewall Entertainer of the Year Award won by 43
superstitions of 149–51
Torchwood news broken to 233
University of Iowa entered by 91
'Wee John' sobriquet of 28, 28*n*, 32, 33, 38, 64
Barrowman, John (father) 21–9, 52–8, 74–5, 95–6, 114, 120–1, 162*n*, 166*n*, 170, 171, 173, 220
accent of 61
arrival of, in USA 60
'Big John' sobriquet of 28*n*
Caterpillar job accepted by 51, 58–9
early life of 38–9
favourite films of 46
golden wedding anniversary of 147
higher education valued by 122

at JB's civil partnership ceremony 145
JB's sexuality and 75–6
Midge and 127–8
work of 46, 52–3, 58–9, 64, 74
Barrowman, John (paternal grandfather) 31
Barrowman, Marion (mother) 21–31, 53–8, 59, 93, 95–6, 120–1, 162*n*, 166*n*, 170, 172, 220
accent of 61
arrival of, in USA 60
birth of 31
golden wedding anniversary of 147
higher education valued by 122
at JB's civil partnership ceremony 145
JB's sexuality and 75–6
Midge and 126, 127–8
Murn's death and 59–60
shop job of 32
singing voice of 30–1
superstitions of 151
Barrowman, Neil (uncle) 30, 38–9, 110–11
Barrowman, Yvonne (niece) 61, 169–70
Barrowman Casey, Clare (niece) 11–14, 21–2, 25, 61, 62–3, 76, 167–8, 171–3, 175–8, 205–6, 222
birth of 167–8
at *De-Lovely* premiere 221–2
first UK visit of 165
JB's bond with 167–8
Torchwood cast met by 238–9
twin of 167
Barrowman Casey, Turner (nephew) 11, 25, 61, 62–3, 76, 165–7, 171–3, 175–8, 215, 222
first UK visit of 165
Barrymore, Drew 244
Bassey, Dame Shirley 42–3
Baxter, Keith 141
Beautiful and the Damned, The (Fitzgerald) 157
Beauty and the Beast 222
Bleeth, Yasmine 67, 188
Bogart, Matt 225
Boss, Hugo 117
Brecon Beacons National Park 237
Broderick, Matthew 116
Brooks, Mel 15, 116–17
Brothers and Sisters 198
Brough, Squadron Leader Gary 46, 47
Brown, Glenn 57–8
Brown, Madelyn 57–8
Brucher, Jim 92
Bryson, Mike 85, 87
Buckley, Betty 153, 155–6, 186, 191, 244
Buffy, the Vampire Slayer 141
Burford, Ian 115

Burnett, Carol 115, 159, 220–1
Burns, Robert 81, 10, 145
Butler, Andrew ('Papa') (maternal
    grandfather) 31, 60, 93
Butler, Murn (maternal grandmother) 27,
    28, 31–2, 33–4, 37, 59, 121, 220
    stroke suffered by 32, 59
    arrival of, in USA 60
    death of 59–60

Caddick, David 203–4
Cannell, Alex 115
Cannes Film Festival 52
Captain Jack (character) 229, 230–1
    Doctor's kiss with 18
    JB auditions for part of 16–17
    JB offered part of 13–14
    popularity of 242
    return of, to *Doctor Who* 231
Cardiff, Wales 53, 146
    Doctor Who set in 17
    JB and SG's civil partnership ceremony
      in 144–6
    production site in 179–80
    tour guide to 234
Carhenge 174
Carol Burnett Show, The 220–1
Casey, Bud 171
Casey, Kevin (brother-in-law) 61, 63, 101,
    127–8, 170–1
    Christmas/New Year celebrations and
      169, 170
    JB's HIV test and 76
Casey, Lois 172
Caterpillar Inc. 51, 52, 59, 64, 74
Cates, Phoebe 244
Central Park West 15, 173, 186–7, 191
Cher 122, 142, 172, 221
Chichester Festival Theatre 141
'City' (Hughes) 206–7
civil partnerships 115*n*, 144
Clowers, Michael 96, 97
Cole, Natalie 52
Collinson, Phil 16
Combe, Anita Louise 154–5, 158
Company 15, 219, 222, 223–6
Connery, Sean 102
Conway, Jeremy 133
Costello, Elvis 52
Coward, Noël 79, 92, 108, 218
Crawford, Joan 24, 226
Cribbins, Bernard 113–14, 114–15, 161–2,
    218
    'Dick of the Week' award given by 161
Crow, Sheryl 52
Curtis, Tony 244

Dallas 51, 66, 186
Dancing on Ice 40, 41, 70, 182
Dankwart, David 81
David-Lloyd, Gareth 52*n*, 145, 180, 236,
    237–8
Davies, Russell T. 16, 176*n*, 230, 231–2,
    233, 242–3
    Captain Jack character and 17
    at JB's civil partnership ceremony 145
Davison, Peter 16
Day, Darren 181
De Palma, Brian 102
Dead Sea 209
Dean, Christopher 41, 182
De-Lovely 15, 52, 152, 221
Denisof, Alexis 141
Dick, Andy 85–6, 87
Dickens, Charles 244
Dickinson, Angie 92
Dickinson, Janice 44
Disney 102–3, 222
Doctor Who 188, 229–31, 233–5
    atmosphere on set of 234
    Captain Jack's return to 231
    Cardiff site of 179
    Jack–Doctor kiss scene in 18
    JB's memorabilia from 66
    JB's name in opening credits of 223
    JB's plea for musical version of 176*n*
    JB sounded out for role in 15
    JB takes up role in 17–19
    Shakespeare depicted in 149–50
Doctor Who aliens:
    Autons 16, 17*n*
    Cybermen 16
    Daleks 16
    Davros 17*n*
    Slitheen 230
Doctor Who characters:
    Brigadier 16
    Captain Jack, *see main entry*
    Doctor, the, *see main entry*
    Jones, Martha 234
    Smith, Sarah Jane 16, 17*n*, 179
    Yana, Professor 234
    Tyler, Rose 16–17, 18, 19
Doctor Who episodes:
    'Empty Child, The' 16
    'Parting of the Ways, The' 18
    'Shakespeare Code, The' 197
    'Terror of the Autons' 17*n*
    'Utopia' 230–1, 234
Doctor, the (character) 18, 230
Donmar Warehouse, London 199
Donner Party 139–40, 142
Doris, Marie 62, 180

Douglas, Kirk 173

Eagle, Barb 83–5, 86–7
Eccleston, Christopher 17, 231, 233
Eden (SG's niece) 148
Egan, Susan 220, 222
Ethel Barrymore Theater 115, 219, 223
Eusebie, Isabel 32
Eusebie, Joe 32, 33
Evans, Sean 137, 149
Evita 62, 112, 143, 172, 203

Fahey, John 15, 130, 131, 158*n*, 163, 226
Fawlty Towers 114
Feestzaal Stadhuis, Belgium 189
Ferrell, Will 116
Few Good Men, A (Sorkin) 197
Fisher, Connie 45–6, 47–8
Fix, The 15, 199–200, 219, 222
Forbes, Emma 180, 182
Forensic Competition entered by 83–5,
        86–7
42nd Street 106–8
Franchitti, Dario 222
Friday Night Project, The 172
Friday Night with Jonathan Ross 44
Frost, Robert 66

Gabriel (SG's nephew) 148, 171, 173–5
Gallagher, Peter 243
Garavani, Valentino 131–8
Garcia, Andy 102
Gardner, Julie 231–3
Gest, David 92
Giammatti, Giancarlo 135, 136
Gill, Scott (partner) 19, 21, 138, 139–47,
        171, 173–8, 200–1, 204, 205–10,
        233, 238
    civil union of 31
    JB's civil partnership with 144–7
    JB meets 141–2
    JB meets parents of 143
    party performances of 170, 172
    scuba-diving by 207–8, 210
    sister's death and 148
Gill, Sheelagh 143
Gill, Steven 147–8
Gill, Stirling 143
Glass, Janet 180
Godspell 181
Golden Girls, The 221
Gorman, Burn 43, 44–5, 145, 229, 236,
        237

Harkness, Jack (character), *see* Captain Jack;
        see also Doctor Who; *Torchwood*

Harper, Graeme 230
Harris, Ed 243
Hawes, James 19
Head, Anthony 141
Hearn, George 222
Hello Dolly! 80, 82
Hemingway, Ernest 165, 191
Hemingway, Mariel 173, 191
Henshall, Ruthie 115, 158–9, 181, 219, 222
Herman, Jerry 115, 222
Hinton, S. E. 51, 64, 65, 227
Hogmanay 29, 170, 172
Holt, Beverly 79, 81–2, 88, 98–99, 101,
        102, 189, 232
    Dreamers Workshop and 88–90
Holt, Jim 81, 101
Hope, Bob 169, 173
Hotel Babylon 145
How Do You Solve a Problem Like Maria? 40,
        91, 219
Hughes, Langston 206
Hutton, Lauren 186

Iowa, University of 91
Iris (SG's niece) 148
Ivey, Judith 243

Jack and the Beanstalk 146
Jacobi, Derek 234
Jeannie, Auntie (maternal great-aunt) 28,
        31–2, 33
Johnson, Juleen 64, 66
Johnson, Kay 66
Johnson, Loreen 66
Johnson, Nadine 64, 66
Johnson, Paul 66
Joliet Drama Guild 79
Joliet, IL 64, 74
Joliet West High School 79, 243
    Dreamers Workshop at 88–90
    JB graduates from 91
    swing choir of 60, 82, 83
    see also Barrowman, John: schooling of
Jones, Suranne ('Sara') 198–9
*Joseph and the Amazing Technicolor
        Dreamcoat* 41*n*
Judd, Ashley 52, 221–2

Kaye, Thorsten 123
Kennedy Center, Washington 189, 222, 225
Kline, Kevin 52, 221

Lake Tahoe 140
Lane, Nathan 116
Lemmon, Jack 243, 244
Lewis 140, 146, 174, 176

Lincoln Center, NY 189
Lion in Winter, The (Goldman) 85, 86–7
Live and Kicking 15, 180–5
    teen magazine of 183
Lloyd-Webber, Lord (Andrew) 15, 75, 90*n*,
    112, 153, 204
Long Day's Journey into Night (O'Neill) 243
Love's Labour's Lost (Shakespeare) 196–7
Lowe, Rob 197–8
Lucas, George 52, 92
Lulu 182

Macdonald, Stuart 145
McKellen, Sir Ian 223, 226–7
Mackie, Bob 221
Mackintosh, Sir Cameron 15, 182, 199,
    200–3, 219, 220, 222
Madonna 203
Mark Taper Forum, LA 220, 221
Marquez, Martin 145, 162
Mary (SG's niece) 205–6
Matador 40, 129–30, 152, 162–3
Mathias, Sean 223
matinee pranks 154–5
Mendes, Sam 15, 119–200, 243
Mickey, Laura 64, 69, 70–1
    JB's sexuality and 77–8
Midge 96*n*, 119–28
    death of 126–7
'Milly, Molly, Mandy' 33
Minerva Theatre, Chichester 141
Miss Saigon 15, 158, 182–3, 184, 200, 203,
    219
Moffat, Steven 16
Molina, Mike 69, 70–1
    JB's sexuality and 77–8
Monroe, Marilyn 244
Mori, Naoko 145, 180, 188, 236, 238
Morissette, Alanis 52
Mount Vernon, Glasgow 23, 28, 37, 72,
    182
Mount Vernon Primary School 32, 34
Moveable Feast (Hemingway) 191
Movie Game, The 15, 183–4, 185–6
Myles, Eve 43–4, 44–5, 145, 156, 179, 180,
    229, 236, 237, 238–9
Mystery of Edwin Drood, The (Dickens) 244

'Night and Day' 15, 52
Norton, Graham 29, 90
'Nothing Gold Can Stay' (Frost) 66
Nunn, Trevor 11, 116, 145*n*, 191–3, 196–7

Oaks, Larry 111–12, 200
O'Connor, Caroline 142
Oklahoma! 96

Old Gold Singers 92, 93–4, 121
    JB leaves 95
Oliver! 85, 243
Olivier Awards 15, 199
Olivier, Sir Laurence 141
Opryland, Nashville, TN 93–5, 96–8, 102,
    225
Oslo Spektrum, Norway 143
Outsiders, The (Hinton) 51, 64, 65, 66, 227

Pagan 37, 59, 73–4
Paige, Elaine 112–13, 114–15, 161, 173,
    186, 218, 239
Partnerships Register, London 115*n*
Penny 138, 145, 174, 176, 183*n*, 201
Perez-Arevelo, Paco 129–33, 142
Pertwee, Jon 16
Peters, Andi 180, 182
Phantom of the Opera, The 75, 77, 101, 204,
    219
Pinchot, Bronson 220
Piper, Billie 17–20
Pizza on the Park, London 189, 232
Police Woman 92
Porter, Cole 15, 52, 79, 156
Powers, Stefanie 40, 130, 152
Prado museum 21
Precious Sons (Furth) 243
Prestbury, Aurora, IL 62, 66, 69, 74
Prick, Peter 106, 108–9, 110, 114, 115–17
Prince Edward Theatre, London 110–11,
    217–19
Principal, Victoria 66–7, 173, 186
Pritchard-Jones, Claire 62, 145, 180
Producers, The 15, 116–17, 149
Pryor, Andy 15, 16, 231
Putting It Together 115, 159, 219–20, 221,
    222–3

QE2 58
Queen's Theatre, Shaftesbury Avenue 129

Ramos, Javier 188–9
Rapp, Anthony 86, 87, 243–4
Really Useful Group 157
recordings:
    Another Side 183
    John Barrowman Swings Cole Porter 99
Red, Red Rose 173
Red Sea 209
Rice, Sir Tim 112
Rigg, Dame Diana 173
Ripley, Alice 225
Rising, Marilyn 95–6, 101, 108, 110–11,
    130–1
Roberts, Doris 221

Rogers, Ginger 92
Rome 207
Rope (Hamilton) 141
Rosenbaum, Dave 184
Rosenbaum, Viv 184
Ross, Jonathan 39
Royal Air Force Tattoo 42, 43–9
Royal Scottish Academy of Music, Glasgow
    111
Russell, Bertrand 242

St Francis, University of, Joliet, IL 89
Saint-Saëns, Camille 99
Sales, Laura 204
Samson and Delilah (Saint-Saëns) 99
Sandie (SG's sister) 147–8, 173*n*
Santorini 205–6
Sarah Jane Adventures, The 179
Savile, Jimmy 32
Schaeffer, Eric 222
Schiffer, Claudia 135, 136
Schönberg, Claude-Michel 203
Scottish play (Shakespeare) 150–1
Sequoia National Park, CA 175, 176, 177
7/7 London bombings 232–3
Shakespeare, William 149–50, 197
Shark Attack 3: Megadolon 210, 212–15
Sharutenko, Olga 41, 70
Sierra Nevada mountains 142, 175
Smash Hits 183
Sofia 210, 212
Sondheim, Stephen 15, 115, 219–20, 222,
    223–4
Sound of Music, The 41*n*
Spacey, Kevin 243–4
Spelling, Aaron 15, 67, 188
'Springtime for Hitler' 15, 116, 117
Stackner Cabaret, Milwaukee 189
Star Wars 51–2, 66
Starr, Darren 15, 191
Stewart, Jacqui 172
Stonewall 43
    JB's support of 77
Stroman, Susan 116
Sunset Boulevard 15, 83*n*, 153–6, 158,
    191–2, 203
superstitions, theatrical 150–1

Tennant, David 188, 230, 231, 233–5
Terrence Higgins Trust 77
Theatre Royal Drury Lane 11, 14, 160, 192
Theatre Royal Haymarket 197
theatrical superstitions 150–1
Thistlegorm 210
Thomas, Barbara 89
Thomas, Wyn Howard 195

Thurman, Uma 116
Tiger 146, 174*n*
Timber Estates, Joliet, IL 74
Titans 15, 67, 173, 186, 188, 210
TM Blue One 133, 134–6
Tomas 136, 138
Top of the Pops 32
Torchwood 184, 229–30, 231, 235–8
    atmosphere on set of 234
    Best New Drama award for 83
    Cardiff site of 179
    'Countrycide' episode of 237
    filming of 236–7
    genesis of 232
    Jack–Ianto kiss scene in 238
    JB's mooning on set of 101
    JB's plea for musical version of 176*n*
    props used on 43
Torchwood characters:
    Captain Jack, *see* main entry
    Gwen 229
    Ianto 53, 229, 238
    Rhys 229
    Toshiko 229
Torvill and Dean, *see* Dean, Christopher;
    Torvill, Jayne
Torvill, Jayne 41, 182
Tracy, Susan 160
Triplett, Sally Ann 160, 193–5
Tygett, Jack 107–8
Tyler, Zoe 204

United States International University
    (USIU), San Diego, CA 16, 94, 119,
    121
    Performing Arts School at 105–10
Untouchables, The (De Palma) 102

Van Dien, Casper 188
Van Outen, Denise 204
Victor Victoria 96
Vinovich, Bret 188–9

Way Out West 96, 98
West End Cares 77
White, Betty 221
Whitticker, Jean 95
Wilde, Oscar 41–2, 165
Williams, Robbie 52
Wilson, Mark 80, 83
Winfrey, Oprah 88
Wombles, The 114

Yap, John 181
Young Frankenstein 116
Yucatán Peninsular 208